Praise for Phil Hutcheon's

"Chronicling the battle against a host of life obstacles from bad grammar, drugs, and crime to paralysis-inducing political correctness, fickle lovers, and domestic violence, *Nobody Roots for Goliath* is a serious-minded, absorbing novel that reads like a true story because it draws so heavily upon harsh reality. Highly recommended."

— *Midwest Book Review,* January 2007

"... [T]he brilliance of this novel is in its style....With a basketball court and player on its cover and written by a male author, *Nobody Roots for Goliath* is, I confess, a book I usually would not have picked up . . . [but] I'm glad I did. I tell my students that we read literature to experience, vicariously, the lives of those who are different from ourselves. Reading *Nobody Roots for Goliath* I experience that very thing. For me this novel is successful most of all because when I read this book, I am taken into another world . . . rooting for Goliath, just like Wade."

—Candace Andrews, *inside english,*
Volume 34, Number 2, Spring 2007

"Awesomely funny. I am laughing so hard, I have tears running down my face. This book is insane! Also witty, nasty, sardonic, ironic, pathetic, engaging, empathetic, realistic. I am in love with Wade. How could such a wormy character be so appealing?"

—Paula Sheil, *The Moon in Three Pieces*

"I laughed out loud on almost every page."

—Anna Villegas, *All We Know of Heaven*

"I enjoyed this book more than anything I've read in a long while. Very inspirational. It should be required reading for burned-out teachers. Maybe a few will read it and remember why they went into the field."

—Greg Greenwood, former Delta
College Publications Center Manager

"Very interesting, very funny, and ultimately, very moving."
—Walter Isle, Clarence L. Carter
Distinguished Service Professor,
Rice University, *Experiments in Form*

"The sardonic tone, established in the opening sentence and carried throughout most of the narration, recalls Paul Giammati's character in the film *Sideways*: Wade's existential angst, his loyalty to his student Marvin, his frustration with his mad PhD advisor, and his literary sense of humor, from the opening page ("the academic calendar stretched out its horrors before him . . . like the lineage of Banquo before Macbeth") to the final moist question ("whether the droplets fell as the gentle rain from heaven or rolled off the end of Marvin's nose"). I give this book an A for its unique development of the theme of interracial friendship, for the aptness of the epigrams, and for the credible, zany overlapping dialogue with an excellent ear for street language."

—Virginia R. Herbert, UC Berkeley,
Harvard University, and San Carlos
High School

"I really enjoyed the flow of the story, like a memorable piece of music: immediately interesting, then building to a crescendo and ending quietly emotional. I do admit to having to look up a couple of words in the dictionary, *yclept* not a term that rolls off my tongue in conversation."

—D. H. Humber, *Varian*

DESPERATION PASSES

A novel of love and football,
not necessarily in that order

by
Phil Hutcheon

Tuleburg Press
Stockton, California
www.tuleburgpress.com

TULEBURG PRESS

DESPERATION PASSES

Published by
Tuleburg Press
Stockton, California

www.tuleburgpress.com

This is a work of fiction. Names, characters, places, and incidents are either the product of the author's imagination or are used fictitiously. Any resemblances to actual persons, living or dead, or to actual locations are purely coincidental.

Library of Congress Control Number 2014939596

ISBN 9780578143675

I dedicate this book in loving memory to my mother, Louise Hansen Hutcheon, who treated everyone she met, regardless of race, color, creed, or sports affiliation, like a member of our family.

CHAPTER 1

I guess I just have to say it: I'm not going to
be the Alabama coach.
        —Nick Saban, Miami Dolphins,
            December 21, 2006, two weeks
            before signing an eight-year,
            thirty-two million dollar contract
            at the University of Alabama

I say, we will have no more marriages.
                            —*Hamlet*, III.i.

"There ought to be a law," Arthur Allenby said, as he poured himself another shot from the bottle of Glenfiddich he had with typical self-sufficiency supplied: "No one under thirty is allowed to get married."

Malcolm Wade slurped his Budweiser from a can, considered the proposal in light of his own experience of wedlock, then nodded. "Or over," he decided to add.

"A one-year window?"

"Works for me. Stay drunk for twelve months and you're home free."

It was one of those years when the new millennium's toddling second decade still appeared to promise improvement upon its filthy first, at least in California, where an epochal Indian summer was bidding fair to extend its splendors all the way through Thanksgiving. While more newsworthy regions of the nation endured the ravages of freezing rain, hurricane, flood, avalanche, and assorted other cataclysms endemic to their blighted climes, unfolding in an obscure Central Valley college town was yet another in a seemingly endless succession of warm, cloudless, perfect days—days perfect for hiking, biking, picnicking in the park, skinny dipping at the lake, nude bathing on the beach. Allenby and Wade were watching football on television.

Onscreen the visiting Cal State team's running back plunged into the mass of tightly bunched San Diego State defenders for the third consecutive carry, gaining perhaps a yard. The camera found Matt Lytle, the corpulent head coach who had sanctioned the play selection, on the sideline. Apparently unperturbed, he waved the punt team onto the field and cued the barrage of change of possession advertisements.

Allenby had come to Wade's condo near the CSU campus after an emergency morning meeting of a committee convened to deal with the dilemma resulting from Lytle's unexpectedly swift success. The coach had parlayed a lamb chop schedule and a roster stuffed with community college transfers and "high risk" admits into a demand that his salary be doubled on the spot. Clemson University and North Carolina State, among others seeking national glory, were rumored to be courting him after seeing the results of his rapid resurrection program. A win today in the conference finale would make CSU bowl-eligible in just his second season and for only the third time ever. The fact that Lytle had signed a five-year contract was widely considered inconsequential in this era of job-hopping opportunism, but CSU was apparently going to try to buck the trend. Allenby had a law degree and had been included on the committee to advise on crafting a covenant, whether for the incumbent or his successor, less likely to be breached. Allenby had his own agenda for accepting the appointment as well: the first African-American varsity athlete to graduate from CSU, he was determined to see that if Lytle left, real consideration, rather than the typical dog and pony show, would be given to minority candidates for the coaching post. While in town, Allenby had also scheduled the task of dissuading his stepson, a CSU sophomore and Wade's student the year before when he was still teaching, from what was by any sane measure an overhasty marriage.

The phone rang. Wade had a fossil, no way to screen. He picked up.

"Why aren't you basking your abs in the sunshine? It's

twenty-three frigging degrees here."

"No one told you to move to Siberia, nitwit."

It was actually Connecticut that Angela Hardy was phoning from, but it might as well have been the far side of Pluto to which she had removed herself as far as Wade was concerned.

After boyhood, adolescence, and early manhood lost lusting in vain for the busty cheerleaders and campus vamps who unaccountably preferred quarterbacks to the geeks who watched them on TV, Wade had wed a woman as desperate for company as he. Many years of chronic mutual disappointment and intermittent suicidal/homicidal fantasies later, he had the previous fall tossed himself into the tempest of a passionate relationship with Angela, a slinky, stirring Columbia PhD and then the shining star of the CSU faculty. When Wade had not acted swiftly to end his marriage, the interval of ecstasy had abruptly ended, and Angela, magically securing on short notice a mid-year appointment, had beaten a retreat not quite to the Ivy League but to the Big East—and to the abusive ex-Buffalo Bill she had left to join Wade.

"Did you and your sparring partner set a date yet?"

"It looks like Ronnie and I might be—"

Wade closed his eyes, held his breath, braced himself for the killshot.

"—separating."

Wade's heart resumed beating. He exhaled, glanced over at Allenby, then turned back to the phone, realized he was squeezing the hell out of it. Iron Man should have such a grip.

"Congratulations."

"Asshole."

"Him or me?"

"Both of you. *All* of you. All men are assholes."

"Of course we are," Wade agreed. "Lincoln, Gandhi, Martin Luther King—"

"They all did shit to their women."

"Is that what you called to tell me?"

"I might be coming back to California."

Wade's heart started to thump harder. Did he dare to believe this? "I thought you were going back to Columbia."

"They want me to come there as an *assistant* professor. Can you *imagine*?"

This was the very rank, though far from the heady realm of Broadway and 116th, that Wade had at long last attained himself after years of groveling in postgraduate poverty and adjunct servitude. "Not possible," he said. "Cannot be humanly imagined. They might as well ask you to pass out tissue in the ladies' loo."

"That sounds more like you at CSU."

Angela had chaired the committee that selected Wade for his new position, officially titled "Compliance Officer," mainly as a result of the rescue mission he had undertaken on behalf of another of last year's students, Marvin Walker, a marginally literate basketball recruit from Harlem, during a series of sometimes public misadventures. After the job had been created at the insistence of the Faculty Senate, Wade had been appointed in spite of his lack of a counseling background, against the wishes of several highly ranking members of the Athletic Department. Strong backing by the alumni group Allenby headed had carried the day.

"Listen, Wade, I was . . . really sorry to hear about your mom."

A month after Angela had left, Wade's mother had died. It had been her late-in-life divorce from his father that had paralyzed Wade, trapping him in his own moribund marriage when he'd had the chance to move on. The irony was that he'd yoked himself to a wife completely antithetical to his mother's common sense, which he heard in his head still, carrying all the way back to childhood: **Marry a girl with a good head on her shoulders,** she'd say, even when he was too young to think of kissing a girl or holding her hand, let alone marriage. He remembered teasing his mother in childish response, "Where *else* could a girl's head *go*?" Then he'd married Brenda and found out.

The figurative scatological contortion Wade ascribed to his bride manifested itself more tangibly in the forms of smoking, drinking, cursing, sleeping all day, eating all night, gaining weight, and blaming him. Her consumption was boundless, in the car, in bed, even once or twice on the toilet. Within two years of the day they exchanged vows, she had put on a hundred pounds. Then she discovered cocaine. An enabling codependent relationship with her younger brother Tommy, who was prone to "visit" for weeks on end, had added to the satisfactions of Wade's domestic life. Tommy shared all of Brenda's bad habits, multiplied them exponentially, and invented many of his own. It was he who had set his sister on the path toward experimentation with crack. Haunted by his father's desertion of his mother, Wade had failed to fully disengage from Brenda even in the face of her various addictions, as a consequence squandering his brief glimmer of bliss with Angela.

The compound effect of mid-life romantic catastrophe and his mother's final departure had proven disorienting beyond any measure that even the worst of Wade's many demons could have conjured. Throughout the spring semester, he had barely been able to eat or sleep, choking down a few bites here and there, tasting nothing, sleeping perhaps two hours a night, losing twenty pounds from a frame less than robust to begin with, staggering in to work. People who barely knew him thought he had cancer; those a little closer guessed he had become addicted to methamphetamine. It was only his new job, guiding the jocks through the rocks, and Allenby's steadily emerging friendship that had sustained him through the roughest stretches, when the bottom of a bottle of Vicodin had murmured siren-like of sweet nothings forevermore.

"You still there, Wade?"

He managed an audible mumble.

"How are things at CSU? Getting used to helping those knuckle-draggers tie their shoes and blow their noses?"

"Usually I just wipe off the powder burns after they finish snorting their party favors."

"Good thing you practiced up on Brenda then. I heard you . . . finally got divorced."

The bright side of the picture was that Brenda had dumped him for the dalliance. In the wake of losing Angela, though, receiving the dissolution decree was like removing the sting of a garden bee after a cobra had clamped its fangs into his gullet.

"The commercial's almost over. Could you call back later?"

"Are you watching fucking football again?"

"It's fall. What the hell else would I be doing?"

"Did you ever stop to think that you should invest your life in something more rewarding than—"

"Falling in love with a heartless blonde who would rip my guts out and then disappear to the ends of the earth with a creep who beats her up?"

"Give me a break, Wade. It was just a black eye. And *you* put more emotional energy into watching baseball and football than you ever did into your relationships, ours included. Don't give me that shit about falling in—"

"You know what really hurts?"

"—love. What?"

"You left out basketball. What's this about coming back to—"

"Next time turn the game off when I call."

Wade heard her hang up, turned to Allenby, shook his head. "Six and a half billion people in the world, half of them female, and how is it that we manage to convince ourselves that there's only one person, one singular soul, whose path we happed to cross by sheer blind stupid incomprehensible chance, that can make us happy? That without whom we'll be utterly lost and miserable, our lives without a single shred of joy or meaning?"

Allenby shrugged. "Think of it this way: the world is full of beautiful women who don't want to sleep with you. Millions of them. Now—"

"Billions," Wade said.

"Okay, billions. You made my point. Now there's just one more: be rational."

Wade wasn't in the mood for rational. "Did you ever hear that first-take recording Sinatra did of a song called 'I'm A Fool to Want You'?"

"When he was mourning Ava. Not a bad record." Allenby knew his music. He was mainly a jazz man, Miles Davis,

Coltrane, but he wasn't a snob about it. Wade could talk to him about other kinds, except for country, of course, which Allenby considered caterwauling, or rap, which both of them considered actionable. "You can hear it in his voice, his guts tearing apart, the real deal."

Wade closed his eyes again, played the refrain in his head. "That's how Angela made me feel."

"Almost worth going to hell and back for, to cut a side like that."

"Sinatra almost didn't make it back," Wade pointed out. "He put his head in the oven."

Allenby gestured at the screen. "Thank God for football. It takes your mind off that crap. Although I don't know how much more of *this* crap I can watch."

CSU got the ball back, ran another dive into the line. The camera found Lytle again.

"Eight in the box and he runs right up the gut again."

"He coaches like McClelland. Lincoln would've canned his fat ass," Wade said. "Or maybe it's Westmoreland I'm thinking of."

Wade had watched the Vietnam War on television. Allenby had been at Kae Sanh. He didn't like to talk about it, though, and didn't take the bait now. "That guy ought to go on a diet. You hate to see a coach who's a hundred pounds overweight."

Wade nodded. *Or a wife.* "Must be great inspiration for his team during two-a-days in August."

"I suppose no chance he'll go now on fourth and short?"

"He likes to punt a lot," Wade said. "That's his favorite play since his quarterback got hurt."

"Some game plan. That's why you let the back-up take a few snaps."

Jake Bonner, CSU's cannon-armed, BB-brained sophomore signal caller, had gone down in a trainwreck sack in the previous game, suffering a concussion and possible brain damage, after holding the ball too long in the pocket in accordance with his annoying custom, which he combined with a penchant for leaving the ball on the ground or throwing it to the wrong jersey at the critical juncture.

Wade didn't want to think about Bonner or his piteously green replacement. Even more, he didn't want to let himself think about Angela. He wondered how much Allenby had pieced together from half of the phone conversation, what he would say about the prospect of Angela's return, wasn't brave enough to find out. "Speaking of game plans, what are you going to tell The Dink?"

This was their name for Allenby's stepson, undistinguished in Wade's class a year ago except by a remarkably volcanic case of acne. He was plighting his insanely premature troth with Jennifer, a chunky, chinless, mildly wall-eyed coed from the same remedial composition crew.

Allenby sighed. "Got to find out first if she's knocked him up. That's the most likely explanation, I'm guessing."

Wade shuddered at the prospect thus entailed, imagined himself twenty years hence counseling the progeny, swathed from head to toe like something out of *The Elephant Man*.

"Probably won't make any difference what I tell him," Allenby said. "He'll do whatever he damn well pleases, just like my daughter."

"That's the one in San Diego?"

"La Jolla. One of my houses, of course. First time I met the deadbeat she's with, five years ago now, I told her three things: don't move in with him, don't marry him, and don't have a kid with him."

"O-for-three?" Wade ventured.

"O-for-four, actually. There's another little bugger on the way." Allenby raised his chin at the screen again as CSU stopped a drive with a corner blitz on third down. "At least this guy has a clue when he's coaching the defense." Then, when Lytle appeared to berate rather than congratulate the tackler coming off the field as the special teams came on, Allenby added, "Unless that was an ad-lib."

"I wouldn't be surprised," Wade said. "That corner's our best player, Marcus Foster. He's small, but he does it all. He and the punter are our NFL prospects."

Onscreen a slender black assistant interceded to calm the still-animated head coach.

"Maybe Lytle didn't know what coverage call was on there. Is that the defensive coordinator?"

Wade shook his head. "Probably up in the booth. Lytle didn't hire a black coordinator on either side of the ball. He kept a couple of black assistants that were already here. I think that's the defensive backs coach."

Two more stuffed runs and a telegraphed screen pass that half of the Aztec nation was waiting to annihilate netted minus four yards. Allenby grunted. "How much you think we should offer the mastermind to come back?"

"What's he making now, six hundred thousand?"

"That's the base. With the perks, he's at about nine."

"Must be tough to feed his family."

"What's that, about ten times your deal as a faculty member?"

"Right. I hit 90k this year." Wade wasn't complaining. After years of making less than a third of that in the part-time pool, he was euphoric about his sudden, if belated, escape from the economic underclass.

Allenby had made a few million litigating Silicon Valley lawsuits, and then multiple millions more in what had begun as a sideline marketing his own legal software, before semi-retiring to his native Los Angeles.

"We got kids kicking down doors in Kandahar making what, thirty thousand a year? Getting blown to bits, coming home in caskets or missing an arm or a leg or a dick, so fatcats like that"— Allenby gestured again at Lytle onscreen—"can get fatter. Some value scheme, huh?"

"How about we pay the Marines nine hundred thousand a year and the football coaches thirty?"

"You got my vote. *Nice* punt."

Wade nodded as the ball sailed sixty yards and bounced out of bounds, preventing a return. The punter came off the field to high-fives from his teammates. "He'll be making nine hundred thousand next year, too."

The game, the season, the bowl bid, and Matt Lytle's career

options came down to a fourth quarter standoff. With the score tied at 7-7, CSU appeared to have an opportunity to settle matters when another punt soared over the head of SDSU's braided return man, who attempted to field the ball on the hip-hop at his five yard line, fumbled, then compounded the catastrophe by trying to scoop the bobble on the run instead of diving on it. He was yanked rudely by his pigtails onto the turf and away from the ball. When the inevitable pile-up at the goal line was sorted out, possession belonged to CSU, apparently at the SDSU two; then, however, a penalty was assessed against the tackler for giving his victim's curls a superfluous twirl. Players from both teams left their benches and headed toward the field. Only the intervention of Marcus Foster, the little cornerback, to pull his burlier offending teammate away appeared to prevent the outbreak of greater hostilities. On the following snap from the seventeen the back-up QB promptly fumbled the exchange. SDSU recovered, drove six yards, punted back to midfield. CSU clipped on the return, ran three times for four yards, punted again.

With less than a minute to go and the prospect of an overtime scoreless nigh unto doomsday looming, Marcus Foster made the day's decisive play, outleaping a taller wideout to deflect and then intercept a desperate downfield heave at the CSU twenty-five. Dipping nearly to the turf after securing his improbable one-handed catch, he steadied himself with his free hand, then spun out of the grasp of the intended receiver and set out across the field, whirling past offensive linemen as if they were statues, hurdling a downed teammate, dodging a discombobulated official, stiff-arming a tight end, juking the hapless quarterback onto his knees, then tight-roping the sidelines until he was finally knocked out of bounds inside the SDSU ten yard line by an angling running back.

"*That* was a helluva play," Allenby said.

Wade nodded. And exactly why you sat through three-and-a-half hours of tedium to see it. *Every down is different*, Joe Montana said. You never knew when something remarkable was going to happen, something you had never seen before. "For a second there I thought that field judge was going to make the tackle."

With only seconds left, there was no need for CSU to risk another fumble. Even the much maligned placekicker, who had missed three previous field goal attempts, could hardly fail now with the wind at his back in the veritable shadow of the enemy goalpost. Except that he did. Sometimes, it was true, you saw what you had all too frequently and only too recently seen before.

"Are you fucking kidding me?" Allenby shook his head in disbelief as the pointblank kick corkscrewed wide right.

"Don't worry," Wade said, spotting the penalty flag. "Defense was offside. He gets to try again. Closer, too."

"I can't stand it. Tell me what happens."

Allenby disappeared into the kitchen. Wade watched the hike, a trifle high, the hurried hold, and the low-flying kick, which he pictured going smack into the vast ass of the Samoan snapper. Somehow the ball climbed just over the fingers of a leaping defender, struck the crossbar, bounced straight up, hit the bar again on the way back down, and then finally fell to earth, barely on the leeward side. No flags. Game over. Allenby emerged from the kitchen, a towel in his hands, glanced at the celebration on the screen, arched an eyebrow.

Wade raised his beer in salute. "A quarter-inch lower, and we'd have been in OT from here to eternity."

Allenby grunted again. "Lytle just made himself another half a million."

After five or six replays of the climactic interception return, ESPN2 cut to the on-field interview in which the victorious coach was assigning credit for his team's latest milestone.

"The Good Lord smiled on us today, when that last kick went though. I'd like to think He rewarded us for a season of dedication and hard work."

Wade mimed a reverential bow, then grinned sideways at Allenby. "You'd think the Supreme Being would have more important work to do than guide placekicks in a CSU-San Diego State game, wouldn't you?"

"Maybe our hero's auditioning for Notre Dame."

"Is he even going to mention Marcus Foster?"

The interview continued, with Lytle somehow managing to exceed the insipidity of the questions with his answers. He explained that his team had played hard, showed character, fought through adversity, and, though not guaranteed a bowl bid, certainly deserved one. The Alamo Bowl was rumored to be interested. The interviewer was more interested in pursuing Lytle's personal future than his team's, however. The coach was unequivocal in response.

"I have no interest in the Carolina job."

"Right," Wade said. "And Nick Saban has never cashed a check in Tuscaloosa."

When the reporter attempted to persist, Lyle interrupted: "I have not been contacted by anyone at North Carolina State."

Allenby snorted. "I swear to God, that fucker's cell phone could ring right now, he could answer it, right there on the field, accept the offer, and he'd still say, 'I have no interest in the Carolina job.' We *know* he's been in contact with NC State. What the hell ever happened to telling the truth? How do we expect our athletes to honor their agreements when their coach is a bald-faced liar?"

Lytle continued: "We have made a commitment to the young men on this team and to this community. My wife and I love the Central Valley, and we fully intend to stay the course right here, not only for the bowl game I believe we've earned with a great win today, but for the rest of my career. Ye of little faith, please note: we just won our sixth game. Two years ago this team didn't win a single game. I like to finish what I start. With the Good Lord's help, I believe we can win a national championship right here at CSU. Let me reiterate: I have absolutely no interest in the Carolina job."

Wade clicked off the TV. "That Christer's goin' to Carolina."

"Yeah, well, he can take his offense with him. There'll be food soon if you want to eat."

Allenby went back into the kitchen. It turned out that on top of all of his other accomplishments he could cook, too. He seemed to be able to do everything. He was, Wade reflected as the aroma of something splendid began to waft into the living room, everything Wade was not: tall, handsome, fit, rich, married to a stunning beauty (Wade had seen a photo besmirched by the pimply stepson's presence), and apparently able to take anything, even the challenges of fathering a bi-racially blended family, in stride. Whatever obstacles Allenby had faced, and Wade knew there would have been no shortage for a black man who came of age in the 1960s, including in this one's case two tours of combat duty, he had survived and surmounted all of them. In a world full of disappointed, unfulfilled, frustrated, neurotic people—people like Wade, in other words—Allenby was an island of serene self-assurance.

The phone rang again. Wade answered, hoping in spite of himself for Angela again, heard instead Allenby's wife ask for him, then complain sharply before he could hand off that Allenby must have turned his cell phone off because he wasn't answering it. Proud of his status as the last primate on the planet without a cellular of his own, Wade had noted with approval Allenby's decision to do that very thing when the game came on, but he was now quickly forming an impression that did not jibe with the demurely smiling blonde goddess he had glimpsed in the snapshot. He waved a puzzled Allenby over.

"Don't tell me she was actually watching the game?"

Wade shrugged, passed the landline, went to see what smelled so good. When he came back, Allenby was back on the couch, staring blankly at the muted TV.

"Nora think we should give Lytle the extra half-mil?"

Allenby drained his glass, shook his head. "Okay with you if I crash here tonight?"

"She's *that* pissed you don't answer your cell?"

Again Allenby shook his head. "She wants a divorce," he said.

CHAPTER 2

I did two tours of duty in Southeast Asia, and
I was married for six months. I couldn't tell
you which experience was worse.
　　　　—Sergeant Mikey to Sergeant Cliff
　　　　in John Sayles' *Lone Star*

I gave him an unlimited budget, and he
exceeded it.
　　　　—Washington Redskins' owner
　　　　Edward Bennett Williams,
　　　　channeling John D. Rockefeller,
　　　　to explain the firing of head coach
　　　　and general manager George Allen

Allenby poured himself another three fingers of Scotch, gestured with the bottle to invite Wade to join him.

"I'll stick with beer, thanks. You look like you're gonna need every bit of that. What the hell happened?"

"Several things." Allenby sighed. "Money, of course."

"Look, if you're strapped, I could lend you a few quarters from my laundry fund."

"Funny. Just as a minor example, she owes $117,000 in interest on her credit cards this month. Or we do, I should say."

Wade knew his friend could snap his fingers and make the 117K go away. There had to be more to it.

"Oh, yeah, way more. Six months ago I put my foot down. I had the temerity to suggest that we cut back our discretionary spending and put more of our income into community projects. There's a shelter that we sponsor, and I wanted to put more into our scholarship fund for kids who aren't going to play their way into a university. Instead of some of the crap that she blows it on."

"So basically what you're saying is you cut her allowance?"

"Right. And then she . . . cut me off, if you know what I mean."

Wade knew what he meant, although in his own case being denied access to Brenda's bulging bundle of charms did not exactly constitute a fair basis for comparison.

"And now you get to pay the lawyers to sort it out?"

"Either that or have her whacked. You think she's worth goin' to San Quentin for?"

"Let me see her picture again."

Allenby dug into his wallet and handed over a photo, minus the pimplepuss this time. Talk about addition by subtraction.

"Not bad," Wade had to admit. "I've never seen teeth that perfect."

"Eighty-four thousand in Beverly Hills."

"You got your money's worth there." Wade's own molars bore testimony to a childhood crammed with Sugar Babies, Jujubes, and jawbreakers, all as often as not washed down the hatch, carrying attached chunks of enamel and composite, with root beer or Coca Cola. Good teeth never failed to impress him. "Did you buy this face, too, or is that the one she came with?"

Allenby shrugged. "A few nips and tucks. Another hundred thousand or so. Nothing major. She's only forty-eight. Twenty years younger than I am. Of course, that's part of the problem, too."

Wade's glance betrayed the usual suspicion.

Allenby shook it off. "Nothing wrong with the equipment. I might be something declined into the vale of years, but I can still fire up the old Howitzer. Even before the big freeze, though, it was just hard . . . finding something to talk about. Like your man Elmore Leonard says, 'There's more talking than screwing in a marriage,' after all."

"The more's the pity," Wade said. "Too bad the ratio couldn't be reversed."

Allenby nodded. "A lot of relationships could be saved."

"If we could cut down on the listening, too, that would really be great," Wade said. "Talking isn't too hard, I mean, I can sort of fake that part, but faking the *listening,* that takes—"

Allenby — 68

"We were all right until I started trying to retire a couple of years ago," Allenby resumed. "We had a deal that when I pulled the pin we'd spend winters on the Cote d'Azur, summers in the Alps, fall and spring here. We were fine when that was just the plan. She'd trot off to Europe for a few months, max out her cards, return with enough crap to fill up our house, then buy another one and start over. It kept her occupied, and I was too busy to pay much attention. Real estate was appreciating like crazy, so it was a win-win. Then when I started trying to cut back on work, we suddenly had all this time to spend together and we . . . found out we aren't all that compatible."

"You didn't sense it before?"

"What can I tell you?" Allenby waved at the photo. "The same old mistake we always make: she was compatible enough with my eyeballs." He sighed again. "You marry them to make them happy—and then they find something else to be unhappy about."

"What will she do now?"

"Go back to Europe, I suppose."

"She misses her family?"

"She misses Maxim's and Harrod's."

"What about you?"

"I've been married three times. The first one was from Africa, the second from South America, and this one's Scandinavian. I'm running out of continents."

"Maybe you should try an American girl next time."

Allenby shook his head. "The hell with next time. All over the world, other women's children are starving, drinking from drainage ditches, sleeping in the streets, dying from diseases easily wiped out at the cost of a few pennies a day worth of preventive medication. American women are shopping for jewelry and shoes."

While American men save the species by dedicating our lives to hops, Scotch, and football, Wade managed not to interject. "You've still got Asia. A well-peopled region, I understand," he said instead.

"Asian women scare me. If you had any sense, they'd scare

you, too."

Wade had been dating an exchange teacher from Japan since the death rattle of his own marriage in the summer. Allenby had met Yoshi when they had all attended a previous game on the CSU campus and gone out for sushi afterward, at Allenby's considerable expense.

"She's way too smart for you, you know. Permanent residence is her agenda. She pushing you to marry up yet?"

Wade, otherwise inactive since the end of his union, largely inert for years before and during it, was not about to give up the only thing he'd had going, however tenuous, since the fling with Angela—at least equally tenuous, as it had turned out—unless *she* was really coming back. He didn't let himself think about that. "I told her I'm still recovering from the divorce."

"Buying some time, huh? Licking your wounds. Trust me, that won't last you very long."

"I know," Wade admitted. "I've got to come up with something else pretty soon. I think I may have to tell her I'm gay. Want to be my . . . significant bother?"

"Now *there's* a dream come true. I knew I didn't make this trip for nothing."

"She's pretty persistent. I might have to give you AIDS."

"Whatever it takes to keep her happy."

"Does this"—Wade paused, tried to find a euphemism, gave it up—"divorce talk mean that you're off the hook for The Dink's decision?"

Allenby shrugged. "I'll still speak to him, long as I'm here. Can't hurt to find out what's going on. Maybe this chick has money."

Wade made a dubious face. Not many prospects in the CSU pool had what Allenby would consider money.

"Or maybe she'll take a powder when she finds out he ain't gettin' any of mine."

"You figure that's what she's after?"

"Well, it's hard to imagine what the other attractions might be."

Wade wondered if The Dink was still scoring coke for her

but decided to keep that speculation to himself for now. "When they were in my class together, he tried to help her with her essays."

Allenby had seen his stepson's sentence structure. "That must have been a howl."

"''Tis the times' plague when madmen lead the blind.'"

Wade's phone rang. He picked up, still hoping for Angela again. This was getting pitiful. Yoshi said hello.

"I'll get out of here if I'm cramping your style," Allenby said when he heard Wade return her greeting.

Wade held the phone to his chest. "One thing about being friends with a man with no style is it's impossible to cramp it. She likes her place better anyway. Much cleaner."

He agreed to meet Yoshi at her apartment, hung up, turned back to Allenby. "She asked me if you want to come along. I think she likes you."

"I think she likes sushi." Allenby hoisted his Scotch. "Thanks anyway. I've got all the company I'll need tonight."

Yoshi answered the bell in a kimono, slit far up the sides of her perfect legs. Wade was aroused before he made it through the doorway. He leaned in for a kiss, but she bobbed, pivoted, and strode straight into the living room, left him standing there in the hallway with a hard-on, watching her perfect ass wiggle away.

"You all day watch football?"

"Not all day," Wade protested, warily following her in, watching for landmines. "I took a nap at halftime."

"You don't call me, why?"

"Allenby came over."

"You like him better than me?"

"He's pretty appealing in a kimono, I have to admit." Wade sat down next to her, not too close yet. "I think you've got him beat, though."

"You like this?"

She folded her legs up under her, the kimono rising almost to her thatch. Wade glimpsed purple lace thong panties, sniffed their jasmine scent. He decided to be brave, leaned in closer, reached a hand toward heaven.

"No touch, please."

Shit. "Okay."

"Talk first."

Of course. "Okay."

"You talk, I listen."

Perfect. "You want me to tell you about the games I just watched?"

"Very boring subject."

"Not much else happening in my life. Since the last time we talked, I mean. Last night."

"You very stupid last night."

"More than usual?"

"You say you maybe never get marry again."

"What's stupid about that? Getting married was the stupidest thing I ever did."

"Your friend Allenby marry, right? He very happy."

Wade smiled. Sometimes the gods were paying attention after all. "He's getting a divorce. Another divorce, I should say. This makes number—"

"Maybe his wife jealous he spend too much time with you."

"—three. Don't be ridiculous. I've never made anyone jealous in—"

"He waste too much time watch football with you, his wife dump him."

"My fault," Wade agreed. "Completely on me. The fact they haven't had sex in six months probably didn't enter into it at all."

"Six months long time no sex. I cannot do."

"Me either," Wade said, conveniently blotting out the memory of six *years* of no sex with his ex during one of her bad moods.

"Next Saturday you call me, we go dinner. Not watch football all day."

"Good idea. Maybe just one game in the morning, one in the afternoon. We'll skip the evening game. Unless of course Oklahoma is—"

"What if I ask you never watch football again? You give up

football for me?"

"But why would you want to deprive me of—"

She reached over, put her hand on top of his, pulled his hand onto her lap, placed it purposefully. "You give up football for this?"

"—so much pleasure? I'd give up anything for this."

"You very smart man."

Wade kissed her, put his free arm around her shoulder, buried his nose in her fragrant perfect bosom.

"You want go bed now?"

"I thought you'd never ask."

"Or fuck me on the couch?"

"We could flip a coin if you like."

"Too much fucking football you watch."

"You ready to receive the kick off?"

"Next time more talk first."

"And listening, don't forget."

CHAPTER 3

Football is not a game but a religion . . . .
—Dr. Arnold Mandell

Anybody who watches three games of football
in a row should be declared brain dead.
—Erma Bombeck

Sunday's weather was even warmer and more spectacular than Saturday's. For Wade, this meant he could keep the sliding door wide open as he watched more football, on the Sabbath the officially professional variety, of course, in keeping with sacred tradition dating back to his childhood. Wade's parents had been Episcopalians, his mother devout, his father less zealous but for a time a compliant churchgoer. Wade had lasted through a year or two of Sunday school but then had been allowed to make his own election which service to attend. It had turned out not to be a choice at all. The first time he stayed home with the hiccups and watched the Baltimore Colts beat the clock in the two-minute drill, his faith was fully formed. Between the healing powers of Jesus and Johnny Unitas, there was simply no contest.

Wade's mother had accepted with equanimity, as she accepted most of life's changes, his defection from her denomination. The church had been a staple of her life, but unlike many other Christians Wade knew, she did not feel the compulsion to impose her faith on others, contenting herself with her own contributions, donating generously even when there was little to spare in her budget. It was hard for Wade to see what she got in return for her patronage. When his father left her, she had uttered one of only two negatively inflected sentences Wade could remember in her lifetime: **My life is over.** Even that had been attenuated by her subtext: *don't worry about me; enjoy* *your own life.* Wade had arranged for the pastor at her church to visit her, hoping he would offer extra projects to fill her time and encourage other members of her congregation to reach out to her. The result: one visit of approximately fifteen minutes, zero projects or contacts, and a 400% increase in mail and telephone solicitations for cash contributions. With quiet resourcefulness, his mother had solved her own problem. She hadn't complained, nor asked his father for money or anyone else for anything; Wade remembered that he'd never even seen her cry when his father said goodbye. She had taken the first job she could get, in retail at barely more than minimum wage, and spun it into gold. One day she started taking cookies that she'd baked to share with her co-workers. The compliments poured in, and eventually she decided to open her own shop. At sixty-five, she became an entrepreneur, substantially supplementing her Social Security income while sharing with several hundred customers something delicious every day, until illness overtook her, her last years darkened, although not destroyed, by gradually increasing dementia. Wade's sister, with some hired helpers, had cared for her at the end in their family home, Wade pitching in to help out on the weekends. He still missed her and mourned her and felt her presence in his life every day, especially on Sundays, her simple, secular words reaching beyond the grave to guide his untempled spirit: **The best way to be happy is to help someone else.**

Allenby emerged from the guest room, shaved, showered and impeccably dressed, as ever. After yesterday's bombshell and the quantity of Scotch that had preceded and followed it, Wade had expected to find him buried under the covers at noon, shit-faced, red eyed, and pleading for euthanasia, but he had started the day with a five-mile run while Wade lay abed after exerting himself well into the wee small hours with Yoshi. Now Allenby sat on the couch, watching in mostly silence for fifteen minutes as Wade fetched coffee, toast, and eggs, pretty much the upper limit of his own culinary expertise. An admirer of the vertical passing game, twice abandoned by his hometown teams, first by the Raiders, then by the Rams, Allenby was still searching for an

NFL team to embrace. Wade's current smash-mouth 49ers were unlikely to fill the bill.

The San Francisco quarterback came to the line, surveyed the defense, bunched to stop the run, and prepared to hand the ball to Frank Gore again.

"If they call another draw on second and ten, I swear I'm gonna throw a shoe through the screen."

"Better throw a sock instead," Wade said. "I don't have six TVs like you."

Gore fought his way up the middle for three hard yards, then caught a third down swing pass for three or four more.

Allenby groaned. "Do they *ever* throw the ball past the first down marker?"

"Why don't you buy your own team? You could hire Daryl Lamonica to be your coach and throw long on every play."

Wade gestured with the remote, offered to turn off the TV; Allenby shook him off, disappeared into the guest room to use his laptop. At halftime Wade switched to ESPN, where there was a cut to a live press conference. Matt Lytle was shaking hands with various dignitaries not affiliated with CSU. Wade amped the volume to reach Allenby. He emerged, checked the screen, and shook his head. One of the reporters at the conference asked about the terms of the new deal Lytle had signed.

"It's not about the contract," Lytle said. "It's about the challenge. It's about the opportunity to compete for a national championship. It's about restoring the great football tradition of a great football university. It's not about the money."

A commercial for a penile erectile dysfunction drug came on. Wade muted, turned to Allenby: "How much money do you think it's not about?"

"The going rate for the power conferences is two to three million per year. Plus perks that could push it to twice that: TV shows, radio, travel budget, housing allowance, car allowance, dogsitter's allowance—it's all part of the package these days. Why can't he just say 'it's five times the salary, and I'm taking it'? Anybody can understand that, accept it, hell, even respect it."

Allenby's cell phone rang. He stared at it distrustfully for a moment before answering. It was CSU's athletic director seeking to convene another emergency meeting of the coaching selection committee on Monday.

Allenby clicked off, then gestured toward the guest room. "Looks like I'll be spending another night at the palace."

"Don't let the luxuries go to your head."

"You're invited to see the A.D., too."

"What the hell for?"

"Update on the academic status of our players before the bowl game, in case we land one."

"I send a report every week."

Allenby shrugged, not his call.

"Great. Another meeting to go to. Please don't tell me I have to get up at—"

"Seven a.m. sharp. We'll go out for breakfast first." Allenby grinned as Wade stitched a death mask. "Don't worry, I'll wake you when it's over."

"Just pass the cyanide now."

In the evening, after savoring Allenby's Bolognese sauce, Wade cleaned up the kitchen and then turned on the Sunday night game, his third of the day. Allenby popped out to replenish toiletries and Scotch, then returned as Wade was settling in.

"Do you ever worry that you watch too much television?"

"Do I criticize *your* form of worship?"

"Didn't your parents tell you you'll go blind if you watch TV all day?"

"Of course they did. Also that it would destroy my brain cells, kill my initiative, and ruin my life."

Allenby nodded. "The 'Vast Wasteland' speech. Right on all counts?"

"Pretty much. I can still see some, though. Could you please move so I can see the whole screen?"

Before turning in, Wade clicked on ESPN again just to check for any highlights of the day's games he might have somehow missed. A brief repeat clip of Lytle's press conference came on, but then was abruptly supplanted by a more recent bulletin from CSU: two of the team's football players had been arrested following a shooting at a campus fraternity party celebrating the awarding of a bowl bid. Both of the players, A.J. Dupree and Thaddeus Marston, were African-American. Wade could see the dismay in Allenby's face when he came out of his room to hear the news.

"I know those guys," Wade said. "I counseled both of them."

"Nice work."

"Marston took forty units of P.E. in JC, and Dupree holds the team record for previous arrests."

"So that's the kind of character Lytle was talking about building."

Wade nodded. "Good thing he's staying to finish the job."

They turned to the late local news but heard no more details about the shooting. No doubt they'd hear more first thing in the morning.

Wade called Yoshi, absorbed the obligatory fifteen minutes of her plan for the rest of his life, went to bed, settled his head on the pillow, closed his eyes, tried to compose himself for slumber.

Sleep was another of the many things in life that Wade was bad at. Weekend catch-up binges provided occasional relief, but when he was required to rise early the next morning, it was not at all uncommon for him to slide around the mattress for several hours like a hophead coming down, greasing the sheets with his own angry sweat. Finally he would briefly go under, only to be blasted back to consciousness by the duty-call of the accursed clock-radio just as he was nearing REM stage, then lurch to work uncombed, half-shaven, and hastily clothed; students would ask if he'd missed a bus or perhaps been hit by one on the way in. Many nights he counted himself fortunate if he wound up with two or three hours of rest. Maybe that nightcap belt of Allenby's Scotch would help knock him out this time. Maybe . . . .

"I'm not getting married."

Wade stared stuporously into the phone that had awakened him, glared murder at the glowing digits at his bedside.

"I heard you the first time, Angela."

"I just thought you might like to hear it again."

"At three a.m.?"

"Oh, sorry, I forgot. It's six a.m. here."

"You forgot which coast you're on?"

"I wasn't thinking about the time difference. I really, really mean it this time."

"I'm really, really glad. And I'm really, really going back to sleep."

"How's Yoshi?"

"Asleep, I would imagine."

"Oh. I just wanted you to know I still—"

"I just want *you* to know I—"

"—think about you."

Pow. Direct hit, right in the heart. From three thousand miles. Smart bombs had nothing on this girl.

"Think about *this*, Angela: I have a meeting at 7:00 a.m.!"

"Oh. Better try to get back to sleep then. I'll call you back when—"

"Pigs fly, the moon turns blue, and the Warriors make the playoffs."

"Not win the championship? That's basketball, right?"

"Right. I'm trying to be a little more realistic in my fantasies. The Lakers are going shopping again. Did you say something yesterday about coming back to California?"

"Could be. I've got a . . . possibility. A couple of them, actually."

"You realize, of course, that I'll never get back to sleep now?"

"You never sleep anyway. Why don't you get up and do some push-ups or something?"

"Why don't *you*—"

"Last time I looked, those biceps of yours needed a little work."

"I'll let you feel my muscle when you get here. Are you bringing Ronnie?"

"I'm *leaving* Ronnie. Good night, Wade. Sweet dreams."

Chapter 4

If you had to identify, in one word, the reason
why the human race has not achieved, and
never will achieve, its full potential, that word
would be *meetings*.

—Dave Barry

The athletic director rose heavily from her chair and extended
a hammy hand toward Allenby as he accompanied Wade into her
fourth-story office. To Wade she merely nodded. Delia Herman
was a stout, florid matron with a combination of features and
garb calculated to bring her visitors' breakfast back up in a hurry.
Here it was barely past dawn and she already had going on a five
o'clock shadow that would have done Richard Nixon proud in
his prime. She had the kind of build that suggested in another
color scheme she could have played pulling guard in front of
Taylor and Hornung. Beneath badly-dyed blonde hair she was
wearing a bright orange pantsuit.

Wade was conscious of but generally unremorseful about his
own conspicuous hypocrisy in judging others for their attire. He
didn't give a shit about his own clothes, as long as they were
clean. He was perfectly comfortable going to work in jeans,
sneakers, and a casual shirt. Some of his shirts, it was true,
probably could stand to be updated from the medieval period—
Angela in her brief residency with him had offered more than
once to cremate the entire collection—but that would involve
going shopping, and Wade did not shop. The amount of time
and effort that other human beings, especially women, devoted
to this enterprise never failed to amaze him, especially when the
result was something like what was on display before him now.
How could sentient creatures justify spending hundreds of hours
and thousands of dollars on the acquisition of apparel when the

flesh it would be attached to was so grotesquely unfit to behold? *Hit the treadmill instead,* he'd often wanted to say when Brenda stuffed herself and a fried egg sandwich into the Toyota to go to Macy's for the latest sale. Or *skip the gym and go straight to the liposuction clinic.*

Wade's attitude in regard to his own wardrobe was in turn a source of some distress for Allenby, who had picked up a couple of suits for him while updating his own extensive collection; they were still hanging in the closet in the plastic covers they'd come home in. Wade could occasionally be talked into a sports coat but steadfastly refused to put on a tie for any event short of a funeral. It was his firm conviction that by the next century, if not sooner, survivors of the species would look back in utter hilarity at the forebears who consented to this absurd constraint. By then, of course, the fashionistas of the day might well be piercing their eyeballs and cladding themselves in garments made of human skin. Wade would hang in there with his sneakers and jeans as long as he could get away with it.

Herman eyed him intermittently and dismissively now while keeping her focus on Allenby, her disdain for Wade's appearance quite possibly equaling his for hers. She had been appointed by a beleaguered university president, under siege for, among other shortcomings, real and imagined, his failure to promote a proportionate total of female administrators. When she had received the position over several indisputably more qualified internal applicants, including a volleyball coach with multiple conference championships and a national reputation, there had been a veritable frenzy of scuttlebutt on the campus. It had been widely bandied about that Herman had threatened a sexual harassment suit in order to gain leverage. Even when he squeezed his eyes closed now, Wade found this gossip hard to credit. He put more faith in the competing rumor that she knew where some of the funds unaccounted for in the president's vast discretionary budget had disappeared to. She had obviously put to extensive use the account she had been given to renovate the office they were now sitting in, including the custom installation into a previously sealed building at a rumored $20,000 cost of a window that would open to admit fresh air. The president, indulging his apparent paranoia with even greater extravagance, had spent twice as much to bulletproof the windows in his chambers, for reasons no one could quite fathom: "Who would waste a bullet on that fucker?" Angela had wanted to know when Wade informed her. The classrooms of CSU might be crawling with cockroaches and the laboratories full of black mold and asbestos, but the executive offices of the institution were proudly and loudly upholding the administration's commitment to expending the contributions of the state's strapped taxpayers.

Bleary-eyed from sleep deprivation to begin with, Wade now inhaled sinus-inflaming fumes from the obscenely plush new carpet and half-listened as the A.D. issued a lengthy account of her recent activities on behalf of the department, the university, and perhaps global harmony as well; Wade wasn't paying enough attention to tell. It was all for Allenby's benefit, as she was obviously courting his millions.

Allenby looked at his watch. Wade got the hint; a lamppost would have got it. Totally oblivious, the blimp kept blabbing. Time's winged chariot could fly by and she probably wouldn't notice that either. Wade tried to suppress his irritation: he had entered the phase of middle age where he was working harder on getting along with the idiots who issued his paychecks. After a while he tuned out completely, started thinking about Angela's call, fought the feeling, fuck her anyway for waking him up, switched to Yoshi, pictured her calves in her latest miniskirt. Moved onward and upward to golden thighs, subtracted the skirt, reached for the thong, jasmine scented, purple lace, and—

"That's where you come in, Dr. Wade. Are you paying attention?"

Herman had been one of several in the Athletic Department who had opposed Wade's hire without ever having met him or knowing anything about him. He'd found out later that she had penciled in for the position the recovering alcoholic/drug addict ex-transvestite son of a trustee whom she owed a favor. Wade emerged reluctantly from his reverie now to find her faintly scowling in his direction.

"I suppose you've heard the latest."

Allenby grunted and beat Wade to the reply. "We watched the news in the morning. Evidently the police have established that no one was hit by the shots. Have our players been charged?"

She shook her head. "Not that we know of. They're still being interrogated."

"They have representation?"

"Of course."

Wade noted Allenby's fractional nod. Both of them were all too aware of the cases where student-athletes, especially blacks, had talked to police without attorneys present. Herman turned back to Wade, managed to downgrade the scowl into something closer to a sneer. "We were hoping you could shed some light on the situation based on your work with these two."

Wade's meeting earlier in the semester with A.J. Dupree and Thaddeus Marston had come about when they had jointly run afoul of the university's academic integrity policy, and he had been summoned to salvage their eligibility.

"I haven't worked with them much."

"But?"

He shrugged. "They came here to play football. They're both planning on the NFL, which is probably a stretch since they can't seem to crack the starting line-up here. They didn't have much interest in the academic counseling I offered them at the mid-term grade review."

"And how were they doing?"

"They were passing their P.E. classes, failing English, dropped the classes they cheated in. Everything else was up in the air."

"Failing English? That's important! Why are they having trouble there?"

You mean aside from the fact that they're ignorant, lazy, complacent, and illiterate?

"They're trying to take it online, which probably isn't the best format for them, considering the level of their computer skills. Plus there seems to be a problem we didn't anticipate with the grading in Professor Hotchkiss's course. I'm still looking into that."

"And the other classes?"

"Dupree hadn't been to one of his for three weeks. And Marston never bought the books for his. He said he needed the money to send to his girlfriend. She's pregnant. Again."

Allenby's turn to sigh. He looked at the wall.

Herman frowned. "What's this about a cheating episode?"

"I sent you a memo about it in September. And they were both included on the list of players with possible upcoming eligibility problems that I sent you in October."

"I can't read every email that every staff member who reports to me generates, Dr. Wade. Surely you know—"

Wade nodded. He wasn't surprised that she hadn't read his email; he was a little surprised that she knew what email was. "I'm just telling you that these are kids with serious academic issues. I have no idea what happened at that party, but—"

"Then I think maybe you should find out."

"Isn't that a job for the cops?"

"I'm making it your job, too."

Herman decided this was the appropriate moment to lecture Wade at some length on the problems and needs of the diverse student population of the CSUs; once more it was all for Allenby's benefit, so he could see just how far out in front of the PC parade she was. Wade's eyes were starting to glaze over again when she asked him to step out while she conferred with Allenby about the coaching committee. He fairly hopped to his feet, trotted into the presumed sanctuary of the outer office; there, however, he found awaiting him another scowl, this one coming at him sideways from a butch administrative assistant who was flirting baldly with the notoriously androgynous department secretary. Wade averted his eyes and amused himself by fantasizing about peeling the pumpkin suit off their boss and parading her naked through the campus with an "All hope abandon, ye who enter here" sign flapping over her bush.

He was starting to wonder if he should give up, go to his office, and pretend to get some work done when Allenby finally emerged half an hour later, looking peeved. The unflappable man was having a tough week.

"Blondie make another pass at you?"

"Never got past the crotch staring phase."

"Got to admit, she's lookin' pretty juicy."

Allenby winced. "That suit: she looks like a fucking pumpkin."

Wade grinned. *Great minds think alike.* "I'm making arrangements for a costume change."

"She hit me up for the new women's locker room. *And* she wants me to chair the committee for the football coaching hire."

"No shit? I thought she was supposed to do that herself."

"Her day to delegate, I guess. There's a chance she might be pushing for a promotion. Moving on to bigger things."

"But she just got this job a year ago."

Allenby shrugged. "Riding Lytle's coattails, I guess. Did you hear your president might be leaving?"

"He's been looking since the day he got here. Nobody wants him so far. You're not suggesting *she* could be the president?"

Allenby shrugged. "The Board of Trustees has done stranger things here. They gave *you* a job, didn't they?"

"Yeah, but I have friends in high places. What did you tell her about the committee?"

"I told her whether I chair the committee or not, there's going to be a fair shake for the minority candidates. And I changed the math a little to make sure."

"Oh, yeah? How did you—"

"I told her I'd consider taking the chair if she puts you on."

"Thanks for consulting me first. You want to do my private investigation work?"

"Hey, you got time to watch a triple-header on Sunday, you can spare a few hours to do this with me."

"But she thinks I'm a shit disturber. Gordon Brooks told her I tried to beat him to death with my bare hands."

"Brooks? That's the assistant chairman of your old department, right? I thought you said that was just a love tap."

Wade allowed himself a second to revel in the memory, still tactile, of the epic moment a year ago when his erstwhile boss had interrupted an intimate moment in Angela's office in celebration of Wade's new job, and Wade had given the ultimate backslapper a taste of his own. "Think Palomalu greeting Gronkowski when he comes over the middle, something on that order. I took my best shot. He's lucky he can still walk. But he's the department chair now."

"How the hell did that happen? I thought you said he was a moron."

Wade shrugged, turned his palms up. "Was, is, and will ever be. But he didn't die, and he wouldn't retire, so they promoted him. His asshole buddy Dean Dedalus gave him the job; those two are tighter than Hoover and Clyde. Business as usual on this campus. Anyway, there's no way Herman will agree to put me on—"

"She said no, all right. That's when I stormed out. I had to get out of that meeting somehow anyway." Allenby paused, looked at his watch, shook his head in disgust. "My bet is she'll come around, sooner or—"

Allenby's cell phone rang. He answered it, listened for a moment, said, "Fine," clicked off, and grinned at Wade.

"Welcome to my team. We meet at three."

CHAPTER 5

Avoid running at all times. It angries up the
blood.
—Satchel Paige

Most of us learn to write at age seven. Then
we move on to more important things.
—Bobby Knight

Wade was learning how to walk. It might have been
reasonably expected that a man of his years would have long
since mastered the act, but Wade was a slow learner. Except
when it came to books, he'd always had to learn things the
hard way, out of long, harsh, and humiliating experience. He
had tried and embarrassed himself utterly and often hurtfully in
many forms of recreation involving bats, balls, nets, rims, and
rackets before concluding that he was meant to partake of these
endeavors as an observer only. Turning to individual sports had
only made matters worse: swimming made his eyeballs bleed
and his few remaining follicles abandon scalp even faster;
jogging made his feet, knees, and back ache for days afterward;
and, Allenby's example notwithstanding, the only emotion even
remotely approximating the "runner's high" that Wade had ever
experienced in that horrifying form of self-abuse was the blissful
relief that came when he stopped.

Some of his CSU colleagues, evidently at a loss unless
affiliated with a bureaucratic superstructure to guide their hours
not devoted to classes or conferences, had formed a campus
walking club. They even paid dues. Wade, by nature not a joiner,
had found his own path lighted when one of his new counseling
confreres, who had been urging Wade to join him in prepping
for a marathon, had dropped dead of a heart attack on mile two

of his planned ten-mile "warm up" run. The wake-up call was clarion: walk, don't run.

One of the simple truths Wade had discovered was that good company made a walk go much faster. (Bad company, on the other hand, could turn it into yet another interminable faculty gassing, as he'd also had occasion to discover.) Today, after a quick bite of lunch, he had put himself safely in the fellowship of his good friend Erica Wiley, a scholar on the Harlem Renaissance nearing retirement but to Wade's good fortune so far declining to embrace it. A few years younger than Allenby, Wade guessed, she had retained a sleek and stylish frame and had a face that could have passed for someone's half her age. They met twice a week at noon for a brisk two miles, which with a bit of practice they had winnowed to just a bit more than half an hour, although neither of them now watched the clock. They walked and talked, and before they knew it, the mileage and the time were gone and the day's cholesterol intake at least partially purged.

Today their topic, after the inescapable diatribe about the athletic director's outfit, had turned to the even more alarming matter of Yoshi's increasingly insistent interest in bearing Wade's child. Wade knew that Erica had been married a couple of times but had no children; he learned now that she had no regrets on that score.

"The truth is, I'm just too selfish. It's too damn much responsibility. I enjoy my freedom. Am I allowed to say that?"

"I could kiss you for saying that."

"In your dreams, Fleischman." His friend wasn't above an occasional flirtation, and that didn't make the walks any less enjoyable for Wade. "Of course some people will tell you that you haven't really lived unless you've had children. Your Delia Herman, for example."

"Really? I thought she was a lesbian."

"Oh, she is *now*," Erica acknowledged, "but she came to it later in life. A second calling, so to speak. But with the conversion came no detachment from the primacy of spreading the gospel of parenting. I have the distinct misfortune to serve on a committee with her, and she never stops yapping about her spawn. Just the other day she said to me, 'You don't know what you've missed by not having children.' This from a woman who drove both of her daughters to the clinic for abortions, one of them three times!"

"That might be enough to turn *me* into a lesbian, too," Wade conceded.

"Not to mention the twin overdoses, one accidental, one deliberate, the pot selling bust, the multiple DUIs, the freeway crash, the shoplifting conviction, or the HIV scare."

"And they probably forget to call on Mother's Day, too."

"Dogs," Erica said firmly, "are the only way to go."

"They shit a lot, though," Wade in all fairness felt obliged to observe.

"True," Erica said. "But unlike children, not *on* you."

Wade, latent uncle and quondam dogsitter, befouled in his day by babe and beast alike, considered silent assent but could not in good faith manage it.

"Actually—"

"At least not every day," Erica emended with a prescient smile.

"Thank you. I was going to say, 'You don't know what you've missed.'"

Wade called to mind the week's headlines: one baby retrieved alive, if just barely, from the dumpster where her teenaged addict mom had tossed her; another scorched by his dad in a microwave; a third, eight months old, whose mother had tried to hang her before stepping into a noose of her own. All three would live; what kind of lives, Wade had to wonder, with that kind of a start? What was it that impelled such misfits to reproduce?

"This Yoshi business: it's all part of the plot to get a certain someone to tie the knot, isn't it?"

"I suppose. Amazing that she'd want to mix her chromosomes with mine, though."

"All the same, I hope you're taking appropriate precautions."

"Oh, of course. The rhythm method and a 'Hail Mary' or two afterwards ought to do the trick, don't you think?"

"You shouldn't mess around with God, Wade. He might give you triplets, joined at the forehead."

"Now that's the kind of God I could get behind. Why didn't they tell me about *Him* when I went to Sunday school? All I ever got was that 'Jesus Loves Me' crap."

"That's why you dropped out?"

"Did I ever tell you about Raymond Berry in the overtime game?"

"Several times."

"Oh."

"You should be careful with this Yoshi, Wade. I have a feeling you're dancing with the devil there."

"What do you mean?"

"You don't love this girl, but you're intimate with her. That's usually a recipe for disaster."

"Well, when I was . . . intimate with the woman I loved, that turned out to be a disaster, too. What's the difference?"

"I know this sounds weird coming from a woman who survived the 'screw anything that moves' '60s, but there's almost always some kind of emotional component to sex, at least for us women. Even when we say there isn't, there usually is."

"She doesn't love me either."

"But she wants to marry you and have your baby?"

"She wants to be a citizen. That's her game plan for getting there. I can't really picture her getting off on changing diapers. I imagine the baby is just a jump start."

Erica nodded. "I'd say that's a good way to make a bad idea a whole lot worse."

"I've made that speech several times myself."

"But the message hasn't been received?"

"She's nothing if not persistent."

"You're in for trouble there, Wade."

"She . . . takes my mind off Angela."

"The heartless bitch who screwed you over?"

Wade had formed the same description a thousand times in his mind but was taken aback to hear it now from his friend. "That would be one way to put it. But . . . I thought you liked Angela."

Erica and Angela had been colleagues, apparently congenial, when Angela had been in the department.

"I do. It was just an exercise in narrative perspective. Gender bending and all that. I was trying to see the world from your point of view."

"Sort of disturbing, isn't it?"

"It's not something I'd want to do every day," she admitted.

"Imagine how I feel."

"You're still in love with her, aren't you?"

"Right. *She* . . . might be coming back."

"You're in for trouble there, too, aren't you?" Erica tsked and shook her head. "Two women, at your age."

Visions of an epic ménage-à-trois flickered briefly through Wade's head. "Oh, I don't know. Maybe they'll get into a fight over me and scratch each other's eyes out."

"Good plan, Wade. Then you can make your move on Delia Herman, see if you can bring her back around to the hetero team."

"Why didn't *I* think of that?"

"Since you mentioned it, I did hear something about Angela's being recruited to apply for an administrative position here."

So *that's* what she'd been talking about. "Getting rid of Gordo? God, what an upgrade that would—"

"I doubt she'd settle for department chair," Erica said. "I'm thinking her sights are higher."

"Shit, I just remembered: isn't this the last year for Dean Deadass?"

Erica nodded. "He's been ROTJ for years."

"Do you think she—"

"Could be."

"She was hoping for Columbia, though," Wade said. "Hard to imagine she'd give up on that to come back here, even as—"

"Maybe it's some*one* she's coming back to instead of somewhere."

"Hard to imagine that, too." *And impossible to think about anything else.*

They'd reached the entrance to the women's locker room.

Wade had one more question.

"What can you tell me about Alden Hotchkiss?"

"Christ. Nothing, really. Is he still alive?"

"Only online, as far as I know."

"In that case I won't waste my time thinking about him in the shower."

In his own shower Wade found himself wondering if Erica ever wasted any of her time thinking about *him*. He'd had plenty of lustful thoughts about her, to be sure, but, as usual, had lacked the initiative to try for anything more than conversation. She was another of the many women who, as Allenby had reminded him, were beyond his reach. Maybe he would introduce her to him, now that Nora was cashing out, see if that could go anywhere. Probably made more sense than running the risk of ruining his own friendship with her.

In spite of reaching this sensible conclusion, Wade found himself becoming stimulated by the mere thought of frolicking with Erica, so he thought about Angela again, then thought about Angela in the shower, then thought about Angela in the shower with Ronnie. Fuck. He drenched himself with cold water that was no longer needed, toweled off, and forced his attention to the matter of Professor Alden Hotchkiss.

Hotchkiss was a retired CSU full-timer approaching his eighties who had been reincarnated as an adjunct professor when the online education explosion had occurred, the English Department had suddenly needed bodies, if not exactly warm then at least not clinically deceased, and the even vaguely sentient emeriti had quickly figured out they could score some easy money without ever leaving their easy chairs. Far from grappling with the ink-stained wretches as in the trenches of yore, they could now log in from Rarotonga if they wanted to.

The Athletic Department was equally delighted with the arrangement, by which putatively academic classes could be conveniently crammed into the schedules of student-athletes without filling up their days with anything that would conflict with their more important activities, such as practicing for several hours a day, lifting weights, studying their playbooks, honing their video game skills, boning their groupies, and getting their beauty rest. Within the English Department, several prime candidates had emerged as favored online instructors for the "academically challenged" members of the football and basketball teams. Especially valued were those faculty known for "student-friendly" policies, meaning that they assigned scant homework, accepted any excuse for not getting it done, and gave out grades like candy for whatever crap came in. As an added bonus in the case of Professor Hotchkiss, his assignments had remained largely unchanged for decades, so there were plenty of recyclable papers floating around that could be downloaded, submitted, and accepted with minimal effort or risk since to all appearances he never bothered to check the authenticity of his students' work.

Until recently the arrangement had gone smoothly, with girlfriends, tutors, and assorted other hired geeks and flunkies cranking out papers, a shitload of A's and B's accruing for the jocks, and no complaints on file. Of late, however, there had been an unforeseen glitch in the process: several of the football players in Hotchkiss's current online sections, A.J. Dupree and Thaddeus Marston among them, had reported getting their essays back with failing grades and uncharacteristically acerbic comments. After meeting with the disgruntled athletes, Wade had attempted to contact the instructor. This had proven futile, as Hotchkiss ignored both phone calls and emails, and no office hours were required of the online faculty. Finally Wade had resorted to contacting a student who had been assigned to assist Hotchkiss in the role of reader, an arrangement typical in the California colleges and universities and carried to an extreme resembling indentured servitude at CSU. For something like $8.00 an hour, advanced students would do the mind-numbing work of deciphering and annotating the disjointed drivel that spewed in epic proportions from the pens, pencils, and personal computers of undergraduates, many of whom had been diagnosed upon entrance to the university as reading and writing somewhere around the sixth grade level (an affront, Wade often felt, to legitimate sixth graders everywhere). With California down near the bottom of the pile next to Mississippi and Alabama in dollars spent per pupil on public education, there was no reason to be surprised by this state of affairs. Asking minimum-wage student-readers to solve the problem while paying coaches, provosts, presidents, and their appointed plenipotentiaries hundreds of thousands a year in salary and perks was apparently the CSU strategy, and it was Wade's lot to deal with the results.

He went to his office, where he had arranged to meet Hotchkiss's assistant. Dixon James turned out to be a short, slight African-American with close-cropped hair and thick glasses. It was hard to tell exactly how old he was, but he would not have looked entirely out of place dodging spitballs on a middle school campus.

Wade fought off the double-take, shook hands, seated his visitor, thanked him for coming. "How did you get matched up with Professor Hotchkiss?"

"I'm in his class."

"You're *in* the class that you're reading papers for?"

Dixon shrugged. "He read my first paper and wanted me to help him. I guess he's pretty busy."

"How many papers does he give you?"

"All of them, I guess."

"He has three composition sections. He gives you all of the papers from three sections?"

"I guess so. It's about ninety a week. Or it was at the beginning. Some of them have dropped. Quite a few, actually."

"Do you evaluate the content or just mark grammar and spelling errors for him?"

"Grammar, spelling, organization, development — everything, really. I mark it all."

"Did he train you?"

"I didn't really need any training. Any fool could mark freshman papers."

Wade had to admit there was some truth to that.

"A monkey could do it, really," Dixon continued. "Sometimes when I'm busy with my other job, my sister helps me. She's eleven."

"How old are *you*?"

"I'll be sixteen in February."

"Shouldn't you be in high school?"

"I skipped it. My father said high school is a waste of time. I was going to go just so I could play football, but they don't take too many guys that are a hundred and ten pounds on the team."

"So you were home schooled? How did that work out?"

"I got 800s on the SAT math and comp, 790 on the verbal."

"Well, I guess you really screwed *that* up."

"They made a mistake on one of the questions."

"I should have known. What's your other job?"

"That's confidential."

"I see." Wade studied the composed face across the desk from him. "Please don't tell me he lets you put the grades on the papers, too."

Dixon shrugged again. "That's not hard. Most of them are D or F."

"Some of the students are complaining that the grading scale is way too tough. Has Hotchkiss talked to you about that?"

"I've never talked to him."

"He just emails you?"

"Mostly I just email him."

"Do you know if he emails the other students?"

"I don't think so. They email their papers to me. I grade them, post some comments, and email them back. He doesn't get involved in that part."

"He doesn't read the papers at all?"

"I don't know. He doesn't need to. That's my job. *I'm* the reader."

Wade clicked on his computer and brought up Hotchkiss's home page. "I checked out his online lectures. They look okay."

"I do those for him too. He had a few on his website that his granddaughter or somebody tried to put on there for him, but they sucked, so I got rid of them and wrote some new ones. Nobody reads 'em, though. They're supposed to, but you can tell from their papers that they haven't even looked at them."

Wade nodded. "Hence the D's and F's."

"That's one reason. Plus they write like crap. I don't know

how much difference it would make if they tried to read the assignments. I can't believe you let these guys into your university."

Wade shrugged. "Actually I don't personally set the admission policies. Anyone with a 2.0 who hasn't shot someone in high school or sold drugs to the principal's daughter is basically guaranteed admission."

"That's fucked up."

"At least it's a job. For you as well as for me. If you're going to be available later today, I'll introduce you to a couple of your prize pupils." The district attorney had declined for now to press charges, pending further investigation, against the arrested CSU players. They were back on campus, and Wade had summoned them for a late afternoon interrogation/strategy session.

Dixon frowned, looked at his watch. "Is *this* meeting about over then? I've got a lot of—"

"Papers to grade?"

"I'm fifteen. That's my excuse. What's yours?"

"What do you mean?"

"I mean, you don't seem too stupid or anything. How did a smart guy like you get stuck with a job like this? Are you actually going to do this for like the rest of your life?"

Wade had asked himself that question more than a few times over the years when staggering home with a briefcase bursting with his students' handiwork. Like anyone else who had ever taught multiple sections of freshman composition, halfway through a stack he'd often felt like constructing a pyre, using his red pen to commit hara-kiri, and jumping into the flames to get the agony over with a little quicker. Fortunately, in the last year his counseling appointment had cut down on his paperwork considerably. "You're not the only guy who can hold down more than one job, you know."

"Oh, yeah? What else do you—"

Wade grinned. Payback. "That's confidential." He stood up. "Actually, I've got another meeting to go to."

"That sounds exciting."

Wade nodded. "I think it's the only thing that's worse than

grading papers. Of course, I've never stormed a beach under heavy machine gun fire or bailed out of a flaming plane into shark-infested waters, so I can't say for sure. When I find out, you'll be the first to know."

Dixon's turn to nod. "Just send me an email, though, okay?"

CHAPTER 6

You came to the University of Miami to play
football. If you wanted an education, you
should have gone to Harvard.
> —attributed to Jimmy Johnson by
> Michael Irvin

Our ancestors risked their lives so they could
read and write. Young kids equate education
as being white. How did it get from risking
our lives, castrated and hung up, whatever, to
learn to read and write, to being ridiculed?
> —Spike Lee, at University of the
> Pacific, February 5, 2003

"There are twenty-eight men's and women's varsity athletic
programs on this campus. Not a single one of them has ever
had an African-American or Hispanic head coach. This is fairly
typical of what occurs nationwide, and football is a case in point.
Nearly half of all the players in major college football programs
are from ethnic minority backgrounds, but fewer than ten percent
of the head coaches are. This committee is going to make damn
sure that qualified applicants of all colors get real consideration
for the head football coaching job at this university."

"We're also going to hire a coach who can keep his players
under control."

After years of enduring the torture of attending meetings
run by the Delia Hermans and Gordon Brookses of the world,
watching Allenby run one turned out to be for Wade a veritable
revelation. For starters, there was an agenda, short and clear;
what's more, it was actually followed. No digressions, diatribes,
or mindless maunderings on topics totally unrelated to the
matter at hand were permitted. Whenever one of the immensely

self-impressed alumni in attendance tried in stentorian tones to interrupt to inject an irrelevance, Allenby would firmly deny the floor and move on to the next item of business.

Wade noted the irony of the committee's composition: for all of her politically correct prattle about diversity in the modern university, Herman had assembled for this task the same core that had hired the last two football coaches, mostly white guys in or nearing their dotage. A few token representatives of other departments had clearly been selected with the expectation that they would mind their own business and keep their mouths shut. The power to be reckoned with in the group obviously was Cal Logan, now a real estate tycoon but previously a quarterback at CSU; he had led the team that last won a bowl game for the school, and there was no doubt that he saw himself leading the charge to get them back to the promised land after more than forty arid years. He had been the driving force behind the hire of Matt Lytle two years ago and had made no secret of his desire to keep the coach in CSU's employ. Wade wondered if the athletic director had even begun to reckon with the change in dynamics she had wrought by putting Allenby in charge of this crew.

When Logan raised at the earliest opportunity the question of renegotiating with Lytle to convince him to change his mind and stay, Allenby simply ran the numbers: the base salary in Lytle's new deal was set at two million dollars, with another two million in guaranteed ancillary income, a million dollar bonus for reaching a New Year's Day bowl, another million for winning it, and yet another million for winning a national championship. North Carolina State had never won one of those in football, so the last part of the deal was perhaps fanciful, but the rest of it looked reachable for Lytle—and totally out of reach for CSU.

Allenby looked around the room. "There's no way we could ever come close to matching that deal, unless you gentlemen want to come up with about a million apiece."

"I'm in," Wade couldn't resist interjecting.

Logan glared at him. Allenby smiled and said, "Anyone else?" He looked at the alums in turn. No takers. "Then let's find ourselves a football coach we can afford."

Having set that gambit swiftly to rest, Allenby divided responsibilities for identifying candidates, assigned progress reports, and set a date for the next meeting.

The whole thing was over in thirty-six minutes.

"Those were some heavy stats you threw out there," Wade said, when the others had left.

"There's a guy named Lapchick in Florida who keeps track of that stuff on the national level. He says football head coach is the most segregated position in all of college sports."

Wade thought about it. "I don't imagine there are too many black coaches in hockey or aquatics either, but—"

"Forty-five percent of the athletes in those sports aren't black."

"At least the numbers for football are improving. Having Obama in office seems to be helping."

Allenby had met the candidate during the primary season in 2008 and had donated substantially to his cause. Wade had blown off a few elections in his time but had made a point of voting in that one and planned to do so again in the next. He'd been a kid when JFK was gunned down and a teen when Bobby and King had joined him in martyrdom; few of the pols who'd followed them into prominence had seemed worth a trip to the ballot box. It felt a little weird now having a president who was younger than he was, but Wade had found himself becoming hopeful again, his enthusiasm attenuated only by the fall-back into holy water after the absurd accusations of a jihadist background.

"I just wish he could have managed to leave The Great Redeemer off his campaign team," he'd said to Allenby at the time of the election.

"He wanted to win," Allenby had bluntly replied. "This country will elect a gay Puerto Rican quadriplegic president before we pick one who hasn't been personally saved by Jesus. You know that—and so did he. He had to win first in order to get the chance to accomplish anything else."

"The question is," Allenby now said, as he gathered his notes from the meeting, "whether we can take the leap from presidential politics to hiring football coaches."

Wade nodded. "Americans take their football a lot more seriously than their country."

"Cal Logan's going to have a problem even looking at anyone but Lytle, I can tell."

"I thought you shut him up really well in there today."

Allenby looked at his watch. "We'll do better next time. I'm giving him ten minutes max for his progress report. He goes over, I'll have Fuzzy come down from the fourth floor and sit on his face."

"Sounds like a photo op there. I'll let PR know." Wade grinned, glad that he had shared his Green Bay vision with someone who could appreciate it. "I get the feeling there's something between you and Logan."

"There is." Allenby thought for a minute about what he wanted to say. "His version is that he beat me out for the quarterback job here half a century or so ago. My version is a little different."

Wade frowned in puzzlement. He knew that Allenby had been a prominent sixth man on the CSU basketball team. "I didn't know you played football here, too."

"I didn't. I switched to basketball after the coach made Logan the starter on the JV team, because I knew that meant he'd get the job on the varsity down the road."

"So you were a quarterback in high school?"

"I was a tailback. I went to one of the last high schools in L.A. that was still running the single wing, so I got to throw the ball a bit. Mostly I was a runner, but I could throw a decent pass, too."

"Better than Logan?"

"He would say no. He came out of a program that was running almost a pro set, so he had more experience reading defenses and finding receivers, that sort of thing. I tried to convince the coach I could learn that stuff, but he wanted me to play cornerback. Told me I'd have a better shot at the NFL that way than trying to play quarterback."

Wade thought about it, tried to put the conversation into historical context. "That would have been the 60s, so . . . given the attitudes that existed, was he right?"

"Probably. But I didn't want to hear it. I just wanted a chance to play quarterback. Besides, there wasn't near the money in pro ball that there is now. I was planning on law school all along. Of course they didn't exactly roll out the red carpet for me there either, but . . . ."

Allenby shrugged, and his voice trailed off. He didn't make a habit of reciting his accomplishments or the obstacles he had overcome. Wade had pieced together most of the remarkable story. After bartending his way through law school at Stanford, Allenby had become one of the most successful African-American entrepreneurs on the West Coast. Not getting to play quarterback would have been one of the lesser impediments in his path.

"Anyway, I walked on to the basketball team, won a scholarship there, so that worked out okay for me. Okay for the football team, too—Logan did all right, too. He was a decent quarterback, just full of crap. Kind of strange I wind up butting heads with him again after all these years."

Wade nodded. "Great job by the A.D. of *diversifying* our committee, wasn't it?"

Allenby shrugged again. "She figured she covered her ass by making me chair."

"You find out anything today you didn't already know?" Wade asked. "Surprised the alums didn't try to say more about the character issues?"

"Not surprised at all. Those good old boys were sick and tired of finishing in last place, so they like what Lytle did. They just want to win. They don't care about the character of the players *or* the coach. Hell, they'd bust Charlie Manson out of Corcoran and put *him* in charge if he could beat Fresno State."

"I hear he's got some great gadget plays."

"He's had a lot of time to work on them. What did you find out about the players at that party?"

"They've been released. I'll hear their story after practice."

"Lytle didn't suspend them before he left?"

"I guess he was too busy."

Allenby nodded. "We'd better get busy and get ourselves a new coach then, too. Let me know how your meeting with his gangbangers goes."

Wade had first met A.J. Dupree and Thaddeus Marston in September, at the behest of the academic vice president, when they were on the brink of suspension for their violations of the campus honor code. They had been scheduled in different discussion sections of two of the same classes, and it seemed that one or the other had come up with the bright idea that they should take each other's tests, Dupree being slightly more adept at the sort of critical thinking that was called for in their Basic Math course, and expectant father Marston, by his own lights at least, something of a Black History buff. The stratagem had backfired when Marston's jilted former girlfriend, also currently enceinte, had exacted her revenge for his more corporeal form of cheating by ratting the two of them loudly out in front of the whole history lecture section. Only the considerable pull of the football program had kept them from dismissal then. They had been forced to drop the classes they'd collaborated in, then thrown into late-starting online classes to replace the units and into a trash-collection detail to repay their debt to society.

Wade seated his visitors in his office, looked across his desk at the dramatically scarred Dupree, who was checking text messages, and Marston, who was stifling a yawn.

"Sorry, Doc," Marston said. "Had me another all-nighter."

"Studying?"

Dupree snorted. "Studyin' pussy. Got his new girl in the room, I can't get no sleep neither."

"That's bull. She was out of there by two. You jerked off, snorin' like a motherfucker long before then anyway."

Marston turned back to Wade. "Helpin' my girl with the baby. She *never* sleep at night."

"You best beat some sense into that bitch. *Her* job take care of the baby."

"Maybe that sociology major you've been looking at will work out after all, A.J.," Wade said. "Have you thought about marriage counseling as a career?"

"Just tell this mofo here to get him a quiet bitch, don't keep me up all night listenin' to her fuckin' moanin'," Dupree said to Wade, then turned and thrust his cell phone toward Marston. "Here what a nigger's dick s'pose to look like."

Wade realized that rather than merely texting in his presence, Dupree had been surfing for porn. No disrespect intended, of course.

Marston threw up a hand to block the undoubtedly mythic organ on display. "You just jealous cause you don't know nothin' 'bout givin' a woman pleasure."

"You sayin' you fuck better than me? With that little—"

"As much as I'd enjoy judging that contest, gentlemen," Wade interrupted, "I think we'd better turn our attention to salvaging your classes if you intend to stay eligible for your bowl game. I know there are still some problems with your English class. I'm working on getting you some help. How are those other online classes going, Thaddeus?"

"Call me Mars, man."

"Okay, Mars, how are—"

"Got it covered, Doc. Computer tutor know his stuff for sure."

"Picking up trash sucks, though," Dupree said. "You never believe the shit people leave on the ground on this campus."

"Plus them orange jumpsuits ain't exactly prime bling."

"Better take your own tests from now on."

Marston grinned, glanced at his former partner in crime. "Online okay. Get some help there, nobody know, nobody care."

Chalk up another triumph for America's educational and criminal justice systems.

"We need to talk about what happened at the party."

"We didn't do nothin' wrong."

"Until you started shooting people, you mean?"

"I didn't shoot nobody."

Dupree snorted again. "What you mean 'I', motherfucker?"

No "I" in team, Wade remembered.

"Didn't neither one of us shoot nobody," Marston clarified. "That's all just media."

"Well, somebody got shot at. I don't think the media did it."

Dupree glared at Wade. "Listen, man, if I shot at some motherfucker, he'd be 10-45D."

"Me, too."

"Bullshit, Marston. You ain't shot shit. Fuckin' Marin County mafia."

Dupree had paved his path to Matt Lytle's defensive line by being expelled for fighting from several high schools in Oakland. He had also earned the rare distinction of being kicked off the football team at the University of Miami. He took a dim view of those less eminently qualified. Marston frowned at the reproof.

"Just 'cause I ain't been arrested twelve times don't mean I can't pop a cap in your black ass."

"Good idea," Wade said. "Maybe later, though, okay? In the meantime the cops have reported that the gun that was fired at the party had both of your prints on it."

"Gun had a shitload of prints on it," Dupree said, then turned his glare to Marston. "*Some*body just brought it to the party for protection. Jokers got high, started playin', passin' it around. Then Bludge got out of line, somebody decide to teach him a lesson."

"Bludge?"

"Motherfuckin' cracker asshole."

"Linebacker on the team," Marston explained.

"You're talking about Louis Blodgett, right? He's the one who made the tackle on the fumbled punt against San Diego State."

Dupree nodded. "Pulled that mofo down by his dreads and—"

"Tried to scalp the brother," Marston threw in. "Bludge the only white starter on D. He start ahead of me. On special teams, too. That's some more bullshit right there."

Dupree laughed. "Maybe Mars shot him to get his spot."

"Shut up, motherfuck. I didn't shoot nobody. Remember where that gun come from?"

"I *told* you not to . . . *you're* the one who—just shut up, motherfucker." Dupree looked at Wade. "You call in Bludge yet, talk to him? He tell you it was Mars or me shot at him?"

"I haven't talked to him."

"Maybe you should."

"What you mean?" Marston objected. "Motherfucker's crazy."

"We'll let Doc here decide about that."

"I'll see what he has to say." Wade looked back and forth between them, sighed. Dupree was texting or sexting again, and Marston was still yawning. "In the meantime, there's someone else I want you to meet."

Wade explained the arrangements he had made for Dixon James to tutor the two of them on their writing assignments and perhaps to help them with other coursework as well.

"You sayin' the same guy been rapin' us on our grades s'pose to help us out now?"

"He still be gradin' us, though, right?" Marston asked. "So if we write what he tell us, we should do okay?"

"Or we could kick his ass, get our grade that way."

Dixon knocked on Wade's open door, right on cue. *Reporting for ass kicking, sir.*

Wade watched with interest as the three of them eyed each other: Dixon impassive, Marston smiling craftily, Dupree putting his penitentiary face on display.

"You the ace tutor we bin hearin' about, huh?"

"How come you got to be such a hard ass on your gradin'? Can't you give a nigger a break?"

Dixon looked at Wade. "Are you sure these guys really want my help?"

"Look like you the one need help," Dupree said. "How much you lift, motherfucker?"

Dixon looked at Wade again. "You told them my name?"

Marston laughed. "That your last name or—"

Wade stood to interrupt. "Now that the introductions are out of the way, I think it's time for you guys to get to work. I'm going to clear out of here and let you have my office for a couple of hours."

"Couple of *hours*? I can't be studyin' middle of the fuckin' day for—"

"My advice is give this man a chance to help you as much as he can. *If* you want to play in that bowl game."

"*Man*? I don't see nothin' here but a little bitty black bookworm."

"Little bitty bookworm with a giant brain, gonna help us out if you give him a chance, A.J."

"Didn't know bookworm come in that color." Dupree glared again as Wade prepared to exit. "Least you could do is get us a tutor with some titties."

Dixon looked at Wade, then back at Dupree, and blew out a deep breath. "I'll show you mine if you shut the fuck up."

Marston cracked up again. "You go ahead, Doc. This little brother gonna be okay with us."

Dupree twisted his lips, glanced at Marston, mean-mugged Dixon, then nodded at Wade. "Don't work out, we'll tell you where to come pick up the parts, 'case you want to donate his giant brain to science, or"—he turned the glare on Dixon again—"his little bitty bookworm dick."

CHAPTER 7

Insanity is hereditary. You catch it from your kids.

— Ronald Reagan

We ought to be paying them *not* to have children.

— Eartha Kitt

Tom Brady threw another perfectly arched pass into the corner of the end zone, far from the futile flailings of the five-eleven cornerback, where only New England's leviathan tight end could reach it. The Patriots upped their lead to four scores.

"Look at those teeth," Wade pointed out in awe as the screen showed the helmetless QB smiling on the sideline. "He's just about perfect, isn't he? You think he's the best ever?"

"Best teeth, maybe," Allenby said. "Hard to beat Unitas or Montana with the game on the line."

Wade grinned, secretly pleased to have this article of his own faith confirmed. "Old fogey."

"Spoken by a man who refuses to get a cell phone."

"Look how much joy and satisfaction *yours* has brought into—"

"Of course, they played in a time when the best athletes didn't usually get a shot at quarterback. Ask me again in ten years when the kids coming along now have had a chance to redefine the possibilities of the position. The only thing that bothers me about your pretty boy there"—Allenby nodded at the screen, which now showed Brady laughing over a photograph of the coverage scheme he had just thwarted—"is why the media give him a free pass about his *filius nullius*. Imagine the trash you'd hear about that if he were black. Remember all the crap that came out about Derrick Thomas after he died in that crazy snow crash? How he'd won the NFL's Man of the Year Award for his community service, but then they played up the pimp daddy angle?"

"Seven kids by five different women," Wade remembered.

"Isn't Clint Eastwood tied with Thomas? Doesn't he have seven kids by five different women, too?"

"That sounds right."

"Nicholson's got extramarital kids, too, right? How come we almost never hear about that shit with those guys instead of all about their Oscar nominations?"

Wade nodded. "Or if we do, it's always what great fathers they are and how they support all of those kids financially."

"As if a signing a check was all it takes to be a father." Allenby sighed. "I'm gonna have dinner with The Dink. Want to ride shotgun?"

"Are you meeting the bride?"

"Not sure. He said she was nervous, might chicken out."

"Out of the dinner or out of the wedding?"

"I like the way you think. Let's hope for the best."

Wade wondered, without much conviction, if it was possible that Prince Pembleton had progressed beyond pubescence since he had doodled and snoozed through Wade's class the year before. Five seconds inside his dorm room was enough to lay to rest that faint hope. The décor was retro-punk-psychedelic, the ambiance a blend of dope, beer, cigarettes, incense, and vomit. Clothes, shoes, CDs, magazines, peanut shells, popcorn kernels, and food wrappers were scattered everywhere.

"My roommate's a pig," Pembleton explained, as Allenby stepped gingerly in, taking care not to brush his shoes, buffed to a sheen that would have passed General Patton's personal inspection, against any of the debris crowding the floor. "None of this crap practically is mine."

Wade lingered in the doorway, surveyed the littered path, searched for improvised explosive devices. "Is any of this stuff wired to blow, or—"

Pembleton grinned fuzzily at Wade. His face seemed a bit

less radioactive than the last time Wade had seen it, although that was a bit like comparing Chernobyl to Hiroshima.

"I'm doing good in English 1B, Doc."

"Well."

"I think I might major in English."

"You've ruled out medical school, then?"

"I got an A in English 1A, you know."

"Congratulations."

"I took it online."

"There's a surprise."

"That C you stuck me with in Bonehead didn't help my GPA any, though."

"He gave you the grade you deserved," Allenby said curtly.

And spared you the stoning you deserved even more.

"Where's your fiancée? She ditching us?"

"Nuh uh. She went to change. She's really uptight about meeting you."

"You tell her what an ogre I am?"

"What's an o-ger?"

Allenby looked at Wade. "Didn't do much vocabulary building in that class did you?"

"We concentrated on putting a period at the end of a sentence."

"I've got that shit down cold now," Pembleton boasted. "Or if I can't figure out if it should be a period or a comma, I just throw in a semicolon. Works every time. You're a great teacher, Doc. Even if you are a hardass grader."

"Thanks for the testimonial."

A timid knock on the door behind them announced the arrival of Jennifer. What she had changed *from* Wade would have paid a month's salary to see. He remembered the various combinations of garments she had worn in a desperate attempt to attract attention to herself when she had been in his class. Having reached the groves of academe in the era when the gods of fashion had decreed that young women should wear their lingerie to class, she had several times exceeded even the considerable self-exposure efforts of her peers. What she was wearing now was a translucent blouse with a black push-up bra, complemented by a microscopic green skirt, stretched tight over substantial thighs encased in black fishnet stockings. She had augmented the effect by applying more make-up than Wade had ever seen one woman wear. It appeared to be enough to take care of a whole classroom full of coeds for a semester, with enough left over to send some to Elvis's ex in case the next face-lift didn't undo the depredations of the last. Wade reminded himself to ask Allenby about investing in cosmetics. Somebody had to be making a killing there.

"Hi, Dr. Wade. Do you remember me? You gave me a C."

"He gives everybody a C," Pembleton announced, generalizing from the two cases known to him and bypassing the handful of honor grades and the many less edifying that Wade had awarded in Developmental English each time he'd had the privilege of teaching it. "Jen, this is my father."

Allenby extended a courtly hand to his future step-daughter-in-law, who placed her own hand into it meekly and then quickly withdrew it. Wade noticed that her fingernails were chewed to the quick. *I'd be eating my own flesh, too*, he thought, *if I were engaged to The Dink*.

"Where are we going?" Allenby asked. "McDonald's okay with everyone?"

"That's super," Jennifer said. "We eat there all the time."

Judging from her physique, not slender to begin with and to which she appeared to have added a good thirty pounds beyond the Freshman Fifteen that Wade had watched accruing, this was probably true. He wondered, as he was sure Allenby was wondering again as well, whether any of the weight gain was attributable to a little Pembleton in the womb.

"He's kidding," her fiancé told her. He turned to Allenby. "I mean, I *hope* you are." Then narrowed his eyes, trying to trust the joke himself. "*You* wouldn't eat in a McDonald's unless—"

Wade waited with interest to see how the sentence would finish. Figurative discourse had not been The Dink's strong suit.

"Unless you were *really* hungry," his better half-to-be finished for him, unmetaphorically, which perhaps was for the best, all things considered. She turned to Pembleton. "Can I have an order of McNuggets for myself this time? You snarfed up practically *all* of them last time!"

"*Scarfed* up, dumbass."

Allenby caught Wade's eye, sighed. Wade contemplated pointing out that in his experience the customary directional modifier for "scarfed" was "down," not "up," but concluded that his pedagogy might, as usual, be lost upon his subjects. The Dink and the Dumbass. Another marriage made in heaven. Wade was beginning to wish he had settled for leftovers at home.

By the end of dinner he was beginning to wish for the swift, pulverizing arrival of a massive meteorite and the instantaneous and everlasting elimination of all traces of the species. Pembleton had also been watching the NFL game, and as soon as they were seated, he proceeded to describe for his betrothed's benefit in elaborate and astoundingly ignorant detail every play she had missed while effecting her wardrobe change. Allenby eventually cut him off and shifted the focus to Jennifer, who, it turned out, was indeed pregnant, was excited about having the baby, and wanted to know if naming it after her father would be a problem for Allenby. The intended namesake had not yet been apprised of the impending honor to be bestowed upon him nor of the circumstances leading to it; Jennifer was hoping that his glory in the former would outweigh his outrage at the latter.

"This way, Daddy might not shoot your son," she giggled to Allenby.

Pembleton winced, looked worried. It was one of the few expressions that he did convincingly. *Stupid, wasted, hungry, worried.* That was about the full repertoire, as Wade recalled, and it didn't appear that much, if anything, had changed.

Allenby reached for his snifter, swirled his brandy blandly, smiled at Jennifer. "Is your father a good shot?"

"I think so," Jennifer said. Then paused to reconsider. "I guess I don't really know. He never shot my boyfriend before. Just threatened to—"

"You said you never *had* a boyfriend before," The Dink protested.

"I didn't have any real . . . experience," she admitted, looking at Allenby with a gooey-eyed, empty-headed expression perhaps calculated to enlist sympathy. Then she turned back scornfully to Pembleton. "But at least I could figure out how to put a fucking condom on."

"Right. That's what you *said*."

"Well, you obviously didn't know what *you* were doing."

Wade pictured Pembleton at the ready: he tries to pull the Trojan on over his ears, curses, tries again, gives it up, throws a fit, flings it to the dorm-room floor, stomps on it; Jennifer scoops it off the linoleum, blows off the typhus, props it on the end of his wiener, tugs him twatward, and—

"They break sometimes," Pembleton pointed out. "It's not my fault."

Allenby cut in again. "I don't suppose you two have considered . . ."

"I can't get an abortion. Daddy would kill *me* then."

Wade didn't really see a problem with that solution from an ethical standpoint, as long as Pops was taking out Pembleton, too; justice, after all, should be even-handed. Too bad about the slaughter of an innocent fetus, of course, but then considering what would emanate from the gene-pool of these two, perhaps it was a grander tragedy forestalled. Maybe not *Elephant Man*, Wade decided; maybe it was The Gimp from *Pulp Fiction* he was thinking of.

Jennifer belatedly suppressed a belch and trotted to the restroom. Wade saw several onlookers at nearby tables crack up as she passed by. He felt a twinge of guilt for his willingness to dispatch her.

Pembleton turned to Allenby, the worried look, absent only during consumption, on display again. "Mom says you and her might be sort of splitting up."

Allenby nodded. "It's called getting a divorce. And please try to say 'you and *she*.' Remember, you're dining with your English teacher."

Pembleton glanced briefly at Wade, then back to where his bread was buttered. "Maybe you can, you know, talk . . . she out of it. *That* doesn't sound right."

Allenby sighed. "Maybe. Any suggestions?"

"She says you're gone a lot. Maybe if you bought her something really cool—"

Allenby laughed. "Like what?"

"I don't know, maybe a Jaguar?"

"She has a Mercedes and a BMW."

"I know, man, I'm just trying to help."

"Thanks."

"I don't want to see you guys break up."

Pembleton had a BMW, too, Wade remembered. Maybe it was a push-down and he was angling for an upgrade.

"Mom was nuts before you guys got married."

Allenby nodded. "Some things never change."

"I just hope you guys can, you know, work it out."

For the first time, Wade had a flicker of pity for Pembleton, started to think of him as almost human. It couldn't have been easy growing up with a neurotic mother and a dipso dad; turning into a teenager with a colonizing complexion wouldn't have made matters any easier, nor would losing now the only source of stability and common sense (not to mention BMW payments) that he had ever known. Of course, now there was Jennifer to share his load.

She came back from the bathroom with fresh mascara caked onto the remains of the primer coat, lipstick gleaming from her chin. Wade hoped she hadn't been refunding her filet mignon and mashed potatoes.

Later, they dropped the well-fed fornicators off on campus arguing heatedly over who'd had the more decadent dessert and went back to the condo. Wade clicked on ESPN.

"Brady threw two more touchdown passes after we left," he informed Allenby.

"Big deal," Allenby said. "Do you think he had dinner with his son?"

The light on Wade's answering machine was blinking urgently. Three messages, all from Yoshi.

"Duty calls," he reported, as Allenby prepared to turn in.

Wade wondered if he was missing Nora at all. En route to his room Allenby stopped to pull a book from Wade's shelf.

"Is that my dissertation you're taking to bed?"

"Thought I'd take a peek, see what kind of crap Berkeley's putting out these days."

"If you want something more gripping, I think I have a copy of the *Faculty Handbook* around here somewhere. Also the refrigerator manual."

"Actually I just need something to put me to sleep."

"In that case you've made an excellent selection."

"Our team has a lot of work to do tomorrow. Don't let the geisha wear you out."

"You sound like Paul Brown."

"Bedcheck at 11:00 p.m. sharp, buster, or you can plan on plenty of push-ups."

Two hours later Wade was gasping for breath and wondering if he should plan on having Allenby draw up a will before he did this again.

"That was amazing. Where did you learn to do that?"

"Just use muscle. Not bad for Jap chick, right?"

"Mighty white of you, I was thinking."

"So you like me better if I am blonde?"

"That could work. Actually I was thinking you'd make a stunning redhead."

"Stupid color for Japanese. Hard to color pussy, too."

"The one hair color I don't care for is green. I've seen a few too many students with that look. They always want to sit in the front row, too, so everyone can see them. It made me want to show them another shade, puke on their papers."

"You bad teacher say that."

"And of course no one really wants to see a green pussy."

"Very naughty man."

"You're right. Since I've been naughty, maybe you should spank me again. Or is it my turn to spank you?"

"No more touch tonight. We talk now."

"Oh. Okay." He glanced down. Just as well. A spank was about all he had left in the tank.

"You ever sleep with black girl?"

"Once. Is *that* what you want to talk—"

"She good?"

"She fast. I paid her."

"You go prostitute?"

"Just the once."

"You never like try with other black girl, no pay for?"

Wade reviewed ruefully the many black and beautiful coeds and several colleagues he had over the years allowed himself to fantasize about but never to pursue. Erica Wiley, of course. He wondered how long it would be before he could shower again without thinking of sharing the stall with her. Then he flashed for some reason to Wanda Wilkerson, the former Athletic Department secretary who had confounded him with a visit to enlist his support after perforating Marvin Walker's ass with a .45. "There *was* a black woman who . . . came to my door one time. We didn't . . . hook up though."

"Just friends?"

"Something like that."

"She cute?"

"Gorgeous. Way out of my league."

"She cuter than me?"

"Nobody's cuter than you."

"Maybe I out of your league, too."

"I wouldn't be surprised."

"I sleep with black guy one time."

"That's nice." Worn out, Wade felt his eyelids start to flutter.

"He twice your size."

"Thanks for letting me know." He was ready to drift off, if she would just—

"Maybe three times. I hard to take his whole cock."

"I see." Wade squeezed his eyes shut, gave it one more try. "Just be grateful you don't have that problem with—"

"He don't want use condom protection."

That opened Wade's eyes. And hastened his shriveling elsewhere. "But you *made* him, right?"

"Not really. He sort of rape me."

"Sort of?"

"He very cute. At first I think okay, I want, then I see . . . down there, I get scared. *So* big."

Wade's detumescence was now complete.

"Your friend Allenby, he big too?"

"I wouldn't know."

"You never see him in shower?"

"There are other people I prefer to see in there."

"I bet he very big."

"I'll see if he has a snapshot I can show you."

"Never mind. Maybe I ask him myself. His divorce finish yet?"

"Just getting started."

"He don't want go Las Vegas, finish right now?"

"I guess not."

"Maybe he need help, someone go with him."

"I don't want to go to Vegas," Wade said. "It's no fun without Frank."

"I'm not talk about you, stupid. Maybe *I* go with him. You think he need new wife?"

"I think we should go to sleep now."

"I think you sleep much better your own bed."

Chapter 8

If black people kill black people every day,
why not have a week and kill white people?
—Sister Souljah

When fascism comes to America, it will be
wrapped in the flag, carrying a cross.
—Sinclair Lewis,
It Can't Happen Here

An inch, perhaps two, under six feet, Louis Blodgett was
a little short for his position on the football field but made up
for it in width. Wade had never seen a neck extend quite so far
beyond the plane of the ears. Blodgett's torso looked like a block
of concrete fitted for a shirt. In his bright blue eyes, even in the
genteel setting of Wade's ivory tower office, there was a glint of
fanaticism. Linebacker eyes, Wade thought. Nitschke. Butkus.
Singletary. Ray Lewis. Don't get ahead of your blockers when
this guy's on the field.

"You wanted to talk to me?"

"Thanks for coming, Mr. Blodgett."

"Call me Bludge. Everybody does."

"Call me Ishmael," Wade said, just because he had always
wanted to. It was the only line he could readily call to mind
from the Great American Blubber Epic, and, in truth, could be
said to represent nearly the full extent of his familiarity with that
purported masterpiece.

"That's *Moby-Dick*. I read that book."

"You're a better man than I am, Gunga Din."

Bludge frowned. "Is that Melville too?"

"I don't think so. Unless Kipling stole it from him."

"Kipling? He's sort of a lightweight, isn't he?"

"Some people think so. A.J. Dupree said you might have something to tell me about the party he and Thad Marston were arrested at."

"Crazy niggers."

Wade winced. "Excuse me?"

Bludge shrugged. "They say it themselves all the time, so I've just decided to skip the bullshit about pretending the word doesn't exist. If they can use it, why can't I?"

"I don't know why anybody wants to use that word, but—"

"They didn't shoot me, if that's what you wanted to know."

"I can see you're not shot. Did they shoot *at* you?"

"They'd be dead if they had."

"Or you'd be."

Another shrug. "I don't think those assholes are half as *bad* as they pretend to be. I know for sure Marston never shot anybody. Hell, he can't even get through drills without pullin' a hammy or gettin' a cramp. That pussy ought to get himself a Maxipad and a bottle of Pamprin to keep him happy on the bench."

"Why do you think A.J. wanted me to talk to you?"

"He knows I was lookin' right at him and Mars when the gun went off. I didn't see who fired it, but it wasn't one of them. Wouldn't surprise me if they brought it to the party, though, stupid ass niggers."

Wade winced again. "You didn't by any chance use that word around them at the party, did you?"

Another shrug. "It's possible. Like I said, they use it themselves all the time. I don't censor myself."

"Could that've been what . . . inspired the shooting?"

"Mars was giving me some shit about that rasta I pulled down by his Jheri curls in our last game, so I offered to give him some of the same. Then A.J. jumped in. Bunch of the other niggers at the party saw us gettin' after it, and one of 'em decided to be a hero, I guess. Like I said, I didn't see who."

"You're admitting you provoked the incident?"

"So now you're saying it's *my* fault those stupid—"

Wade held up a hand to cut him off. "I'm just trying to clarify what happened at the party."

"Okay. Here's what happened: I didn't get shot. I didn't see who didn't shoot me. I did see that it wasn't A.J., 'cause I was beatin' on his ass, and it wasn't Mars, 'cause he was right there watching, like always. Clear enough?"

Wade sighed, figured the interview was over. He stood up. Bludge didn't.

"There's actually something else I wanted to talk to you about."

"Oh? What's that?"

"A few of us on the team and some others on campus have formed a new organization. We're a little . . . different. We're looking for a faculty advisor. We heard you don't go for that political correctness crap. We're hoping you'd be interested."

Wade sank back into his chair, managed a feeble pretense of a smile. He had against his better judgment allowed himself to be talked into advising several previous student organizations, even in his adjunct phase: a film society, a Faulkner club, a recycling program. The film group had quickly degenerated into all-out war between the avant garde arthouse crowd seeking Student Body Association funds to screen subtitled obscurities deservedly unseen in their countries of origin on one side, and, on the other, the mainstream braindead-and-proud-of-it contingent who wanted to reset the bar on campus arts to include *Dude, Where's My Car?* A faction of out gays and lesbians had pointedly pressed their own agenda on the fringes of the battle, and Wade, caught in the crossfire, had managed to alienate all of them at once, not to mention the administration, in the single semester of the organization's incarnation. The Faulknerians had foundered on Benjy's section of *The Sound and the Fury*. Wade had tendered his resignation when the film version featuring Yul Brynner's Russified Jason Compson had been substituted for the "reading" discussion. The recyclers had actually made some headway in their initial efforts to clean up the campus, but the fevered enthusiasm of the resumé-building phase had soon burned itself out and left Wade literally holding the bag. He was pretty sure that his days of volunteering for such off-the-clock duties were done, whatever inducements were offered up. Even the guilt-trip approach wasn't likely to sway him.

"The thing is, nobody wants to help us."

"I take it you've asked some other faculty."

The strategy here, of course, was to insinuate that he was insulted not to have been the first to be asked. Solid grounds for refusal right there, really, when you factored in the prototypical professorial ego.

Bludge recognized the gambit and countered calmly. "Oh, no offense, you're still our top choice. We just figured you'd be so busy, with all the athletes you've been helping. So we—"

"It does take a lot of time," Wade jumped in to agree, just to buttress his position.

Bludge nodded. "I understand. Keeping us dumb jocks in class, out of prison, and on track to graduate to the unemployment line, that's got to be a ton of work. Especially some of those niggers on the D-line, like A.J. It's hard to imagine how he got out of the third grade. Unless he threatened to kill his teacher."

Wade shrugged. "I think he said he only had to break her leg."

Bludge grinned. "So anyway we asked a couple of other faculty, more than a couple actually, who we figured wouldn't be as busy because they're like, you know, two hours a day in class and then they're out of here, haul ass to the parking lot like their house is on fire or Teri Hatcher's waiting for them in the sack, but they all turned us down. I think they're a little afraid of us. Of our honesty."

"And what is it that your group is being so honest about? If you're trying to get all of the gay administrators and faculty to come out of the closet and join you on the front lines of the AIDS walk, I've already been there and done that."

"I heard about your film club. Those faggots got you in some deep shit with that S&M flick they tried to show, didn't they?"

Bludge grinned again as Wade blanched at the vocabulary and at the memory.

"I guess they're calling themselves 'queers' again now, aren't they? It's hard to keep up. But don't worry, our club is nothing like that. If anything, we'd like to round up those perverts and send them to—"

Auschwitz? Guantanamo?

"San Francisco. They'd be happier there, and we'd be a lot happier here without 'em."

"But that's *not* what your group is—"

"We want to form a European heritage club on this campus."

It was pretty much what Wade had expected after hearing "niggers" and "faggots." He closed his eyes, breathed out, let it sink in. His kinky cinephiles were starting to look pretty appealing in retrospect. "White Power, you mean."

"*No.* That's exactly the reaction that everybody has. That's not it. We're not a bunch of skinheads or KKK assholes that want to kill black people or bring back slavery or—"

"Well, that's a good start."

"—anything like that. We just want the same rights that everybody else on this campus has. There's a Black Student Union and a Hispanic Students Association—there's even a branch of MEChA, which you probably know advocates the violent overthrow of the U.S. government. There's an Asia Club, and a Filipino Club, and a Muslim Club for the towelheads—there's a club for everybody except us white Americans. Tell me how that's any kind of justice? Who fought and died to create this country?"

"A few million Native Americans, rough estimate, just for starters."

"There's a Native American Club, too. They have six members."

"I guess we won't be building a casino on campus any time soon then."

"Look, I'm not stupid. I know about the Native American genocide. But guess what: I didn't have anything to do with it. I wasn't there. I missed it by a couple hundred years—okay, a hundred and thirty, last chance. It wasn't my fault. You get my point?"

Wade put his head down, folded his hands.

"Let me tell you something else," Bludge said. "Let me tell you what happened at my old high school, just this year. My little brother goes there now. He's borderline retarded, you know, CP, not full-on mongoloid but has a real hard time learning things. Good kid, though. Loves everybody, tries real hard in school. So my parents let him try to start high school with the 'normal' kids. You ever heard about 'White Wednesday' at the urban high schools?"

Wade shook his head but could guess what was coming.

"That's the day of the week all the ghetto kids get together and beat the crap out of the white kids. First Wednesday of the year comes along, guess what happens to my brother? He's minding his own business, trying to buy a coke from the vending machine, and these black assholes, wannabe gangsters but too chickenshit to pick on anybody who might fight back, they grab him up, take his money, and throw him in a garbage can, start rolling him across the campus. He falls out on the cement, cracks his glasses, cuts his face, breaks his arm. You think life isn't hard enough for him without dealing with that shit?"

Wade didn't know what to say. "I'm sorry that happened to him." It sounded even lamer than he'd worried it would.

"*I'm* sorry I wasn't at that school that day. Those niggers would be fucking dead."

"And you'd be in prison. And your brother's arm would still have been broken." Wade could tell he wasn't making much headway. "What happened to the . . . perpetrators?"

Bludge snorted. "They got suspended for two weeks. Their parents complained, about racism of course, and the suspension was lifted. They were back at school two days later. Still there. Of course, that's just until they drop out and start dealing drugs full-time." Bludge slowed down, drew a breath. "If we're not going to put those assholes in prison where they belong—"

"Plenty of them are in prison already," Wade pointed out. "It doesn't seem to be solving our—"

"—guys like me are going to have to do something about it."

"—problems. Is that why you're trying to form this club?"

Bludge breathed deeply again, tried to change the tone with something resembling a smile. "Look, all we want to do is get together and have a meeting, or throw a party, where we know we'll be with our own kind, where we won't have some crazyass nig—'brothers'—crashing in and shooting somebody, just like all those other campus groups get to do all the time. That's all we're asking."

"I believe the activities of the other campus clubs are open to all students."

"Sure they are, officially—but how many Caucasians do you think you'll find celebrating Cesar Chavez Day with the spics?"

Wade shrugged. "I had some killer pork at the Hawaiian Club's luau. I saw a lot of people there who didn't look like Kamehameha."

"Hawaiians: that's not a club—that's a barbecue. Bunch of those island pussies are on the team. Don't want to hit, don't want to lift, won't go over the middle to catch the ball—all they want to do is eat and 'lay back.' The Samoans, now, those boys will hit you. They eat *and* hit. But the Hawaiians, they're just lazy."

"Maybe if you invite them to join the European Heritage Club, they'll shape up."

Bludge laughed. "We need a faculty advisor first. Did you know you get a partial release from your workload if you take a club advisorship?"

Wade knew. The release was half-a-unit per semester. In other words, three years of dealing with this psychopath, his pals, and whatever lynch-mob level lunacy they might drag him into, and Wade would have earned credit for the equivalent of one course's worth of work—when he wasn't teaching any more anyway. What a deal.

"I'll certainly take that into consideration," Wade said, injecting a tone of finality intended to transport the supplicant out of the chair, out the door, and out of his life. He stood up again to reinforce the message.

Bludge didn't budge. Apparently intonation and body language weren't going to suffice. Wade wondered what to say next: *don't you have some niggers and faggots to string up?* crossed his mind. He found himself staring at the elaborate tattoo on Bludge's massive forearm, got caught in the act.

"It's a snake swallowing a Bible. I had this Satanism thing going on for awhile when I was in high school, before I became a Christian. Stupid, huh?"

"Which one?"

"What do you mean?"

"Getting the tattoo, or becoming a—"

"That's not very funny."

Wade shrugged. "You part of Lytle's God Squad, then?"

"No way. That's just a scam. That man's a hypocrite."

"Why do you say that?" Wade asked, deferring at least temporarily consideration of the hypocrisy-judging qualifications of a nigger-faggot-Hawaiian-hating Christian.

"Well, for one thing, that party you were just asking me about?"

"Yes?"

"You got a lot more research to do, Dr. Wade."

"You have something more to say?"

"Nothin' to do with the shooting, but are you aware that Lytle was there?"

Wade's jaw dropped. "Wait a minute. Coach Lytle was *at* the party where Dupree and Marston—"

Bludge nodded. "Ever wonder why he didn't suspend those guys?"

"You saw him?"

"That's not all I saw."

"What do you mean?"

"Better let A.J. and Mars tell you about that."

CHAPTER 9

I saw what seemed a mere shrimp mount upon
the table; but as I listened, he grew, and grew,
until the shrimp became a whale.
—James Boswell, on William
Wilberforce in the House of
Commons

I wouldn't give a damn if he was green with
red breath. I'm hiring a motherfucker to play,
not for what color he is.
—Miles Davis, on hiring Lee
Konitz to play in his band

When Sherman Slate walked into the room to be interviewed
by Allenby's committee, it was impossible not to notice how
slight he seemed. He appeared to weigh about a hundred and
sixty pounds, wore glasses, toted a nerdworthy briefcase. Wade
thought of Dixon James twenty-five or thirty years down the
road. It was hard to imagine Slate taking on the monsters from
Nebraska when he had played for Oklahoma. It also would
have been hard to guess that he had commanded a company of
infantry in the invasion of Iraq.

Slate was the CSU assistant responsible for the defensive
backs, the position coach Wade and Allenby had seen intervening
between Lytle and his cornerback in the San Diego State game.
It had been Wade who flagged Slate's impressive resumé from
the stack of applications, and Allenby had insisted on adding
him to the list of candidates to be interviewed for the job Lytle
was vacating. The committee had already interviewed Lytle's
coordinators and two coaches from outside the program, with
a resulting general impression that all of them appeared to be
competent but none had separated himself from the pack. One

of the external coaches, like Slate, was black, and Allenby had initially held out high hopes for him. He had briefly held a previous head coaching job in another conference, and it was hard to tell if he had botched it or if the opportunity for success had simply not been there; in any case, his interview had been lackluster, as Allenby had been the first to acknowledge. The applicant had also not helped his cause by carrying seventy or eighty extra pounds into the interview. "A heart attack waiting to happen," one of the committee members had sniffed, and Wade knew from Allenby's remarks about Lytle that he would share this concern.

There was no such concern about Sherman Slate, nor were any other deficiencies, apart from a lack of head coaching or coordinating experience, apparent as he moved smoothly and impressively through the set list of questions that each candidate had been asked, striking a particular chord with Wade when he spoke about his philosophy of preparing quarterbacks.

"I believe in playing two quarterbacks, every week. Don't just send your second guy out there to kneel on the ball in the last two minutes every Saturday if you want him to win a game for you when the other guy goes down. He needs to play and move the ball in a competitive situation that you can't fully simulate in practice if you want him to do it in a game when it matters. It's also more stuff for the defense to prepare for, and it gives you better options to have a good runner as well as a good passer if you don't have one guy who's great at both."

Wade saw Allenby and several others nodding in agreement, no doubt recalling the stagnation that had set into Lytle's offense after the injury to Jake Bonner.

The nods continued as Slate addressed the issue of conditioning. "We've got to get the players on this team into better shape. We've prioritized bulk, especially on our offensive line, at the expense of agility and endurance. Some of our players can barely catch their breath by the second half. What's more, some of them have body fat ratios that are going to make them prime candidates for all kinds of health problems a few years ahead. We've got a guard who's three hundred-and-sixty pounds and can barely touch his toes or finish a forty-yard dash without throwing up. That's no way to train student-athletes to prepare themselves for football games or for life. I want to build a lean, fit team that can go full bore for four quarters on the field now, and one that will carry forward the habits of conditioning learned here for the rest of their lives."

Wade was impressed anew. Without mentioning Matt Lytle's name or discounting his achievements, by invoking the image of a fat guy puking on his shoes on the sideline, Slate had made it clear that he would chart a different course for the team.

Slate continued: "The biggest question we have to address is the behavior of the players, on the field and off. I personally will not stand for the kind of incidents that have been associated with this program in recent years, and especially in recent days, and I would hope that the university as a whole will not stand for them either. There'll be no guns, no parties with alcohol, and no second chances for players who get arrested or otherwise embarrass the program."

Cal Logan, perhaps sensing that this *was* a shot at Lytle, jumped in: "Can you really maintain those rules and stay competitive in the current environment of college football?"

"We'll lose a few studs in the short term," Slate conceded. "In the long run, though, we'll become a program that kids want to play for and that parents want to send their kids to play for. This job is not just about Xs and Os. It's about setting an example for young men, teaching them the values of hard work and teamwork and leadership. What are we teaching them when we encourage them to fill up their schedules with junk classes just so they can play football? What are we teaching them when we encourage a culture of celebrating when they score a meaningless touchdown at the end of a game that they are losing as a team?"

Wade looked around, saw heads nodding again. Slate saw the same, kept going.

"Another issue that we need to tackle is the social dynamic of the team. You've got the whites, the blacks, and the Hawaiians and Samoans in essentially three different factions, doing their own thing. We've got to bring them together. I was on the staff at Arkansas when Houston Nutt came aboard there. The first meeting he walked into, he saw the black players sitting apart from the white players. He put a stop to it right away. I'll do the same thing here."

Slate had scored again, Wade could tell. Easier said than done, of course, but clearly the right thing to say.

At the end of the interview there was an open question that allowed the candidate to frame a response that summarized his case. "Give a man enough rope and he'll hang himself," Allenby had said sourly, after one of the interviewees had gone off the rails here with a bitter rant about how he'd been betrayed by a reference and screwed by the selection committee in a previous interview. Conversely, one of Lytle's coordinators had apparently been so confident of the quality of his earlier responses that he'd said nothing in this opportunity. The committee had not trusted his self-satisfaction. Wade wondered what Slate would do now with the opportunity to make a final impression on Allenby and a pack of mostly white senior citizens.

Slate glanced at his notes, looked around the room calmly, exhaled, and began.

"The last thing I'd like to do is talk to you for a few minutes about a plan for winning our upcoming bowl game."

Now he's taking his shot, Wade thought. The end of the regular season had brought an almost unthinkable development. After beginning the season with its usual national championship aspirations, a loaded Southern California team had been upset by UCLA in its last game and had consequently fallen behind two other Pac-12 teams and out of the New Year's Day bowl pairings. A rumor that several All-Americans might be suspended imminently for taking cash and other favors from prospective agents had further dimmed the Trojans' luster. Wade had even seen one report speculating that they might be forced to forfeit all of this year's victories and last's; in the meantime they had just this morning stunningly settled for a second tier bowl berth against lowly parvenu CSU—whose previous coaching candidates had expected to be facing Southern Mississippi. The committee members, while salivating over the prospect of an unprecedented payday and a quantum leap in prestige for the program, were anticipating a hopeless mismatch: the early betting line had USC favored by five touchdowns.

"Aren't we getting off track here?" one of them interjected. "Shouldn't we put our focus on something more practical, like how we're going to raise money for our weight room upgrade?"

Allenby squelched the objection. "Let's hear what Coach Slate has to say. If he has a plan to beat USC, maybe we can forestall grilling him any more right now about how he plans to participate in our fundraising projects."

Slate smiled softly, nodded at the committee member who had spoken up. "We *do* need a new weight room for that conditioning plan I mentioned. I figured that the money for it will come a little easier if we put up a W in this game."

"Dream on," someone muttered.

"Go ahead," Allenby said to Slate, silencing the interrupter with a glare.

"Here's what I'm proposing. Thanks to UCLA, we now have a historic opportunity to play a great USC team. Let me coach our team for this game, and then make your decision about whether you want to hire me permanently."

The weight room advocate jumped in again. "Are you saying you can beat USC? Aren't we getting a little off into Fantasyland here?"

"I'm saying it can be done. I can't guarantee a victory, but I can guarantee that you will get the very best possible effort out of the talent that we have. And a plan that will maximize our opportunity."

Cal Logan snickered. "Sounds to me like playing USC is an opportunity to get slaughtered. I've heard they have seven potential NFL number one draft picks on their defense alone. Do you realize how many high school All-Americans they have on their bench? Half of them don't even get into the game."

Wade thought about Matt Cassel, the QB who'd put up 400-yard games for the Patriots the year Brady was out with an injury, after never even starting a game for the Trojans. This year's crop had something like five tailbacks who would be starting anywhere else in the country.

"They have great talent," Slate acknowledged. "They're also very likely to come into this game disappointed to be in what they will consider a minor bowl and very overconfident about playing a team that lost half of its games."

"They might come in pissed off and try to hang half a hundred on us in the first half," Logan said.

"That could happen, too. But I doubt it. They have a tendency to play down to the level of what they think the competition is. How do you think Stanford beat them a few years ago, on their home field, with a team that had gone one-and-eleven the year before Coach Harbaugh took over? There were probably not ten players on that Stanford squad who could crack the eighty-man roster at USC."

"And not ten on SC's team who could even get admitted to Stanford," Allenby, Cardinal alum too, couldn't resist pointing out.

"Well, we're not as smart as Stanford," Slate said, "but we can do a few things to give ourselves a fighting chance. What I'd like to do now is outline my plan for the game so you can get a sense of how I'll approach it if I'm given this opportunity."

Allenby nodded, looking around the room to make sure that his assent was noted by all, then gestured for Slate to continue.

"Coach Lytle made a commitment to putting his best athletes on defense, and that's not a bad way to start. Now, though, it's time to try something different. I'm going to take our best player, our fastest man, Marcus Foster, pull him off the corner, and put him at quarterback, which he played in high school, and which is the position he was recruited to play here. We've got about a month to get him ready for this game. We'll put Marcus in the shotgun, run some motion in front of or behind him on most plays to spread the defense, let him look around, throw the ball quickly if there's an open receiver, and if not, pull it down and take off. The one component that most college defenses can't account for is the running quarterback. It's tough to play a whole season that way, of course—you get your guy beat up so much, he's bound to go down for a few games—but it's possible to get through one game. A game like this."

"Can he throw the ball at all?" Logan wanted to know, his inflection conveying his low expectations.

"He's rusty, of course, hasn't been taking any snaps since he got here and was moved to DB, but I've tossed with him after practice enough to see that he's got the arm and the touch. If you saw him in high school, you'd know he wasn't just a runner. He threw twenty touchdown passes his senior year in a tough league."

Slate waited a beat for that stat to register and then continued: "He's also really, really smart. He's not going to kill you trying to force the ball into tight coverage just to show off his arm, which has been one of the problems with our starter. If Marcus sees his receivers are covered, he'll tuck it and go. That's where we'll get our chance to win the game. We'll give him the ball twenty-five or thirty times and give him a chance to get outside the defense. Then I want to take our running back, Frank Jackson, who's pretty fast, and split him out wide. He's actually got pretty good hands, although you'd never know because we've almost never thrown to him. He's not super elusive, which is why he can't shake several tacklers at the line of scrimmage, but he might be able to make one guy miss and run by him if we split him out. We hit that pass once or twice early in the game, they'll have to loosen up in the middle, and then maybe we can run a little bit more effectively than we've been doing. Actually, I hope, a lot more effectively with Marcus carrying the ball. We'll also keep all this quiet, let them prepare for our big stud QB and the drop back pass attack we've been using."

Allenby looked at Logan, then back at Slate. "Bonner's been cleared to play. How's he going to handle not being the starter?"

"I might start him," Slate said, smiling again. "His teammates are always accusing him of throwing all those interceptions on purpose just so he can hit somebody. Maybe we'll line him up at wide receiver and see if he wants to throw a block against one of those two hundred and sixty pound linebackers. And he'll get a few snaps at QB, too, just to give their defense a different look."

"What about *our* defense?" Logan's turn again. "How are

you going to stop all those All-Americans on that side of the ball?"

"Their offensive line is going to outweigh our defensive line by forty or fifty pounds per man. The only chance we'll have is to blitz from every angle, run blitzes as well as pass blitzes, seven or eight guys coming on some, maybe most, downs. We'll use our whole squad, keep guys as fresh as we can, keep them coming after the quarterback."

"Isn't stopping the run even more problematic with the size disadvantage you were talking about?" Allenby asked, Logan nodding a second to the question.

Slate smiled again. "It should be. In all honesty, if they were to commit to running the ball fifty times, like John McKay or John Robinson would have, there's probably no way we could stay on the field with them—just like Stanford couldn't have with that first team Coach Harbaugh took into the Coliseum. But they tried to throw the ball all through that game, even after their quarterback broke a finger, because . . . because they're USC. They wanted to run up the score. They expect to win by a bunch. They'll expect the same against us. That's what gives us a chance. We'll put pressure on the passer with our blitzes, get a few sacks, maybe a few picks, a few fumbles—then keep the ball in Marcus's hands on offense, run the clock as much as we can, keep our defense off the field. We'll give up a few cheap touchdowns; that's inevitable. They've got a good quarterback and great receivers."

"Aren't you going to miss Marcus on the corner then?"

Wade had been wondering how Allenby was processing this plan to weaken such an important position. Slate was ready for the question.

"He's a great athlete, not a great corner, at least not yet. His technique is still pretty raw. He's gotten away with a lot of stuff just out of sheer talent. We can replace him, and the rest of the secondary has played together long enough and well enough so that I'm not worried about that."

The answer seemed to satisfy Allenby, Wade thought, or maybe it was the confidence Slate projected that was making his case.

"One other thing I can promise you is this: you will never see from me in this game, or any game I ever coach in, the prevent defense. You might as well just put the points up on the scoreboard for the other guys and walk off the field."

Wade noted heads bobbing around the room at this. The only thing these two-percenters hated more than Obamacare was the prevent defense.

Logan spoke up again. "You talk as if you expect to be protecting a lead with a chance to win at the end of this game instead of losing by five or six touchdowns like most of the other teams they've played."

"That's exactly where I hope to be. And when we get there, I promise we won't rush just two or three, drop everybody else back in coverage, and let the quarterback pick us apart. We'll keep comin' after him, from every position: linebackers, safeties, corners, everybody. If we get a shot at him close to our sideline, I might even send a cheerleader after him."

Around the table Wade saw a few actual smiles now. Even the weight room fundraiser seemed to be getting into the spirit. "Go down with your six-guns blazing, huh?"

"I don't expect to go down, sir, but we'll definitely . . . throw everything we have at them."

Allenby smiled, and, sensing the moment, stood to bring the interview to a close. Slate stood as well, but raised a finger for a final word.

"Look, there's one other thing I'd like to say. I want to thank you for the opportunity for this interview. I especially appreciate the work that Mr. Allenby is doing to make sure that equal chances are going to be given to all candidates, which still unfortunately does not happen on all campuses as it should. But I want to make this perfectly clear: I don't want you to give me this job because of the color of my skin. If my plan makes sense to you, if I've convinced you I can lead this team the way you want it to be led, then that's the reason to hire me. Talk to my players, talk to the coaches I've worked for, and I believe they'll tell you that I'm the right man for this job."

Afterwards, Wade drove Allenby to the airport. With the interviews concluded, he had to make a quick trip back to L.A. to tend to business and family matters, or as he phrased it, "to put out some fires and start a few more." En route, Wade took the first opportunity he'd had to tell Allenby about Bludge's revelation that Lytle had attended the party where the gunplay broke out.

"Good riddance," Allenby muttered. "I guess he can't coach a party any better than he coaches a game."

Then, expecting to rehash in detail Slate's performance in the interview, Wade found Allenby surprisingly quiet. In deference to his passenger's preferences, Wade put on *The Cellar Door Sessions* and concentrated on dodging the usual gang of road warriors conspiring to annihilate them. After Allenby stepped out of the car to head into the terminal, he leaned back into the window.

"I think we found ourselves a football coach."

Wade grinned. "Next thing you know, you'll be telling me we can beat USC."

"There's a black man in the White House," Allenby said. "Anything is possible."

In the evening as he was heating up leftovers and watching the news, Wade was thinking about the pride and pleasure Allenby would take from Slate's appointment and wondering how much opposition he would face from Logan or others on the hiring committee. Suddenly there was Matt Lytle's unprepossessing face on the screen again. What the hell was he doing now, jumping to the NFL?

"My wife and I have prayed on it, and we've decided that the Good Lord's plan for us is to finish our work here at CSU. I have told the folks at Carolina that I will not be accepting their very generous offer but will be returning to coach the team here."

Wade stared at the screen, shook his head to clear the cobwebs. The phone rang. Wade muted and picked up.

"Did you see what I just saw?" Allenby's outrage was electric. "What does that jackass take us for?"

"Well, a little less than the four million Carolina was going to give him, apparently."

"And he has the gall to say it's God directing his decision."

"I guess the Almighty called an audible."

Wade heard a click on Allenby's phone. "That's the A.D. I've gotta take this. I'll call you right back."

Wade unmuted, changed channels, and listened to the brief, inane analysis of Lytle's reversal by the cartoonish announcers on ESPN. How was it, he wondered, that mouthfarters like these got high-profile, high-paying jobs for jabbering gibberish that wouldn't have entertained a six-year old, when there was a nation full of serious sports fans investing precious hours of their otherwise meaningless lives every week in pursuit of commentary relevant to their one sustaining passion? Were there viewers who actually preferred the infantile banter and the nursery school noises to intelligent, informed discussion? Maybe they were the same people who listened to talk radio hosts dismissing their callers as "garbage" or "scum" instead of rationally disputing them. Wade muted again and reminded himself of Mencken's epigram: *no one ever went broke underestimating the intelligence of the American public.* It was this kind of pandering to the lowest common denominator that had made a media icon out of muddle-mouthed John Madden— when fans could have been enlightened by the erudition of commentators like the late Bill Walsh, the greatest football tactician of his era, and actually learned something about the strategy behind the game they were devoting their lives to.

Allenby rang back. "You still watching?"

"I turned the sound off. I was thinking about Bill Walsh."

"Too bad he's gone. We could've used his advice."

"Maybe we could just get his playbook."

"Fuzzy wants us to take Lytle back. Can you believe that? After the stunt he pulled?"

"She thinks he's better than anyone else we can get?"

"She thinks we can knock his price down and save some money. Carolina must have had a reason for backing off."

"The party?"

"Could be. See if you can find out what he was doing there,

okay? Let's not be the last to know."

"We still going forward with the background check on Slate?"

"Hell, yes. If Fuzzy tries to block that, she can find herself a new committee chair. Who's to say Lytle won't change his mind again before breakfast anyway? Aren't the 49ers looking for a new offensive coordinator again?"

"Bite your tongue *off* and speak no more, forever."

CHAPTER 10

Recruiting is like getting married. When you
finally decide you're going to get together,
you better not have told too many lies.
　　　　　　　　　　　　　　—Joe Paterno

Allenby took on personally the task of communicating with
Sherman Slate's most impressive references and asked Wade to
talk to some of the players about him. Wade decided to start with
Marcus Foster.

Most of his time in his new job Wade had so far spent trying
to get scholar-athletes like A.J. Dupree and Thaddeus Marston
to remember what classes they had signed up for, visit them
occasionally, sit on their cell phones, and look over the shoulder
of someone who was taking notes. He had addressed the football
team briefly in meetings that Marcus had attended but had never
spoken with him privately. From a couple of feature stories about
him in the local newspaper during this break-out season, Wade
had learned that Marcus had never met his father and had lost his
mother at age ten. He'd grown up being shuffled from relatives
to friends and had even lived with his coach's family during
some of his high school years. He seemed to have survived the
challenges of his disrupted upbringing remarkably well: a little
computer research now told Wade that Marcus was carrying a
3.4 cumulative GPA in an Economics major. That explained why
there had been no pressing need for a counseling appointment.

Wade had initially expected to find Marcus housed with
most of his teammates in the varsity athletes' main dormitory,
better known on campus as "The Zoo." He discovered instead
that Marcus had moved the previous semester into a dorm
designated as a quiet study facility. When Marcus told him over
the telephone that he was preparing for an exam but could take a

short break to talk with him, Wade offered to meet him there. He walked into a sparsely-furnished room that was a little smaller and a lot neater than the rooms he'd seen other football players occupying.

"Too hard to get any studying done there," Marcus said when Wade asked him about the move.

"Too many party animals?"

Marcus nodded.

"What are you studying for?"

"Test comin' up in Poly Sci."

Wade waited to see if he would amplify, talk about plans for law school or an MBA, but nothing more came forth.

"Coach Slate said you might be a good person to talk to about his candidacy for the head coaching job."

Marcus nodded. "Great man. Great coach. He'd do a great job for us."

"Great."

Wade paused, waited for more. It wasn't called the quiet dorm here for nothing. "Anything else you'd care to say?"

"He made a decent cornerback out of me."

"He said you were recruited to play quarterback."

Marcus chewed his lip, looked away, then back at Wade. "Didn't work out that way, though."

"Coach Lytle had other plans?"

"I don't want to say anything bad about him. He's coming back to coach us again, isn't that right?"

Over Allenby's dead body, Wade thought, but he nodded. "It's a possibility."

"He said I'd have a better chance to play in the NFL if I move to corner."

Wade thought immediately of Allenby's getting the same message nearly fifty years ago. Some things were very slow to change. "Is that what you want to do?"

"Of course I'll go if I get the chance, if they draft me. A man can make enough money in a few years in that league to set himself up for life, and—"

Other things had changed a lot. The 49ers had signed a

cornerback to an eighty million dollar contract.

"—help his family, too, which I definitely need to do. I got some cousins in New Orleans still living in cardboard boxes," Marcus continued. "I couldn't pass up an opportunity like that. But—"

He paused. Wade waited for a moment, then prompted him. "But what?"

"I just wish Coach Lytle would have been honest with me when he brought me here. He should've told me he was bringing in another quarterback, building the offense around his game. Then I might have had a chance to go somewhere else where they'd let me play . . . my position. The thing is, I *am* a quarterback."

"I understand you put up some pretty good numbers in high school."

Marcus shrugged. "We had a good team."

"Did you try to talk to Coach Lytle about it?"

"I talked to Coach Slate, and he talked to Coach Lytle for me, asked him to at least give me a chance to compete for the job, but he didn't get anywhere. I appreciated what Coach Slate tried to do for me, though. Thing about that is, you got to remember he's my position coach, and I'm starting for him, doing pretty well, but he wasn't worried about making himself look good. He wanted to do the right thing to help me, help the team."

"Did you think about transferring?"

"I thought about it a lot, actually, but I talked to my high school coach, and he said better just keep your mouth shut, work hard, make the best of it. So that's what I've tried to do. And it's worked out okay for our team. We made a bowl game."

"Indeed. Against USC."

Marcus nodded again. "I know what you're thinking: we could get killed. But nobody on the team thinks that way. This is our chance to show what we can do against the best college football players in the country. We're all fired up for it."

"Coach Slate said there are some problems between the different racial groups on the team. Is that something you've seen?"

"I think he's a little more sensitive to it, bein' from the South, than the rest of us are. Most of the white players are cool. They know the black players are good athletes, usually better athletes than they are. They respect that. They see how hard we work in practice, how much we want to win. There's a couple of guys that are a little ... different, but—"

"Louis Blodgett?'

"Bludge? Yeah, he might be a little . . . out of control."

"Good linebacker, though?"

Marcus weighed the judgment, then delivered it. "He's good for our league. He's not fast enough to cover anybody from USC, so that might be a little ugly unless we change our scheme."

Wade decided to find out what Marcus knew about the party. "I wasn't there—I don't go to fraternity parties any more."

"Did you know that Coach Lytle was at the party?"

"I've heard that. I don't know anything about it, though."

"What about the confrontation between Bludge and Dupree and Marston?" Wade could tell Marcus wasn't eager to address the subject, but decided to persist. "A lot of your teammates were there. You must've heard some talk from some of them. Anything you can tell me might help me sort this out. Do you know if Coach Lytle was there when it happened?"

Marcus sighed, met Wade's eyes, made a decision. "I heard he was gone by then."

"What else did you hear?"

"All I heard is A.J. and Mars were ragging Bludge about pulling the hair of that San Diego guy when he tackled him—and then again after. You saw it, right?"

"Right. Pulled him down by his pigtails. That's legal, isn't it? Not very *nice*, but—"

"If somebody's stupid enough to wear his hair like that on a football field, he deserves whatever kind of take-down he gets. But then Bludge had to go and give him another yank."

"That was you that pulled Bludge off the guy, wasn't it?"

Another shrug. "He already got one penalty. I didn't want him to get kicked out."

"He didn't seem too happy about it."

"He didn't like me putting my hands on him, I guess."

"Was there any more to it?"

Marcus looked away again, then back at Wade. "He might've used the 'n' word to the guy."

"Not to you?"

"Maybe that, too. He uses that word a lot. Of course, so do A.J. and Mars."

"Do you think he said it to them at the party?"

"That wouldn't be too surprising. I guess they were gettin' on him, saying he pulled that brother's hair 'cause he didn't like his 'do. Mars is always on Bludge anyway, pushin' him, hoping he'll screw up, so he can get his spot. I guess maybe Bludge said something back, they started shovin', and somebody pulled a gun."

"Somebody *fired* a gun," Wade pointed out.

"Like I said, I wasn't there. I don't know whose gun it was or who fired it. Not my place to guess. That's all I know."

"You know Dupree and Marston got arrested."

"Yes. But I heard they're not going to be charged."

The team had closed ranks, stonewalled the cops. Wade wondered if Bludge was on board with the plan and if the D.A. would decide against prosecution.

"That's still up in the air. What do think is going to happen to them here?"

"Depends on who the coach is," Marcus said. "I don't think Coach Lytle will do much. Maybe make them go to church or something."

"What if Coach Slate were making the decision?"

"That might be a different story."

Wade decided he had gotten as much as Marcus knew or was willing to tell. On his way out of the apartment he stopped briefly to study a framed photo of Marcus arm-in-arm with an attractive young black woman, both smiling radiantly.

"My fiancée," Marcus said. "We're getting married when we graduate."

"Easy on the eyes," Wade said.

Marcus nodded. "Smart, too. She's at Howard now in premed. She's why I don't go to parties."

"You're pretty young to have figured that out."

Marcus nodded once more. "My high school coach again. He cared about more than just football. He talked to us a lot about how to be a man. 'Find a good woman and treat her right,' he said. He said that's the most important thing in life. 'Find a good woman and treat her right,'" Marcus repeated.

Marry a girl with a good head on her shoulders. Wade felt like he was hearing the countersign. "That sounds like something my mother would say."

Marcus looked at the photo again. "That's what I plan to do. I don't need to go to parties and get shot at."

Upon returning home to make his report on the wings of this image of impending domestic bliss, Wade found Allenby on the phone with his wife's attorney.

"Tell her I sold the company for a billion-five, went straight to Vegas, and blew the whole wad on strippers and slots."

The rest I wasted, Wade thought. R.I.P., Dino.

Allenby listened for a moment to the response, then replied. "She can go to hell. And you can go with her." He clicked off his cell, spun it on the coffee table.

Wade parked himself. "Sounds like she wants to kiss and make up."

"*He* wants to be paid. Her funds are frozen by the pre-nup. No money for a divorce attorney."

Wade nodded admiringly. "You learn from your mistakes, don't you?" *Find a good lawyer and treat him—*

"Right, but I seem to keep making new ones. What'd you find out from the kid?"

"Pretty much what we thought. He loves Slate. Thinks Lytle's a liar and a jerk, although he wouldn't use those words. What'd the coaches say?"

"Stoops and Nutt gave Slate a big thumbs up. Good recruiter, good fundamentals, works hard, willing to take a risk. No skeletons in the closet. Switzer said he'd be proud to have him for a son. I think it's a go."

Wade set his DVR for the local news while they ate dinner,

then fast-forwarded to the sports segment when they finished. The featured story was about the melee that had broken out in a high school playoff game over the weekend. Footage showed both teams and their fans attacking each other, with numerous injuries, some of them serious, including several to women and children.

Allenby was angry. "Why are we surprised when this happens? Remember that crap that went on a few years back when the kids from Miami and Florida International started swinging their helmets and stomping each other? If high school kids see college players doing that, what do we expect *them* to do?"

Wade nodded. "Our game against San Diego State could've turned into something like that if Marcus hadn't stepped in."

"You're right. Both sides were ready to fight." Allenby paused, shook his head, then smiled as if dredging up a sacred memory. "You ever see the footage of Willie Mays pulling John Roseboro away after Marichal took that bat to his head?"

"Of course. Many times. I was listening to that game on the radio." Wade played the tape in his head again, saw the Dodger catcher's bleeding scalp, Mays's outrage and compassion blending as he jumped in to stop a brawl. "One man can make a difference, huh?"

"One man like that can. Do you remember how that game was decided?"

"Do you think I'd forget *that*? Mays hit a home run. Off Koufax."

Allenby smiled again. "Did I ever tell you about the time I met him? *Times*, actually."

"Willie Mays?"

"Yep. A friend of mine introduced me to him at a charity event a few years ago. I told him about a catch I saw him make near the end of his career. I was home from 'Nam, after my second tour. The Giants were running a promotion where they let servicemen in for free at Candlestick, that old bedpan of a ballpark, trying to get a few fans in to fill the place up after the A's moved to Oakland and stole half of their attendance. I saw Mays play against the Big Red Machine, early days of it anyway. Saw him run all the way to the fence in right-center, a ball hit by Bobby Tolan. Jumped up, got his glove on it at the peak of his leap, crashed into Bobby Bonds, a big man, on the way down, and somehow held onto the ball. Greatest play I ever saw live. He was nearly thirty-nine years old."

Wade remembered. "I saw that on TV."

"After the game, they let a few of us grunts into the clubhouse to get autographs. Mays wasn't crazy about signing that shit, I could tell, but when he saw my uniform, he gave me a fist. He'd been in, too, done his bit. Biggest hands I ever saw. When I met him again at that fundraiser, years later, I told him that was some catch he made off Tolan. You know what he said to me?"

"Let's see: if it was *Barry* Bonds you were talking to, it probably would've been something on the order of 'Get the fuck out of my chair.'"

"Mays said, 'Bobby Tolan was a great ballplayer.' Not one word about himself."

Wade nodded, then thought again about Marcus's intervention, how the 170-pounder had pulled big bad Bludge away from the fray. "When I praised Marcus for what he had done, he just said, 'I didn't want him to get kicked out.' When I asked him about all those touchdown passes he tossed in high school, all he talked about was the team."

Now Allenby nodded. "The kid's got something in common with his coach, then, too. Switzer told me Slate's father died when he was just getting started at Oklahoma. Switzer drove him to the airport, gave him a few bucks—somethin' he'd be busted for now—put him on a plane. Slate gave up his scholarship, went home, took care of his family, helped his mother raise five siblings, finished a degree at night. Never complained. Joined the Army, went to the Gulf War, got called up again as a reserve after 9/11, did a tour in Afghanistan and another in Iraq, got a Bronze Star there, never talks about it."

"All the resumé says is 'U.S. Army veteran,'" Wade recalled.

"Apparently he was in the thick of it in Basra, got his unit through some tough stuff."

Allenby's phone rang. His face told Wade it was Fuzzy again. "I thought you said he faxed a letter of resignation." Allenby shook his head wearily and spent the rest of the conversation listening, then brought Wade up to speed.

"She's insisting that we reconsider Lytle. I guess she thinks he'll dazzle us into ignoring his flip-flop."

The committee reconvened the next day, forestalling for the time being any deeper digging into events at the party or other complications Lytle might have run into in his negotiations. The coach had been on good old boy terms with Cal Logan and a few of the other committee members, but Wade could sense from their greetings that their affection for him had been strained by his flirtation with Carolina. Lytle had another ally, though, in Delia Herman, who, after skipping the previous meetings of the committee entirely, had now to Allenby's consternation reclaimed her position as a voting member. Wade was reluctant to consider the possibility that she was a whisker brighter than she appeared, but it did occur to him now that by yielding her chairmanship she had given herself this opportunity to cast a ballot. Allenby wouldn't have a vote except to break a tie.

Allenby moved the process swiftly through most of the set questions but pressed a little harder when the opportunity for cross-examination arose.

"What's your record on hiring minority coaches?"

"I'm proud to say that there's two African-American coaches on my staff. You've interviewed one of them for this position. He's still a little green, I'd say, but—"

"Both of them were on the staff when you were hired."

"Well, I kept 'em."

Allenby paused to let the heft of that response be measured. *Wipe my butt and praise my doody*, Wade was thinking. He tried to figure out how he could work in a question about promises made to Marcus Foster during recruitment, but couldn't decide how to do it without jeopardizing Marcus's status if Lytle retained his job.

Allenby wasn't ready to let the race issue go. "This committee has heard that there are some signs of racial disharmony on your team. Are you aware of that, and if so, what steps have you taken to address the problem?"

"That's just media hype. There's no problems on this team that every other team in America doesn't have."

"Gunfire at a party on campus doesn't alarm you?"

"Of course that was a disappointing episode. We're taking appropriate steps to make sure it doesn't happen again."

Wade looked at Allenby, who nodded a go ahead. "I understand you were present at that party."

Herman glared at Wade in shock. Lytle's eyes widened briefly, and then he drew a deep breath. Wade leaned forward to listen. "I stopped by for a few minutes, to check on a few of my players. Everything was under control while I was there."

Wade leaned back, looked around the room. So that was it. Hard to tell how the answer had gone over.

When Allenby asked about the issue of disciplining the players at the party, Lytle said that would be dealt with as soon as the outcome of the interview process was announced. He knew what he wanted to say when the open question at the end came. He made eye contact with each member of the committee but kept his comments short, and, Wade noted, dialed down the Jesus jive for the capitalists in this audience.

"I came here to win football games, and I've done that. If you want to keep winning football games, I would encourage you to think long and hard before making a change. This program could very easily be right back where it was two years ago. I know I've caused some confusion with my talks with those folks at NC State, but I've realized this is the best place for me right here. You don't mess with success."

Allenby stood to show him the door, closed it behind him. Wade was thinking that if the committee hadn't met Sherman Slate, Lytle's performance might have been enough to save his job. He looked around the room, guessing that others were thinking the same thing, wondered who would say it.

It was Delia Herman who spoke up: "I move we vote to reinstate Coach Lytle."

CHAPTER 11

In that moment he saw the world in its true
light, as a place where nothing had ever been
any good and nothing of significance done: no
art worth a second look, no philosophy of the
slightest appositeness, no law but served the
state, no history that gave an inkling of how
it had been and what had happened. And no
love, only egotism, infatuation, and lust . . . .
—Kingsley Amis, *Jake's Thing*

I'd rather get a brain tumor than go back to
teaching.
—Cliff, in Jim Harrison's
The English Major

"There were some substantial irregularities in your hire. I
don't know how this ever happened."

Wade knew he had antagonized Delia Herman by interjecting
the question about Lytle's appearance at the frat party, but he'd
failed to anticipate that retaliation would be so swift or so severe.
After Herman's motion, Allenby had declined to hear a second,
which Cal Logan undoubtedly was ready to make, and had put
off a vote until the next meeting after more research on the
candidates could be conducted. In the meantime he'd gone back
to L.A. again for a few days. Facing the A.D. behind a tower
of donuts in her office now without his benefactor's protection,
Wade stared bleakly at the innards oozing from the half-
consumed specimen in her grasp, then back at her, wondering
how he was going to extricate himself from this latest fiasco.
Maybe give charm a try: *have I told you how sexy you look with
that custard in your mustache?*

Herman paused for another substantial chomp, didn't bother

to swallow or close her mouth before continuing. "You don't even have a counseling background. I'm sure if you did, you would have been a little more respectful at our committee meeting instead of . . . harassing Coach Lytle. A little discretion wouldn't have killed you."

Watching her feed, on the other hand, might. Wade closed his eyes, kept his own mouth shut, *the better part of valor,* hoped she would she get to the point before he became sick to his stomach.

"I'm afraid it's going to be necessary for us to reopen your position to fresh competition."

And there it was.

"You're welcome to reapply for the position yourself if you wish, of course, but I think it's only fair to let you know now that we expect many other candidates with excellent credentials and a *much* more diversified background. As you know, we're working hard to diversify our faculty, and honestly, as a white male, your chances are—"

As good as Heinrich Himmler's.

"—slim. I honestly don't see any way that you could hope to compete. I just thought you should know so you can consider carefully whether you want to invest the time and energy in reapplying. Time and energy that could be so much better spent—"

Strangling and dismembering fat-assed administrators. Wade pictured Herman's head after a month or so in his freezer. Couldn't hurt that face, might even help. Get rid of the glare from that orange lip gloss anyway. *Honestly.*

"—elsewhere. Of course you might be able to get your English job back, as far as I know; that's under Dr. Brooks's supervision. Assuming that he was satisfied with your work."

She smirked, crammed in a final clump, smacked her lips, and waved him to the door, cruel intention evident in her dismissive suggestion. Everyone on campus knew the story of what had happened last year between Wade and Gordon Brooks, the short, fat, bald, lame-brained, stink-breathed, wart-faced Polonius who had sucked his way up the ladder to low-level management and now chaired CSU's English Department. It was possible, of course, that Brooks was senile enough to have forgotten the thumping that had sent him out of Angela's office gasping for breath and stumbling back to his own. In any case, it was apparent that Herman was determined to end Wade's counseling role, and while he still had it he needed to sort out the Hotchkiss situation anyway, so at the same time he might as well force himself to put out a feeler, see if there was any chance of reestablishing his former composition load. Maybe he could line up something for next semester, enough to get by on, if he started pimping himself now. It was a goal consistent with what had long ago become Wade's general strategy for getting through life: aim low and settle for less.

The prospect of conversing with Gordon Brooks had the approximate appeal to Wade of taking a bubble bath with the brothers Bush. Since the SEALs' hit on Bin Laden, only Assad, Ahmadinejad, and Bill O'Reilly outranked him on Wade's list of people the world would be better off without, although Delia Herman was bucking to jump the queue. Brooks was one of the few life forms extant who could rival the repulsiveness of the A.D.'s appearance. His most prominent feature was the massive, cauliform tumor projecting from his slimy forehead. It was a wonder that anyone could bear even to look at him, let alone exchange words, once having heard the crap that came out of his almost equally unsightly pipe-fouled mouth. Wade plodded now at death march pace to the English Department's headquarters, half wishing to learn upon arrival there that Brooks was booked solid with complaints, petty grievances, and assassination plots for the rest of the month. A lot could happen in a month. Assad could unleash his chemical weapons, or A-jad his nuclear mouth, and launch Armageddon; al Qaeda could target California, crash a plane into CSU, nerve-center of the western world. Delia Herman could choke to death on a baker's dozen. There was always hope if the appointment could be put off.

"Jesus shot your dog and fucked your wife, am I right?"

Clara Shelby, the English Department secretary, greeted Wade with her customary cheeky cheer. Better known as God's Grandmother, she had been on the job since the Johnson

Administration and knew everything about everyone who had ever worked there or applied to. She could tell you to the second when it was that the two cross-dressing full professors had found each other's underwear in their mutual lover's knapsack, or to the penny how much the previous department chair had paid in hush money to the faculty wife to whom he'd conveyed Chlamydia. It was only Clara's universal expertise and command that allowed imbeciles like Brooks or those who'd preceded him to carry out the charade of doing their job. For some reason she had taken a liking to Wade in his adjunct days and had even alerted him a couple of times to cancellations by other instructors that allowed him to pick up an extra section. When he told her his purpose now, she clucked in sympathy, then buzzed Brooks in the interior office, to no effect.

"Probably popping zits in his private john. Guess I'll have to go in there and see if he tripped and fell into the toilet again."

She spun in her chair, strode into the chairman's lair, came back out a moment later.

"No sign of him. Ever since he got the promotion and has no more classes to teach, he spends most of the day wandering around the campus spilling coffee on himself and yakking about his new pooper to anyone he can corner."

For a moment Wade wondered if Brooks's proctologist had enlarged his asshole or perhaps presented him with an extra one, no doubt medically warranted; then Wade remembered hearing the rumors, rife with sexual innuendo, about Brooks and his new Chihuahua.

"I swear I'm gonna have to put a bell on that man. I'll tell him that you stopped by to beat him up again. This time you have to let me watch."

Mission accomplished, sort of, Wade slunk back to his own office. He was killing time there mentally transposing Delia Herman's headless corpse into the dog-eared *Sports Illustrated* swimsuit issue he'd pulled out of his desk when Yoshi popped in for a visit, caught him in the act.

"You like to see the naked girls?"

"They're not quite naked, actually."

"You busy man in office."

"Just keeping up on the latest fashions."

"That is February, I think," she said, gesturing at the evidence. "We are almost December now."

"Almost," Wade said. He smiled and took in the view, forgot for the moment about Herman. Yoshi looked like she could have posed for the magazine herself. The miniskirt she was wearing didn't cover much more than the bikinis in the pictorial. "Are you my Christmas present?"

"You always thinking about make love to me?"

Wade flipped to an article at the back of the magazine, held it up. "Almost always. Sometimes I think about football."

"This is good transmission. I have new idea."

"Transition? What is your i—"

"I want work with football players to improve his study skills."

That sounded suspiciously like something that was supposed to be Wade's job.

"I thought you were here to teach Japanese. We don't have too many kids from Tokyo on the football team."

"Ex-panding my job, see."

"I see. Well, how do you plan to get football players to study?"

"Actually, athletes has higher GPA than rest of student body. Why you not know that, Dr. Wade?"

Actually, Wade *did* know that, knew also that, dismal graduation rates for CSU's football players notwithstanding, there were dedicated student-athletes like Marcus Foster on the team and even some brilliant ones who somehow qualified for medical school or completed engineering degrees while devoting fifty hours a week to their sport. There were also plenty of others like Dupree and Marston who filled out their schedules with P.E., pottery, and sociology classes, seldom went near them, and still somehow managed to stay eligible.

"My job just temporary. Only one year. Not so good. But maybe I find better job while I here. How you like *your* job?"

"I love my job," Wade said, and, now that he was about to lose it, for the first time in his life he could say this almost sincerely. After surviving the indignities of high school teaching, a dead-end journalism career, and then years of sweatshop wages as a part-time instructor while completing his PhD, Wade had felt as if he finally had it made. If his was not exactly the pinnacle of professorial eminence he had envisioned while thrashing out his dissertation on the heroic code in Hemingway, it was nevertheless a vast improvement upon his prior fortunes. It was true that he was still trying to figure out exactly what he was supposed to be doing, which could be confusing at times and frustrating at others, and working with coaches who were routinely obsessive-compulsive workaholic megalomaniacs indifferent to the realities of the rest of academia could be trying as well. If a kid got a bad grade, it was never, "Tell him to study more"; it was always, "Find him an easier class." Nevertheless, there were many compensating factors. He had his own office, flexible hours, and that salary of ninety thousand dollars a year, which, if unimpressive by the wider world's standards, was still a hell of a lot more than he had ever made before. He could even supplement that sum, in the role he had declined to reveal to Dixon James, by working in the summers as an odd-jobs editor on computer publishing projects for Allenby, who overpaid him handsomely for reasons Wade could not quite fathom but declined to question. Even with ex-wives, step-children, and indigent progeny of his own piling up, Allenby was still making money faster than his many dependents could squander it. All in all, for Wade it was a pretty damn good deal. "The only problem is, they're trying to take it away from me. I might have to apply again."

"I hear rumor you got job not right way."

"Really? Where did you hear that?"

"Not important."

Yoshi looked around, surveyed the office she'd been in many times, once or twice in less than she was wearing now. Why, Wade wondered, did he get the feeling that she was looking at his station with different eyes today?

"I think maybe I apply this job."

"You're kidding, right?"

"You think I no can do? I think this job very easy. Have time watch football all weekend, read dirty magazine in office."

Wade pushed aside the bikinis, made a mental note to show her what a dirty magazine looked like. "But why do you think they would hire *you* for this job?"

"I have two Master degree. I have ESL credential. I have counseling certificate."

"Yes, but I have a PhD."

"In literature," she scoffed. "You know about Shakespeare, Faulkner, Hemingway. What good that do—"

"Don't forget Sherwood Anderson."

"—when you talking to students who cannot read or spell? He not so important, I think."

"I think so, too," Wade had to admit. "But why would you want to do this to *me*?"

"What you mean?"

"We made love to each other *last night*."

"That was just sex. This is business. We talking about my *career* here."

"But what about *my* career?"

"That is *your* business."

Wade stared, tried to digest this. Suddenly the miniskirt wasn't doing anything for him.

"Your country all fucked up, you know that? Vietnam, you drop napalm, feel guilty, let Vietnam people come here live, let whole family come. My country, no napalm, you drop fucking atomic bomb, two of them, but we can't come here live. Only visit."

Wade thought it impolitic to point out that Japan had in fact also seen its fair share of napalm in the spring of 1945. "A million G.I.s might've died without those A-bombs. One of them might have been my old man, and I wouldn't even have been born, so who would you be asking to marry you then? And how many civilians in your country would have survived a full-scale invasion?"

"Don't give me your sick history. You know about literature

only—I think you not qualify for this job." She paused, looked at him shrewdly. "If I get this job, I stay U.S. Don't have to get marry. You don't want marry me, right?"

"Well, trying to screw me out of my job is certainly enhancing your attractions."

"I think maybe you all mix up. You the one screw *me*. Maybe I tell your boss you touch me at work. You harass me."

Wade gaped, nearly gasped. Was he really hearing this?

"Maybe I tell her you think she big fat dyke, too."

"I never used that word, and you know—"

"Okay. You call her cunt, twat, douche ball. Very nice."

"*Douchebag*. What do you do, take notes? If you're going to quote me, at least have the decency to—"

She startled him by reaching right in front of him and snatching the *Sports Illustrated* off his desk. Wade didn't give a shit about the SI, it was hardly irreplaceable, but he had never liked grabby people, he didn't like Yoshi's grabbiness now, and the tenor of their conversation hadn't improved his mood a bit. Without even thinking about it, he jumped out of his chair, leaned far across his desk, and grabbed back; in the process he miscalculated the momentum generated by his fury, lost his balance, and plunged all the way over the desk, disengaging the telephone and dragging it in his wake. He landed head-first in a heap on the floor, clutching the torn-off front cover of his souvenir edition, at eye level with both the hem of Yoshi's skirt and the garbage can into which she now tossed the desecrated remains of the supermodels.

"I think we talk enough now. No more touch, okay?"

"Don't worry about it."

"Enjoy magazine."

She jerked her head at the garbage can and turned toward the door. Wade started to pull himself off the deck, weighing whether to go home and get drunk first or get it over with now, twist Yoshi's head off and put it next to Herman's melon in his cooler. Before he could make up his mind, Gordon Brooks, eyes on a swivel, on the lookout as always for another ass to kiss, barged through the door and plowed into Yoshi, knocking her fanny-first straight into Wade's face. Wade got a brief whiff of jasmine before he banged his head against the desk behind him and the air exploded into a thousand stars.

"Dr. Brooks!" *What the fuck are you doing here?* "Have you met Ms. Yamamoto?" he managed to stammer—then had a sudden spasm of terror at the thought that Yoshi might choose this moment to recite some of the various terms of endearment she'd heard him bestow on *this* former and possibly future boss.

Instead she merely nodded curtly to the new arrival, smoothed her scandalous skirt, shot Wade a final murderous glare, and darted out the door and down the hallway.

"What in the world are you doing down there on the floor, Dr. Wade?"

Wade reached over next to him, picked up the phone, checked for a dial tone. "Just waiting for your call, actually."

"Is that the swimsuit edition?"

Wade let go of the phone, looked at his other hand, which still gripped the portion he'd clung to when Yoshi had grasped the magazine. "It used to be."

"Hardly the time or place, wouldn't you say? I mean, I like to peek at the ladies myself once in a while, but only—"

Through the keyhole into the crapper.

"—where and when appropriate, *sabe*?"

"Sorry about that," Wade said. He stood up, brushed himself off, started over. "Did you get my message about the online English 1A problem?"

"That's why I came over. I understand you've got the skinny for us on what's going on with Professor Hitchcock."

Wade sighed. "Professor *Hotchkiss*. I was asking *you* for information about what's going on with him."

Brooks frowned. "That can't be right."

"I was hoping *you* could tell *me* what—"

"Well, maybe the secretary got it mixed up." Brooks scratched his head, fiddled with the wart. "She gets things backwards once in a while. Got to keep a sharp eye on that old gal."

"Right."

"Well, shoot. I was hoping you were the man to get this

harangle with those online sections cleared up. You are familiar with our online instruction program, aren't you?"

Wade didn't know what a harangle was and didn't care to find out. He nodded, hoping there wasn't a lecture about Gordo's partnership with Al Gore in the invention of the Internet forthcoming.

"Great opportunity for the U, for the shut-ins, people who are busy at work. Major boost in our productivity."

Pretty good deal, too, for slackers who want someone else to do their work and teachers who can't stand the sight or stench of unwashed undergraduates.

"As you must've heard, there've been some complaints about our old compadre's grading this term. Not sure exactly why, never had any issues before. He's had some health concerns previously. I suppose they might be recurring and even interfering with his judgment. I have a call in to him to try to find out what the heck's going on, but we've been having a devil of a time getting ahold of him."

Wade speculated briefly on the size and variety of the pharmaceutical cocktail Hotchkiss must be consuming daily to cope with his various afflictions. A kidney replacement and a quintuple bypass were merely the latest of his many medical procedures. Wade pictured the hyper-medicated geezer behind the steering wheel trying to aim his land yacht in the right direction, find a lane, find the campus, park without scattering pedestrians or ramming into a retaining wall. Maybe it was just as well that he was computing instead of commuting these days.

"So how're things in the head shrinking game?"

Wade wondered if Brooks had heard something already, possibly from Herman herself, about his status in the Athletic Department. He began a dispirited attempt to provide an update.

Brooks interrupted. "Hope you know I put in a *bon bon* for you when that job came up, gave you some props."

*Bon **mot**,* Wade knew he meant. The man could mutilate more than one tongue at a time. Wade eyed the wart, thinking, if al Qaeda ever did send a suicide plane this way, there would be a perfect landing place. Evidently either Brooks's accelerating dementia or his terminal self-absorption had somehow convinced him that he had been responsible for Wade's appointment as an advisor, having conveniently forgotten that in fact he had tried to fire Wade from his teaching job. Was it possible that the oaf had forgotten too even about that epic lick that Wade had laid on him?

Wade bit his lip and tried again. "It looks like there might be some . . . complications with my appointment."

"Sorry to hear that, amigo. What seems to be *la problème?*"

Le problème, idiot. The fat cow who runs that department is a clueless doofus just like you. Almost as butt-ugly, too.

"Testosterone purge," Wade muttered.

Brooks nodded sagely. "Not easy to work for a sensitive gal like DH. Takes a lot of . . . sensitivity. Have you ever thought of attending a sensitivity-training seminar?"

Have you ever thought of exchanging brains with a hamster?

"I've got a couple of buddies on campus I could steer you to, change your whole mode of communicating. Tap into your inner—"

Where was Bludge when you needed him?

"—feminine side."

Fuck it. Wade gave up trying to figure out how to broach the topic of coming back to the English Department. Better to beg for pennies in front of the 99 Cents Only store. Even starving couldn't be worse than going back to work for this cretin.

Brooks flashed tobacconated teeth in a hideous grin. "Wondered if you'd be interested in picking up those comp sections yourself if our old pard decides to let them go."

Wade blinked. He hadn't even had the stomach to ask, and now it was being offered?

"Actually, that might work out well for me next semester, if this counseling appointment doesn't—"

"No, no, bro. I'm talking about *this* semester. In case we need to—"

"You want me to add three sections of English composition to my workload? *Now?*"

"Just until the end of the semester. If we need you. Is that a problem?"

"I *have* a full-time job now."

"Heck, some of our people teach three or four overload sections. Moonlight at the JCs and so forth. I'm not asking you to do it for nada, you know. Great way to make yourself some extra moola. Give you the prorated pay for the rest of the semester, be another two, three thousand bucks in your kitty when it's time to do the Santa thing."

"I think I identify more with Scrooge."

Wade paused, realized he had dropped an allusion that Brooks might actually recognize. No way to know for sure, of course, unless you gave him a quiz. This, after all, was the man who at an MLA convention meeting had once introduced Joyce Carol Oates as Joyce Cary.

"It's all online, you know. *And* there's a reader."

"So I've heard."

"It's a"—Brooks raised a hand airily, attempted to oppose a pair of pudgy digits, couldn't quite produce an audible snap—"breeze."

Why don't you do it yourself then, dipshit?

"Might help keep you in the loop for next semester if"— Brooks paused, showed that he could still connect a few of the dots—"there's other cuts. Wouldn't want to find yourself with no work at all, now would we, old buddsky?"

"I'll think about it," Wade said, thinking already about the drudgery of digging himself out of all the crap that would be piling up on him again if this turned out to be his only employment option. "Thanks for the offer." On a whim he stepped nearer as if to move within backthwacking range, noting with some satisfaction a sudden glimmer of anxiety in Brooks's cloudy eyes. "It's good to be remembered."

Brooks went away. Wade went home, found a note taped to his front door. Eighty-something Ellen Partridge, two condos down from him, was renewing her invitation for Wade to join her at evangelical services bright and early Sunday morning. Wade wished he could say his neighbor reminded him of his mother; the truth was that she reminded him more of Cotton

Mather. In her note she also wanted again to know if he would join her in filing yet another complaint against the neighbors in between them. She had already complained to the Homeowners' Association, the Police Department, and probably the FBI and Interpol as well, about Julio and Simon. Sort of the flip side of Delia Herman, they were guys who, after siring their wives' children, had discovered they were gay, and they were celebrating their new lifestyle long, loud, late, and often. They had installed a hot tub on their patio, and they were doing their best to keep it busy. It was fine with Wade that they had found each other; he hoped they paid their child support, but he had no problem with their choice—to each his own as long as the disinclined were left alone—and unlike Mrs. P., they had not tried to press their persuasion upon him, although he suspected they were promiscuous, and not just from the constant parties. Much to his friend's amusement, both Julio and Simon had attempted to hit on Allenby. Wade wasn't quite sure whether he should be more relieved or insulted that they had found him unworthy of their advances, but he knew which way he was leaning.

Wade crumpled the note, went inside, then remembered: no Allenby, hence no dinner. He had a few beers instead. He fell asleep in his chair, was strangling Yoshi in a dream when the phone rang and saved her life.

"Wade, it's Angela. Are you in some kind of trouble?"

Wade woke up, took stock. "Let's see: my boss wants to revoke my tenure-track appointment, I've been accused of sexual harassment *and* harassing the football coach, the campus lunatic fringe is recruiting me again to sponsor them, Gordon Brooks wants me to add three sections of composition to my workload, my neighbor wants me to speak in tongues, the 49ers are averaging two hundred yards of offense per game, and the woman I yearn for is three thousand miles away with her head up her ass. Other than that, life is perfect."

"You say the sweetest things to me. Why don't you think about coming out here to spend Christmas with me?"

"You'll meet my flight in a snowmobile, right? And then where do I bunk, with you and Ronnie, or—"

"Ronnie and I are finished, Wade."

Wade sang into the phone: "'It's Over, It's Over, It's Over.'"

"Sinatra?"

"Of course. TOSTM. How come you're not marrying him this time? Did he hit you again?"

"Let's not talk about Ronnie, okay? Let's talk about you. Allenby said—"

"Allenby called you?"

"From L.A. He said you might need a letter to explain the circumstances of your hire. That committee I was chairing, we wanted it to happen fast, so we kind of . . . cut a few corners."

"And my balls."

"That's gratitude for you. You know, Delia Herman wasn't too thrilled about hiring you in the first place. I actually schmoozed with her a little on your account. Of course, I figured I'd be around to defend you in person. I didn't expect the offer from Connecticut, or—"

"To shack up again with the bastard that smacked you in California?"

"Remember when I said I might be coming back to California, Wade?"

Wade felt his heart leap in spite of himself.

"I have an offer from Berkeley, plus CSU wants me to come back. They're inviting me to apply for dean."

So Erica had been right. Wade's hopes were surging now. He tried to resist, played devil's advocate. "Why the hell would you want to be a dean? Do you have any idea how many meetings you'd have to go to—and the kind of morons you'd have to go to them *with*? Not just go to, *run*? You *hate* meetings. Why would you put yourself in that position?"

"I'd be closer to you."

Wade's heart jumped again. A big one this time. Stop that. That *hurts*.

"Better tell me about Berkeley. No one leaves UConn for CSU."

"I left Stanford for CSU, didn't I?"

"Yeah, because they fired you."

"Because I wouldn't sleep with that Jamesian creep."

"Correction: I believe the record will show that you *did* sleep with that Jamesian creep. He fired you when you wouldn't *keep* sleeping with him."

"Thanks for refreshing my memory. I see you're still keeping score. How's Yoshi?"

"That sexual harassment charge I was telling you about?"

"You're kidding."

"If only. She wants my job."

"Poor Wade. I'll get a letter into the mail."

CHAPTER 12

Given half a chance, every man becomes the
hero of his own detective story.
—Douglas Grimes, in Irwin Shaw's
Nightwork

Sometimes, just when I think you're the
shallowest man I've ever met, you somehow
manage to drain a little more out of the pool.
—Elaine to Jerry, on *Seinfeld*

In years gone by Wade had devoted countless hours to reading
detective fiction. Chandler, Hammett, Ross Macdonald, John D.,
Ross Thomas, Elmore Leonard—he had compulsively consumed
every title cranked out by each, even when one plotline differed
only minimally from the last. It had all started, he supposed, with
flashlights under the childhood bedcovers to finish *Freddy the
Detective*. In high school, where first exposed to the edification
of serious literature, he'd saved his real enthusiasm for Ed
McBain and Mickey Spillane. Even in graduate school, when he
was supposed to be figuring out what to chuckle at in *Tristram
Shandy* or misting up over Proust's *petite madeleines*, he had
often turned for relief from excruciating boredom to the pages
of his police or private eye procedurals. Indeed, as he looked
back now across the years to count the return upon investment
of the various enterprises to which he had committed his time
and spirit, apart from the hours devoted to watching television or
listening to his teams lose on the radio, it was quite possibly his
most prevalent activity. What did he have to show for it? Well,
hours of utter absorption, pleasure, and distraction from the
dismal nonsense of his real life, one side of him wanted to argue;
to which the other typically replied, exactly—and a deserved life

of dismal nonsense in result.

Now, retracing his investigation of the circumstances of the fraternity party and Matt Lytle's role in it, Wade tried to remember if he had absorbed from all those pages any lessons in detection he could apply to the project at hand. He pictured himself browbeating hopelessly overmatched suspects in an interrogation room, cleverly separating them and getting them to rat each other out. Perhaps that was worth a try with Dupree and Marston. The other recourse, he recalled, was to put them together and goad them into betraying each other and themselves. He decided to give it a shot when they returned to his office for their next appointment with Dixon James. Wade had the players report a few minutes early. Maybe he'd try the good cop/bad cop routine, draft Dixon to be the enforcer when he turned up.

"Louis Blodgett told me I should talk to you two about Coach Lytle and the party."

"Bludge say that? What else he tell you?"

"He backed up your story about not being the ones that shot at him."

"No story, Doc. God's honest truth."

"Like I told you, before, if I'd shot at that cracker mother-fucker, he wouldn't be doin' no talkin' to you now."

"That's pretty much the same thing he said about you." Wade turned stern, tried to imagine what kind of countenance would make an impression on someone with Dupree's rap sheet. "You guys realize I can recommend your suspension from the team for the bowl game unless you cooperate fully with my investigation."

"What you talkin' about?"

"We already cooperated, Doc."

"You haven't told me everything you know. I can tell from what Bludge told me that there's something about Coach Lytle that you left out. I need to know what it is. No one else needs to know it came from you."

"Fuckin' Bludge. Can't keep his fuckin' mouth shut." Dupree clamped his own jaw.

Okay, Wade thought, try the sweet innocent kid.

"Mars, you know that your prints were found with others on the gun that you said—"

"Couldn't keep your motherfuckin' mouth shut either, could you? Worse than a white boy."

"Fuck you, A.J."

"Fuck you, too."

Well, Wade thought, we seem at least to have succeeded in sowing the seeds of dissension. Wasn't that step one in the manual? But what did the manual say about the advisability of jumping in to break up the fracas if two guys who outweighed him by a total of four hundred pounds started beating on each other more than verbally, as seemed imminent?

"Can't we all just get along?" Wade couldn't stop himself from saying.

"Very fuckin' funny, man." Dupree glared at Wade, then at Marston, who looked puzzled. "Rodney fuckin' King, idiot. Mr. Black History."

"Don't call me a idiot, idiot. You the one got us in this mess. I'm gonna tell Doc here what he needs to know, get us out of it. I got to *play* in that bowl game."

"Yeah, like your ass is gonna get off the fuckin' bench."

Marston tried the Marin County version of fuckface on Dupree, then turned to Wade. "Coach Lytle told us to bring him a girl."

Wade exhaled. "At the party?"

"*From* the party. Coach see the one he want, tell us to pick her up, bring her to him."

"To his house?"

"Fuck, no, you crazy, man?" Dupree couldn't stand to be left out. "To the motel, place where we stay nights before the home games so nobody be out chasin' pussy till 6:00 a.m."

"Doesn't sound like the policy works too well."

"It don't apply to the coach staff."

"Don't apply to me neither," Marston said. "Got plenty in that motel myself."

"Yeah, got your ass busted, too. Cost you twenty laps."

"Worth it. That Shaniqua bitch got a sweet mouth on her."

"Don't need but half a mouth for that Asian dick of yours."
Dupree sneered at Marston, then at Wade. "His daddy half—"

"My condolences. Let me make sure I have this straight:
you're telling me Coach Lytle told you to bring a girl to him at
the motel?"

"That's right."

Wade tried to envision the scene, square it with Lytle's public
pronouncements. "Maybe he just wanted to talk to her, keep her
away from the players?"

Marston laughed. "Or invite her to a chapel meetin',
somethin' like that? Sounds like how he might try to say it. You
want to believe that shit, I guess that's your choice."

Dupree shook his head, sneered at Wade again. "He paid for
it, man. He wanted a damn lap dance."

"That doesn't sound like something Coach Lytle would be
interested in."

"You ever seen that wife of his? She weigh more than me.
That bitch sit on his stick, he be out for the year. No doubt."
Dupree looked at his teammate for confirmation.

Marston nodded. "Need him a dick transplant if that fat thing
ever bounce on his business. I seen her havin' dinner with the
team one time. Had half a chicken in her mouth in one bite, I
swear to God. Almost made me sick to watch her eat that shit."

Wade flashed to Delia Herman, shuddered, turned the page.
"Let's get back to the party."

Dupree shrugged. "He told us which one he wanted, told us
to bring her to him, drop her off, come back in a couple hours,
pick her up."

"That's a long lap dance."

"Maybe he was buildin' in some prayer time afterwards."

"How did you approach the girl? Did she go willingly?"

"She went," Dupree said. "Fifty up front, promised her a
hundred more. She didn't put up no fuss. That's good money for
a damn cocktease."

"You s'pose to give her a hundred up front," Marston
protested. "Hundred and a hundred, that's the deal."

"Kept fifty for us to split. Commission."

"I never saw no fuckin' commission. Where my twenty-five, nigger?"

Maybe two weeks in Basic Math had paid some dividends after all. Wade wiped his brow. "So you dropped her off at the motel?"

"That's right."

"And then you picked her up later?"

"Nobody there when we went back. We just went back to the party."

"Did anyone hear you make the arrangements with the girl?"

"You think we broadcast that shit on the P.A., man? We tryin' to be sly."

"We din kidnap nobody, Doc. She glad to get the money."

Wade nodded slowly. "I guess I'd like to believe that's true. Why don't you tell me the name of the girl you . . . escorted, and I'll see what she has to say."

Dupree and Marston looked at each other.

"I'll find out sooner or later. You might as well tell me now."

Marston spoke up: "That new sister on the volleyball team? Look like Tyra Banks?"

"He wanted a black girl?"

Dupree's turn: "The man got good taste, I'll give him that. That's one thick chick. Look more like Beyoncé, you ask me. Taller though."

"Does she live on campus?"

Marston again: "Far as I know. We just took her from the party. Haven't seen her since."

Dixon James knocked on the door. Didn't need the brass knuckles after all. Wade waved him in and turned the office over to him for the day's tutorial, then went to see what he could find out at volleyball practice.

Women's volleyball was one of the few sports in which CSU had achieved national distinction. The head coach, Marilyn Porter, in place for twenty years, had built the program from scratch into a consistent powerhouse, winning a dozen conference championships, making several long runs in the NCAA playoffs, for which the team was headed again this year, and pulling off a string of implausible upsets against such high profile programs as Stanford, Pacific, and UCLA. She was the most distinguished coach at CSU, and clearly should have been the president's choice to be the new A.D.; probably he had been intimidated by her accomplishments. She'd passed on several offers from competing universities that would have meant more prestige and money, in order to raise her family outside the megalopolises. Unlike Delia Herman or Matt Lytle, she also set an example for her student-athletes by keeping herself in perfect shape, as Wade had noted admiringly when he met with her in the fall in his new counseling role. She'd offered her support for and appreciation of his services, but, at least until now, appeared to have had little use for them: the girls on her team rarely needed the kind of burping and weaning that the football and basketball players required. They went to class, did their homework, graduated on time; Porter made sure of it.

A contributing factor to that pattern Wade again noted now as he sat down in the bleachers to watch: this sport was still mostly the province of the upper classes. Most of the girls at practice were white. Girls from moneyed families who could send them to summer camps and support year-round club teams had a leg up on everybody else when it came to trying out for the varsity, even at the high school level now. Anyone playing at the college level would have been heavily scouted and recruited, and the camps and clubs were an integral part of that process, too. Wade didn't see anyone matching the description Dupree and Marston had given him. There were a couple of black girls on the floor, but one was short, obviously a setter, and the other was tall but brawny, not confusable with a model or rock star. Wade had always thought that African-Americans would dominate volleyball as soon as they began to play it in numbers, just as they dominated other sports. Now, though, looking at the team on the floor, he was reminded of the have/have not dichotomy polarizing the nation as a whole. Even baseball, historically a gateway to affluence for shoeless country boys and ghetto waifs, was turning into a country club sport: most of the players on the high school and college varsities had the summer camp pedigree there now, too. Very few of them were black. Where, Wade wondered, was the next Willie Mays coming from?

He watched the highly charged practice for perhaps half an hour, tried to share the spirit, couldn't quite get into it. Wade couldn't really concentrate on watching women play ball unless they were half-naked. He knew it was a stupid prejudice and he wasn't proud of it, but there it was: it was almost like it was hardwired into your system, like religion or homosexuality. You couldn't do anything about it. He could spend three and half hours in perfect absorption in front of the television watching a football game between, say, Ball State and Eastern Michigan, even when he had no connection whatsoever to the schools involved and no rooting interest in the outcome, but he couldn't seem to keep his focus on the drills unfolding right before him now even though he could see that the CSU girls were skilled, superbly conditioned, intensely competitive athletes. Their practice uniforms were an improvement at least upon what the women basketball players wore—those baggy jerseys and the accursed Fab Five carryover calf-length "shorts" that should never have been allowed to adorn any female form outside of a maximum security prison—yet Wade as usual found his attention wandering and himself wondering what these girls would look like in something more seductive.

Wherever it came from, his attitude was certainly not rooted in any sense of his own inherent superiority. Once, after a few hapless hours of trying to maim themselves on surfboards, Wade and a college pal had staggered in to the beach to find two girls in skimpy string-and-thongs setting up a volleyball net on the sand. Dumbstruck by their luck, they offered to help, and the girls offered a game. Wade's friend suggested mixed doubles, tried to claim the more buxom of the pair as his partner, but the girls demurred, preferred to play in tandem. They said they'd played in high school but claimed to be out of shape now, an assertion transparently belied by the showcasing threads of their barely-there attire. Wade had read an interview in which Chris Evert had confessed that even when she was ranked as the number one women's tennis player in the world, she could not beat her own brother, who was not ranked among the top *thousand* male players, so he figured the benefits of comparative anatomy would kick in here and compensate for lack of practice. Both girls were knockouts, and sporting with them under the high summer sky seemed to offer the promise of a little slice of heaven. Another harsh life lesson, alas, awaited Wade: it was hard to appreciate the beauty of women's bodies while they were kicking your ass. Sun-scorched, dehydrated, and exhausted before they even began, the proud peacocks had insisted on playing a full three-game set. Neither could consistently bump the girls' serves, set with accuracy in the slight sea breeze, or gain purchase on the shifting surface to spike with any velocity. The final tally: bikinis win, 15-2, 15-1, 15-0.

When the third game ended, the girls' boyfriends showed up. Hirsute almost beyond belief, they were packing pot and a twelve-pack, none of which they offered to share with the vanquished pair. Wade had been hoping to score at least a phone number; instead, he dragged home a shattered ego along with a bent skeg, a sprained ankle, and incipient bubble blisters no doubt due to metastasize in later life as full blown melanoma. His humiliated pal, who as far as Wade could tell had failed equally to cover himself with glory in the match, had put the capper on the afternoon's abuses by pronouncing Wade the worst surfer *and* volleyball player who ever lived and banning him from the beach for the rest of his life. In the crowded annals of Wade's personal athletic infamy, the day was down at the nadir next to wetting his pants in Pee Wee League and hanging at the bottom of the climbing rope in freshman P.E. because he lacked the muscles to pull himself to the top.

Coach Porter rescued Wade from his ignominious perch in the past when she called a brief halt to the drills and approached him in the bleachers. She told him the girl he was looking for was Larashawndria Lewis. The redshirt freshman had called in early in the week reporting flu symptoms and had not been at practice for several days. The other girls on the team had not seen her in class, and Porter had been about to contact Wade to see what he could find out. She sent an assistant back to her office to get telephone and dormitory information for Wade, thanked him briskly, and whistled her charges back to work.

Wade went to lunch and then back to his office, where he found Dixon by himself, two hours after having left him with his projects. "So, how long did they last? Ten minutes?"

"Naah, they were here until a few minutes ago."

"Make any progress?"

"They're not as stupid as they pretend to be, but—"

"Nobody is."

"—it's going to be hell getting them through this semester. They've got this big research paper due in their history class, and they're freaking out about the source notes and the bibliography when they haven't even done the reading to understand the topic."

Wade nodded. It was a familiar sinkhole on an oft-trod sidetrack. For students at Dupree's and Marston's level of "development," for want of a better term, worrying about the fine points of documentation format in a research essay was tantamount to fretting over the brand of dinner mints you put out for your guests after serving up a main course of spoiled pork.

"What are they supposed to be writing about?"

"World War II."

"That should be enlightening."

"They don't know anything *about* it: how it started, how it ended, even who was *in* it. They don't know *anything*. When I asked them who made the decision to drop the atomic bomb, A.J. said, 'Rose Bell.'"

Wade laughed. "Our first female Chief Executive."

Dixon shrugged. "Maybe a hermaphrodite."

Wade nodded. "You know she must have had some big balls on her to make that call."

Wade's father, like millions of others of his era, had given three years of his life to World War II. To face a generation of high school graduates ignorant of its importance or even of its occurrence seemed on the surface incomprehensible. On the other hand, Wade reflected, he lived in a city where the featured columnist of the single surviving newspaper had once reversed the lineage of Yogi Berra and Yogi Bear, informing a readership of a hundred thousand or so that the Hall of Fame catcher had been named after the Hanna-Barbera creation. This of a man, no more than five-and-a-half feet tall, who had gone in on a rocket boat with the first wave on D-Day before earning three MVPs as the linchpin of the most enduring dynasty in the history of American sports, the only damn Yankee it was impossible to loathe. Cultural illiteracy, obviously, was everywhere, even in print, when the heroes of Omaha Beach were forgotten or turned into fucking cartoons.

"And Mars thinks it was Ronald Reagan who—"

"Oh, Christ, they're saying *he*—"

"—*started* World War II. You'll never guess how."

Ben Affleck's video game version of *Pearl Harbor* apparently hadn't improved matters much either.

"They're . . . street smart. You can tell," Dixon continued. "But they're like . . . idiots when it comes to school. I don't see how anyone can expect them to take college classes. They can't even read the textbook for our English class."

"Of course, *buying* it before deciding they can't read it might be helpful," Wade said.

"It's part of their scholarship scam. All their books are paid for by the Athletic Department. They just take them back to the campus bookstore, sell them, get the money back, and then borrow someone else's book."

"Or, more often, go without."

"Or sell *them*, too. Mars told me he made six hundred bucks that way this semester."

"Probably thinks he's an entrepreneur. Great long-term planning in place there, huh?"

"I think their long term plan is four walls."

"That's what we pay our taxes for."

Dixon shook his head. "I don't pay taxes."

Wade laughed. "How do you manage that?"

"You should meet my father. Or at least meet his accountant." Dixon paused. "You know that other job you were asking me about?"

"Yes?"

"You've already guessed, haven't you?"

"Why do you think I would know what you—"

"I work for a drug dealer."

He paused again, waited for a double-take that Wade managed not to provide.

"What's *your* other job, anyway?" Dixon asked.

"I'm a hit man for the Mafia. Mild-mannered academic by day, cold-blooded assassin by—"

"You don't believe me, then?"

"Let's just say I can't see you—"

"I'm a pharmacy tech. I can't get my license until I'm eighteen, but I took a course and learned all that shit so I could work for my father. He's a—"

"Pharmacist."

"That's right. One of two black pharmacists in town. He does a lot of business. You wouldn't believe all the crap black people buy to put on or into their bodies to make their problems go away."

"Sounds a lot like white people," Wade said.

"We sell plenty of shit to them, too. Instead of go on a diet or get some exercise, all these crazy people want to take a pill. And then of course there's all the old dudes like you that want to get something so they can walk around with a hard-on all day long."

After the last round of Yoshi's ministrations, Wade had indeed found himself wondering if his days of seeking pharmaceutical enhancement might not be too far off. At least that was one problem he didn't have to worry about right now.

"Mars said if I give him an A in English, he'll get me laid. Maybe he'll give you the same deal."

"If he offers to pass along one of his harem, be careful. Very high fertility factor there."

"They invited me to a fraternity party."

Wade grinned, pictured the mix.

"I know what you're thinking: I'll be the mascot."

"I thought maybe they'd use you to stir the punch."

"I told him I can't be bought that cheap. My integrity is—"

"Good for you."

"—worth at least a car. He said he'd try to get me a Mustang."

"Maybe he should wait until you're old enough to drive."

"A.J. said he's full of shit. He says Mars couldn't jack a car if a naked lady came out smiling from behind the wheel, handed her his keys, and said 'Pretty please.' He says Hondas are much easier to steal, anyway."

Wade nodded, put a hand on Dixon's shoulder. "Who says a student like you can't learn anything at CSU?"

Chapter 13

When I think of most people's lives,
especially women's lives, I don't know how
they bear it.
—Robyn Penrose, in David Lodge's
Nice Work

"I'm at the hospital," Allenby said when Wade picked up the phone in his office.

What the hell. "Are you—"

"I'm fine. It's Jennifer."

Wade drew a blank for a moment. Then, "Oh, right. The Dink's—"

"Apparently they decided to get rid of the baby after all."

Wade put it together. At the hospital, not at a clinic, so . . . . "Christ. I hope not with a rusty—"

"With a twelve-pack of Pepsi."

"This I gotta hear."

"Apparently she tried to induce a miscarriage. The Dink read a news story—or more likely saw it on TV, in between his video games—about a cola overdose being adverse to pregnancy, and so, in his inimitable way, he turned it around and told his betrothed to—"

"Drink up?"

"Exactly. One flaw in the plan: he forgot to tell her the part about the crucial ingredient being the caffeine. All she had on hand was the caffeine-free crap she drinks to keep that svelte figure of hers, so she downed that."

"A twelve-pack?"

"The whole thing in half an hour. Almost hydrated herself into a coma. No harm to the fetus, though. Now I think she wants to keep the baby—and kill *him*."

"Well, at least you'll get *some*thing out of this. You still planning to have his mother bumped off, too?"

"Negotiations continue. I'll fill you in later. And you can let me know what you learn from the volleyball star. If she confirms what those players told you, it should be enough to keep Herman and Logan from cramming Matt Lytle back down our throats."

Larashawndria Lewis had declined to find Wade's office and had also rebuffed his offer to meet her in the lobby of her dorm. She'd finally agreed to a cup of coffee. When she slouched through the entrance of the Starbucks where Wade had sat waiting for half an hour beyond the appointed time, he instantly had to adjust the top end of his list of the most spectacular women in the world. Lately he had been alternating between Angela and Erica Wiley, now that Yoshi had shown her true colors, but here were a face and form to make a man forget . . . everyone else. She was 6'2", slender but stacked, with perfect ebony features. It was easy to see where the Tyra and Beyoncé comparisons had come from. The only thing missing was a smile.

Wade was familiar with the look if not with the face. Often when he first talked with the current crop of black female students, it was very hard to get past the wall they put up. Sullen, frowning, pouting, pissed off before the first words were exchanged between them, they often answered with monosyllables his good faith attempts to engage them and looked anywhere but into his eyes when he spoke. *The world is out to use me, screw me, fuck me over. Why should I expect **you** to be any different from everybody else?* Often they were overweight, sometimes obese, even grossly so, and they were pissed off about that, too. Wade remembered Marston's and Dupree's description of this girl, and it had seemed reasonable to hold out hope that being drop dead gorgeous might give her a different perspective; as she neared his table without altering her froward expression, he began to have his doubts.

He had been raised to address people by their names whenever possible, so he gave it a try as he rose to greet her. She put up a hand, corrected him curtly before she even sat down.

"You don't pronounce the 'i' near the end."

"Oh." *Of course not. Why wouldn't I have known* **that**? "Sorry."

"My parents got a little too *creative*"—she sneered the word—"when I was born." So she was pissed at them, too. Popped out of the womb and started looking for someone to be mad at. Okay by Wade: spread the blame around, less to fall on him.

He smiled agreeably, tried again: "It's—"

She put her hand up again, almost in his face this time. "*Please* don't tell me how 'unique' or 'interesting' my name is."

—*very nice to meet you,* Wade didn't get to finish saying. As a man with no use for the first name he'd been stuck with himself, he'd had no intention of risking such a presumptuous compliment—with good reason, it turned out.

"I'm *sick* of having an interesting name. I swear to God, when I have my kids, if I have a girl I'm going to name her 'Ann'; if it's a boy, he'll be 'Bill.'"

Wade was still smiling. "Mr. Cosby will appreciate that."

No return smile. "My sister is 'Toshiba.' Can you believe that shit?"

Wade shrugged. "I hear they make a nice 3D screen."

She grunted. "I guess she should be glad they didn't name her after a car. Are we gonna order?"

Wade habitually made a cup of coffee for himself in the morning, in the winter another when he came home from work. **Savor life's simple pleasures**, his mother had taught him, and in this instance he had followed her always excellent advice, relishing the routine, especially now that he no longer had to listen along with it to Brenda's crunching her Sugar Pops or swilling her cocktails. He had long since joined the masses of American consumers in buying and grinding fresh beans. He considered it a mild extravagance after his parents' contentment with Maxwell House or, Christ, those fucking freeze-dried crystals from Folgers his father used to buy that looked (and tasted) as if they'd been chipped from rabbit turds, and he didn't often fork out for the overpriced pour at coffee shops. He'd see students all the time carrying their brand-name paper cups all over campus, into class if you let them, slurping and sloshing away while ignoring the lecture and texting their friends. Many of them made multiple caffeine runs every day. How the hell could they rationalize spending money that way *every day* while complaining endlessly about the cost of tuition, books, gas, and rent? How many future-delinquent student loans were funding this addiction? How many of these frivolous sippers would wind up in bankruptcy or foreclosure because they were too short-sighted to buy a fucking coffee pot and brew their own?

Larashawndria seemed to be spending a long time placing her order. Maybe she was having a hard time deciding. There seemed to be fifty different choices listed on the menu board behind the counter. Wade started to pay more attention when she began arguing with the bored, lanky teenaged "barista" on duty and then demanded to talk to his supervisor.

"I *am* the supervisor," he said. "I'm telling you, we don't *have* that drink."

"I get it all the time at the other Starbucks."

"Maybe you should go get it there then."

It's a fucking cup of coffee. Order something else, for Christ's sake.

"Fuck it. I'll order something else."

Now we're getting somewhere, Wade thought. Then watched in something approaching awe as she ordered a combination of specialty preparations, flavor shots, and sprinkles that brought the tab for her beverage to nine dollars. *It's a fucking cup of coffee*, he thought again. She added an obscenely expensive muffin to bring the hit to fourteen bucks, then pointed at Wade, and said, "He's paying."

Always pay your own way. Wade flashed to his mom, a week before she left the world, mind and body almost gone, spirit still strong, core values intact, on the night he had taken her to get her last ice cream cone, Dairy Queen, as usual, instead of Baskin-Robbins: **Get your money's worth whenever you can**. She'd reached into her purse and pulled out the cash Wade had secreted there an hour earlier while she was napping, knowing what she'd say when they arrived: **Thank you for bringing me.**

I want to pay for this. My treat tonight.

Back in the brave new world, Larashawndria snatched her muffin off the counter and plodded back to their table, picking en route at the premium cornmeal she'd added to Wade's bill. Wade ordered his own cup from the standard daily brew pot and awaited the creation of the pièce de résistance.

"Someone must be on the rag today," the barista condoled, as he finally pushed the towering, fizzing, foaming, tricolor concoction toward Wade with a glance at the table where Her Majesty awaited. "I hope she's not diabetic. Even if she isn't, there's enough sugar in there to send her into toxic shock."

Wade wondered if there was any coffee in there. He thanked the kid and put a dollar in the cup that was marked "Tips" apparently so Wade would know he wasn't making a contribution to the elimination of sub-Saharan poverty.

"Thank *you*. I hope she's worth it, man."

No further thanks were exchanged. "*That* took long enough," Larashawdria said when Wade placed the vessel before her. "It takes forever to get a fucking cup of coffee in this pit."

He shrugged. "Some of the orders are more complicated than others." He hoisted his own proletarian cup, offered an ironic mock clink.

"So you want me to pay for that, is that what you're saying?"

Actually, I want you to pay for **that**. He forced himself to look away from the Triple Jumbo Caramel Mocha Deluxe Clusterfuck with Muffin and said, "My treat. Why don't you tell me what happened at the frat party?"

"You really want to talk about that *here*?"

He tried out *No, I wanted to talk about it at my* **office**, *but you wouldn't get your buns out of bed to meet me there*, but it didn't exactly capture the tone he was hoping to set. *No, let's book a flight to Florencia, and you can loosen your tongue with a real cappuccino.* Better, but still not quite where he wanted to go.

"Sure," he said. "No one's paying attention to us."

"Yeah, right." She rolled her amazing violet eyes. "Look around."

Wade looked around. Everyone in the place was staring at

them. He heard Erica's voice in his ear, shifted the narrative perspective, adopted the onlookers' point of view: *a short, bespectacled, balding white geek who'd be lucky to get a date with Rosie O'Donnell is sitting alone at a table with the most beautiful girl in the world, a glorious Amazonian goddess dwarfing him by at least half a foot.* So what?

"Just ignore them," Wade said. "I'll sign autographs for everyone later."

Another eye roll over the straw as she sucked down Wade's life savings.

"They probably think I'm Joe Montana," he explained. "I get that all the time."

He wondered if she knew who Joe Montana was. Coach Porter had said the girl was not even eighteen yet. Joe had finished with KC in 1994. His last Super Bowl had come after the 1989 season, when she hadn't even been conceived, let alone born and abusively misnamed.

"Or Tom Hanks," he offered. "Some people tell me I look more like him."

"You look more like Humpty Dumpty to me."

"Thank you. I get that quite a bit, too."

He was hoping for at least a giggle or the beginnings of a grin. She shook her head contemptuously in dismissal instead. "Let's get this over with then. How much did the . . . guys tell you?"

"A.J. and Mars, you mean?" He'd wondered if they knew more about her than they'd let on, perhaps trying, after their own fashion, to protect her.

"I didn't even know their names, those guys I . . . went with. I just met them at that party." She paused, looked down into the remnants of her drink, directed her words almost into the dregs: "I can't *believe* I let them get me drunk and take me to that motel."

Wade tried to ease the pain. "You're not the first freshman who ever had a little too much to drink at a fraternity party and—"

"I didn't 'have a little too much to drink,'" she said fiercely.

"I got fucking drunk, okay?" Wade noticed heads pop up around them again. She noticed, too, lowered her voice but not its intensity. "I passed *out* on the way." She paused, shook her head. "Do you have any idea what those guys are like?"

Wade had an idea, decided to hear hers. "What do you mean?"

"I mean there's only one thing they're interested in."

Wade nodded. "Resolving the crisis in Darfur, you mean?"

A tiny sliver of a bitter laugh. "Most of these guys, even though they're African-Americans themselves, they couldn't pick out Africa from a map of the world if you crossed out Europe and Asia. They don't give a shit about Sudan."

"They don't know much about World War II either, I understand."

Another derisive little laugh. "I don't know too much about that myself. We kind of skimmed over that in high school." She looked away from the table, off into space, back down into her drink, then studied the menu board once more. Wade wondered if she was going to bail out the international economy and order another of the same. The next time he came into this clip joint, not that it would be any time soon given today's damages, he would see her drink listed up there with the others on the menu, named in her memory: the Double Trouble Meet Your Maker Toxic Shock Express. She looked back in his direction, almost met his eyes. "I guess that was a pretty important war, huh?"

Wade said gently, "Are you trying to change the subject?"

She blew out a huge sigh that crossed the table, redolent of whipped cream. "It's just that it's such a fucking stupid subject. These guys, they expect you to go down on them on the first date. They don't want to put a condom on when they get inside you, and then they want to throw you down and do it doggy-style. And you're a 'bitch' if you don't let 'em do exactly what they want." She paused, sneered across the table. "Isn't it romantic?"

"I haven't seen the Hallmark card with that storyline yet," Wade said. "But"—he couldn't stop himself from asking—"don't girls know what they're letting themselves in for if they go out with guys like that?"

"I *told* you, they got me *drunk*. They could have done *anything* to me. Christ, *he* could have done anything to me, that fat piece of shit coach they took me to. I didn't have any protection. I'm not on the pill or anything. I could've gotten a disease, or gotten pregnant with that man's baby. *God.*"

She started to cry. Wade reached for a napkin, extended it to her, too late. She'd wiped her eyes with both hands, smearing all over her face a combination of mascara, eye shadow, and snot. Hers was the only face Wade had ever seen that could absorb this new make-up scheme and still look alluring, even with the tears still coming. She saw the perplexed way he looked at her, laughed, perhaps at *his* discomposure, a little louder now than before.

"You know what the funniest part of all this is?"

Wade hadn't realized he was in a comedy, told himself to pay more attention. The genre crossovers were getting tricky these days. He pressed the napkin on her after all; she used it to wipe her hands, then balled it and thrust it savagely into her cup.

"I didn't *do* anything. If I lose my scholarship over this, I'll ... fuck, I don't know what I'll do."

"I don't think you're going to lose your scholarship," Wade said, hoping this was true even though he had no power to promise it. "Why don't you start over and tell me exactly what happened?"

"Could you hand me another napkin first, please?"

Wow. Manners. A breakthrough. Wade complied. She scoured her face, blew her nose, stuffed the cup again, and began her recitation: "I've had a really hard time here, fitting in. My boyfriend was supposed to come from home with me to play football here, but he couldn't make the grades. So I came here by myself."

Wade knew exactly how bad someone's grades would have to be to keep him off Matt Lytle's roster, but he didn't interrupt to inquire about other attributes the absent boyfriend might possess. He nodded, encouraged her to continue.

"I don't really have any close friends on the V-ball team. They all know each other from the club teams, but I hang a little bit with some of the girls who play basketball. Me and a couple of them—"

Wade stifled a grimace over the grammar, reminded himself that this was not the time or the place, and he wasn't an English teacher any more anyway. Someone else's problem now.

"—went over to Kappa Chi. We knew it was risky, but it's just so dead around here on Saturday night except for the frats, so we took a chance. We didn't know the football players would be there. They were all stoked from winning their last game and getting to a bowl game after all those loser years."

Wade nodded. "I imagine they were celebrating . . . liquidly."

"They were drunk off their asses. Some of them were stoned, too. They were peeing on each other and fighting over any chick that showed up. They practically—"

"Wait a minute. Back up. They were *peeing* on each other?"

"Yeah, outside on the patio, some of 'em had their dicks out and they were whizzing at each other. I guess they thought they were showing off."

Wade shook his head in almost disbelief. The mating rituals of a new generation. "That's almost as inspiring as the dating shows on TV. Then what happened?"

"Like I was saying, they practically tore our clothes off when we came through the door. They wanted us to take pictures: you know, take our tops off, *Girls Gone Wild* style. We told them to get lost."

"But they . . . didn't?"

"We had a few drinks, and . . . then a few more, and . . . I'm not really much of a drinker. I guess I went way over my limit. I know what you must be thinking, but I'm *not* a party girl. I just came here to play ball, earn my scholarship, get my grades, get my degree, and move on to a good job. I never meant to get in any trouble, cause any problems for anyone. Coach called my parents when I missed practice, and now they're so worried about me, they're talking about making me come home, go to the JC in town even though their V-ball team sucks. I can't believe how messed up everything is."

Wade nodded. "Let's get back to—"

"This is my ticket, my chance at some kind of a life. I got friends just started having babies in high school, never got married, never finished school, now they got no chance for any kind of life except Welfare. That's not what I want. Do you understand that?"

"I understand."

"Your job is to keep those guys on the football team, right? And cover for the coach. Why would you want to help me?"

"My job is a little broader than that," Wade said. "First, I'm not trying to 'cover' for the coach. I'm . . . investigating to find out what he did. As you might know, he's still a candidate to come back and keep his job here. Second, I try to help the athletes on all the teams, not just the football players. If they did anything truly wrong, I certainly won't be trying to help them stay on the team. And I want to help *you* because I don't think *you've* done anything wrong, and I want you to stop punishing yourself for . . . somebody else's misconduct." He paused. "Look, we all make mistakes when we're . . . going out with other people; we just have to figure out how to get past them." On an impulse he decided to tell her an edited version of the tale of Yoshi's threatened harassment suit.

"Oh, great. So now they're letting the fox investigate the wolf who ate the chickens."

"I don't think I know that story," Wade truthfully reported. "I *can* tell you, though, that I'm being actively considered for the advisorship of the New Hitler Youth Group on campus, in case you'd care to put a word in for me there."

"You trying to tell me you fuck up sometimes too?"

Wade nodded. "Like I said, we all make—"

"All you wanted from that girl was a little pussy?"

A lot of pussy, actually, but . . . Wade nodded, fell back into self-defensive mode: "And all *she* wanted from me was—"

"Shame on you."

Wade stopped, took the blow, forced himself to feel it.

She hit him with it again. "You a grown-ass man."

He nodded now, accepted it. Yoshi was a grown-ass woman, too, but still . . . . **Love truly, with all of your heart**. "You're right. Okay. Shame on me."

She studied his face, looking into his eyes, something different in hers now. She sighed. "At least you didn't get her all drunk and send your house niggers to pick her up."

"Why don't you finish telling me what happened?" He paused, then prompted, "You were passed out in the car, on the way to see Coach Lytle, and then . . .?"

"I really don't have that much more to tell you. The rest of the night is really . . . sketchy. I guess those guys, those *assbags*—"

Wade hadn't heard that one before. Always good to get a vocabulary lesson. Maybe class was in session today after all.

"—woke me up when we got to the motel, gave me some money, pushed me through the door. I remember that he didn't come to the door. He just left it unlocked. He was sittin' on the bed wrapped in a towel. He was pissed off when he saw I was alone."

"Why was he pissed off?"

"They were supposed to bring a white girl, too. He said he ordered chocolate and vanilla."

"Who was supposed to be vanilla?"

"*That's* the girl you want to talk to."

CHAPTER 14

A cute girl knocks on the door. What do you
do?

—Joe Paterno

Dixon James had printed out and left at Wade's office for
his inspection a stack of unmarked essays from the survivors of
Hotchkiss's online classes. Still debating whether to take Brooks
up on his offer to pick up the sections if it turned out Hotchkiss
could be persuaded to let them go, Wade was managing so far
to ignore the pile on his desk. He had found his way to Jenna
Jones's website when a sharp rap on the door announced her
appearance in the flesh. Spiky bleached blonde hair with raven
highlights, piranha eyes, lots of lipstick, a "do me" top, no
bra, short shorts, harem sandals: the perfectly coordinated late
autumn ensemble. She bounced into the room looking like she
could eat Napoleon's army for breakfast. Wade felt like a table
scrap.

She peered around him, saw the screen, grinned as he
initiated introductions. "You probably didn't recognize me with
my clothes on, did you?"

"I was just doing some . . . research on . . . you."

"Like my . . . body of work?" She gave him a little twirl, then
stepped closer—much closer, almost snuggling range—to him,
leaned in to see which of her many images was up on the screen.
She smelled like bubblegum and rum. Wade wondered if crystal
meth had been added to the mix.

She threw herself into a chair as if she were diving onto a
water bed.

Wade closed his eyes for a moment, tried to refocus. "Thanks
for coming in to see me. Your friend Larashawndria told me you—"

"I hope you didn't call her *that*," she interrupted with a laugh.

We settled on **sugar booger** *after the first few enchanting moments.* "There was a little confusion over—"

"She goes by Lara."

"Oh. That's . . . good to know. As I was saying, your friend said you might have some information about—"

"So, do you dig porn?"

Wade blinked. "Excuse me?"

"It's an easy question."

"I asked you here today to see what you can tell me about—"

"And I asked *you* if you dig porn."

"I hardly see what that has to do with—"

"Fine. Be that way. I'll be that way, too."

"What are you—"

"If you won't answer my question, I won't answer yours. Fair is fair, right?"

Wade blew out a breath. This was going to be harder than grilling Dupree and Marston. "What was your question again?"

"You know what my fuckin' question was. DO YOU LIKE PORN?"

He shrugged. "I've been known to take a look."

"See, that wasn't so hard, was it? Take a look at this." She pulled her top up, flashed him.

Wade gaped, gulped. What the hell was—

"Do you think my tits are too small?"

Wade snorted, in spite of himself, then cleared his throat and leaned forward, as if speaking into the microphone at his congressional investigation hearing. "For the record, I have no opinion on that subject."

"Maybe you should take a better look." Before Wade could respond, she had pulled the top over her head and tossed it aside. She stood up, stepped toward the desk, stretched forward onto her tiptoes, gave Wade an unrestricted view.

"Off the record then?"

"I think you'd better put your blouse back on."

"It's a T-shirt, not a blouse, dork. Did you see any buttons on it?"

Wade concentrated on trying not to stare at her nipples. "I didn't see . . . anything."

"You're no fun, are you?"

"So I'm told."

She narrowed her eyes, leveraged his discomfort. "Can you imagine how much trouble I could get you in if I ran to Security right now just like this and told them what we've been talking about? You realize I could be recording this whole conversation on my phone? I could put this shit on the Internet as soon as I get home."

Never be alone in your office with the door closed with a female student, staff person, or fellow faculty member, Wade remembered being counseled during mandatory sexual harassment training sessions when he was hired. It was probably an especially good idea to observe this policy when the visitor had recently escaped from a psychiatric ward.

She stepped back, sat down again. "Maybe you don't get off on this. Maybe you're gay."

Maybe I should be, Wade thought. *Maybe this crazy person will go away if—*

Arms akimbo, she tapped a toe, thrust her pelvis forward. "You like to look at pussy or not?"

"I don't see how that—"

"Want to see mine?"

Wade gestured limply at the computer screen. "I already have, remember?"

"Those are just pictures. You should see the real thing."

Now shorts came off. No panties. Another grin. "I never wear underwear."

Wade swallowed, nodded. "I understand Hillary has the same policy." He did his best to study the paint on his walls.

She grinned again. "This is sort of like Clinton and Lewinsky, don't you think?"

"The parallel escapes me."

"What did you think about all that? I mean, I was just a little girl, but you must've been keeping up on that stuff. Did you get pissed off at the prez, or did you wish that was you? Even though she was kinda chubular, not nearly as hot as me. Be honest, now."

Wade realized she actually expected a response. "It seemed that there might have been other matters to occupy him."

This time she laughed in his face. "You're lying your ass off."

Wade blushed. "How can you tell?"

"What's the big deal? It's no mystery. Men like to get their dicks sucked. If I had a dick, I'd like to get it sucked, too. Hillary was probably too busy fucking up her health care proposal."

"Nevertheless—"

"Are you telling me that if I was to offer you a blowjob right here, right now, you'd turn me down?"

"I'm afraid I am." Limp no more, Wade fought off his untimely arousal by forcing himself to speculate about how many varieties of venereal diseases were orally communicable.

"It would be good for you. Keeps the prostate gland from getting backed up. You know what they say: a BJ a day keeps the doctor away."

"Sounds like a good campaign slogan," Wade said. "Maybe Monica can use it when she runs for Congress, or—"

"*President* Lewinsky. How do you like the sound of *that?* The first woman in—"

Don't forget about Rose Bell.

"—the Oval Office."

"Well," Wade conceded, "it's not like she hasn't been in there before."

"Damn straight. Fuck affordable health care: she could run on the 'Oral Sex for Everyone' platform. Maybe put a porn star in the Cabinet."

Wade had to admit, the idea had its attractions. "I'll bet John McCain wishes he'd thought of that. Instead of—"

"Now *there's* another guy who *really* needs a blowjob."

More dire need . . . than any white man in history. Wade had laughed long ago, like everyone else in the theater, at Robin Williams' gash of the martinet in *Good Morning, Vietnam*, but in the intervening years he had often enough wondered if the line didn't apply just as well to himself.

"You've probably haven't had a real one in a while yourself, have you?"

Christ, was she psychic, too?

"You probably mostly get the half-ass kind where they reach for the towel and spit you out, am I right? I mean, if you're not going to swallow, you might as well leave the room, right?"

Wade looked at her carefully, tried to assess his options. "Actually, leaving the room seems like a pretty good idea right now," he said, standing to seize the opportunity to show her out. "Maybe you should put your clothes back on and go home now, and I'll call you another time"—*after the next Ice Age or two*—"and we can talk about—"

"Anal sex, how do you feel about that?"

Wade collapsed back into his chair, rubbed a hand over his eyes.

"Oh, don't go all Dr. Laura on me now, like you're disgusted that I even mentioned it. It's not my favorite thing in the world either, but what the hell, if the price is right, I'm game. Sixty percent of Americans have tried it. A lot of 'em like it. Some of 'em do it that way every time. Didn't you ever hear her ranting on the radio about it?"

Wade figured out that she was back to Dr. Laura. He shook his head.

"I'll bet you've seen her naked on the Internet, though. She's probably just your type: a big vocabulary and no tits."

He shrugged. "It was hard to say about the vocabulary from the pictures I saw."

"I'll bet you've tried anal yourself. You said you're gay, right?"

"Actually, I'm—"

"So you know what it feels like to have a ten-inch cock rammed all the way up your ass."

"—not," Wade said with a wince, flashing to the shower scene in *American History X.*

"You teach English, don't you? I thought pretty much all English teachers were gay. It seems like a pretty gay thing to do for a living, for a guy I mean, don't you think?"

"That's what my ex-wife used to say. Actually, I *don't* teach English any more. I—"

"If you don't teach English anymore, what are all these fucking essays doing on your desk? It says English 1A right here. 'Professor Hotchkiss': is that like your pen name or something? I thought your name was Dr. Wayne."

"Wade."

"Whatever. So do you guys like trade papers with each other then? God, what a gay thing to do."

Wade didn't have the energy to explain.

"*Ex*-wife, huh? You *sure* you're not a fag? *Hotch*kiss sure *sounds* like a faggy—"

"I could summon witnesses," Wade said.

"Just because you fucked a few chicks doesn't mean you're not gay. You could be bi, I guess."

"I believe 'metrosexual' is the term of choice now."

"You've got a big-ass vocabulary yourself, don't you, Dr. Wade? That probably means you've got a tiny little dick. They usually go hand in hand. Of course, it's probably your own hand you usually go in. I could help you with that, you know. If you're tired of wanking, I could get you off, any way you want it." She paused. "I'll be honest with you, I don't mind a small dick. I mean, not microscopic, but small is okay. It's better for anal actually."

"Thanks for the . . . tidbit," Wade said. He stood up again, threw up his hands. Time to surrender. "Okay, then. If you're not going to go, I guess *I* will." He paused, wondered what kind of risk he was taking abandoning his office to this wacko. "I'll leave the door locked. Could you please just be sure it closes behind you when you leave?"

"Sure, Doc." She came out of the chair, slipped by him, rubbing his leg in transit, claimed the seat he had just abandoned, pushed off from the floor for a 360 swivel, repeated it, then scanned the room from behind his desk. "Want me to grade any of these papers or anything for you before I go?"

Wade gestured to the pile. "Help yourself. Don't forget to ream them for the run-on sentences."

"People write like crap nowadays, don't they? They write like they're retarded. How hard is it to put a fucking period between two independent clauses?"

Hand on the doorknob, Wade paused, twisted his lips. "You know what an independent clause is?"

"Is that getting you hot? Just because I'm sexy doesn't mean I'm stupid, you know. Have you ever heard of MENSA?"

Wade blinked. It was *possible*, he supposed, but—

She grinned. "So have I. *Gotcha!*"

Wade shrugged, turned the knob. "Who says you're sexy?"

"Yeah, right, like you don't wish you had the balls to climb over this desk and fuck me six ways from Sunday right now."

"The last time I climbed over this desk it didn't turn out so great." Wade pointed again at the pile of essays. "I might be able to scare up some money from the reader budget if you actually want to give this a try. Have you taken English 1A?"

"Let me get this straight: you don't want me to suck your dick, but you'll *pay* me to grade your papers?"

"That's right."

"You've *gotta* be gay. That's *sick*." She picked up the top essay off the stack, glanced at it, mimed a retch, tossed it aside, picked up another, tossed it quickly as well. "I was gonna be an English major before I decided to switch to Business and learn something useful. Don't you get tired of reading this crap?"

"Never," Wade said. "I wake up with a hard-on every day just thinking about all the great papers I'll get to read." It was much easier to lie about now that he didn't have to *do* it any more.

"How 'bout this: if I find a great paper in this stack, I'll fax him my ass. That's gotta beat the hell out of an A."

"What if him's a her?"

"I do chicks, too. You're not the only metrosexual in this burg, you know."

"I told you, I'm not—"

"I'm bipolar, too. Also ADHD. You *sure* you don't want me to blow you before you go?"

Wade turned away to conceal the erection that seemed to have persisted in spite of his best intentions. He nodded at the papers.

"I wouldn't want to distract you from your labors."

She snickered. "Haven't you ever heard of multi-tasking?

I'm a woman—W-O-M-A-N. You think I couldn't suck you off and mark this shit at the same time?"

"As . . ."—Wade flashed to Larashawndria, scowling in the coffee shop—"*romantic* as that sounds, I think I'll have to—"

"Fuck romantic. You just need to get laid. And *I* need to get paid."

"—take a raincheck."

"I'm a bitch, not a ballpark, Doc. I don't do rainchecks."

"Well, in that case—"

"Shame to waste that soldier." She pointed at his trousers. "And don't give me that bullshit about waking up that way every day. What do you get at your age, like one of those every two weeks?"

Wade pulled the door open just enough to squeeze through, surveyed the terrain, put one foot out, said back over his shoulder, "We pay eight bucks an hour. I don't have a time sheet with me, but you can write your hours down on that pad there next to those papers when you get done."

He had almost pulled the door closed behind him when he heard: "Don't you want to hear about what happened with Coach Lytle?"

Wade sighed, stopped, came back in, closed the door, picked up her clothes, handed them to her, motioned her back into the visitor's chair, reclaimed his seat behind his desk, exhaled, composed himself as she quickly, casually put herself back together.

"Okay, tell me what happened."

"What's in it for me if I tell you?"

FUCK. I won't report you to Campus Security or the Mental Health Association.

Wade did a quick think, tried to guess how much Allenby would authorize from the hiring committee's funds to cover this expense. Fuck it. Not his game. He threw a dart at the board. "How about a hundred bucks?"

"Make it two hundred and I'll throw in that hummer."

"Okay, two hundred. Pass on the hummer. What happened?"

"Two hundred it is, then. That's the same deal I gave the

coach." She grinned at the symmetry. "I made him pay me extra not to tell the cops or the reporters. For now, anyway. It's nice to get paid twice for the same gig. Let's see the green."

Wade looked into his wallet without much optimism, found seventeen bucks, handed it over. "I don't carry that kind of cash around with me. Here's a down payment. I'm good for the rest."

"Do I look like the kind of girl who gives credit?"

"I'm good for it," Wade said again. "Besides, you can always blackmail me with the pictures on your iPhone if I don't pay up."

"Okay, I'll trust you. Trust *me*, though: if you *don't* pay up"—she jerked a thumb at Wade's computer screen, where she was still displayed in all her glory—"you'll be all over that World Wide Web with a monkey sucking on your dick."

Better that than the other way around. "Fair enough. Tell me—"

"Lara called me and said could I come over and help her out. She had a . . . situation."

"Why did she—"

"She's a good kid. Just really, really new to all this party stuff. She had a couple of drinks with those fraternity assholes, and then the football players talked her into going to see the coach. I think she actually thought she was just going to do a couple spins for him, collect her money, and go home. She's been really lonely here, and she ran up a four hundred dollar bill calling home to her idiot boyfriend last month. I know she was freaking out about it, and she probably figured she'd clear it or half of it anyway in a few minutes. Anyway, when the coach figured out she wasn't going to give him what he wanted, he told her to call a friend, she picked me, and the cavalry came to the rescue."

"How did she know to call you?"

"We met in our Intro to Biz class, and I told her about some modeling jobs and a porn shoot I had lined up. She's awesome looking. I told her to quit wasting her time with volleyball. She could make a fortune as a lingerie model. Sky's the limit if she's up for some porn. God, if I had her rack and her ass, I'd be famous by now."

"So what happened with the coach?"

"Nothing. Nada. Zippo. But not for lack of trying."

"What do you mean?"

"Do I have to draw you a picture? I sent Lara out to wait in the car and tried to get down to business. I gave it my best shot, Doc. Sat on his dick, stuck my tits in his face, teased him, squeezed him, rubbed him, sucked him, licked him—Limp City. He couldn't even get it up long enough to put a condom on."

"He couldn't . . . perform at all?"

She leaned her head back, tipped a cartoon bottle into a corner of her mouth. "He tells his team booze is the devil's tool, but I guess he doesn't listen to his own sermons." She paused. "You want more details?"

Wade nodded slowly, not sure if really did.

"He said he wanted to try anal. Like I said, not my favorite thing in the world, but he had the cash, so we tried that, too. Zipperoo. I even whispered naughty football words in his ear. I'm sure you know the ones I mean: *double reverse, naked bootleg, stick it in the end zone*, all that shit. Nothing."

Wade digested the report, pictured the scene.

"You look sort of disgusted, Doc."

Wade nodded.

"Do you know what really was really disgusting to *me*?"

*Let's see: **more** disgusting than a drunk, married, blubber-bellied, Bible-thumping blowhard three times your age trying to fuck you in the ass but he's impotent so he can't, you mean?*

"I give up," Wade said. "Unless you're going to tell me he asked you to pee on him. That seems to be popular around here these—"

"Worse than *that*."

"Oh." What could be worse than—

"The fat fuck wanted me to *pray* for him."

Nymph, in thy orisons, be all my sins remembered.

"For forgiveness, you mean?"

She nodded. "At first I thought he wanted me to pray him up a hard-on."

Wade laughed. "That sounds like quite a trick. I might even

go to church again if—"

"I told him to try Cialis. I mean, the laying on of hands wasn't working any miracles, was it? Of course, it turns out he can't use the leadlifters because of his high blood pressure. He's also got off-the-charts cholesterol, of course, whines about it like a big baby. Like you want to hear about all that crap when you're trying to get a guy off. The man's a total fucking, flopping mess."

Wade couldn't fight off the image of the frantic fat-ass defying doctor's orders, popping a pill or two—and then detonating right on top of Jenna, even as she sends forth her supplication for the ascension of his sullied flesh and/or the salvation of his immortal soul. The cleaning lady shows up in the morning, lugs the guts to the garbage can, finds Jenna cowering beneath, barely breathing.

"So, did the Good Lord forgive him?"

"Beats me. I don't do that praying shit. I gave up on that stuff when the minister at my mom's church tried to feel me up when I was ten."

"Christ," Wade blurted. "Did you . . . tell your mother?"

"Wouldn't have done any good—he was doing her, too."

Of course. The great American clergy's SOP. "What did you—"

"I told the jerk I'd tell my brothers and they'd beat the crap out of him unless he gave me fifty bucks. He paid up, too."

"Wow." Wade couldn't believe how inane that sounded, couldn't figure out what wouldn't sound the same.

"It didn't exactly work the way I planned it, though. I told my brothers anyway, thinking they would mess him up. What the hell, I had my fifty bucks, right? They had other plans though."

"What other—"

"The younger one held me down and the older one fucked me; then they traded places."

Wade found himself gaping again, couldn't help himself.

"Some family values, huh? You look a little shocked." She shrugged. "It didn't kill me."

Wade felt his throat tightening, his stomach lurching. Five minutes ago she was trying to talk him out of his pants; now she was tearing his heart out. Bipolar indeed. Maybe she wasn't the only one, though: five minutes ago he was fighting off a hard-on; now he wanted to puke.

Jenna got out of the chair, came over next to him again, not quite as close this time. She glanced at the essay now atop Dixon's stack, perused a paragraph or two. "This stuff really blows, doesn't it? Probably rots your brain to read it. You should look into working in the sex industry, Doc. It pays way better and it's hella interesting."

She leaned across in front of him, closer again now, knees touching, tapped a key on his computer, which had gone to screensaver, brought back up her slithering naked beckoning image, planted a perversely chaste kiss on the top of his head, and slipped out the door.

Wade watched her go, pushed the pile of brainrot onto the floor, put his head down on his desk for a long time. Then he went home to share the news about Lytle with Allenby, who met him at the door with news of his own.

"Your Japanese friend? The one that wants to marry you?"

"Yoshi. Only she doesn't—"

"She came by."

Wade frowned. "She knew I was at school, so I don't—"

"She wasn't looking for you."

"Oh. What was she—"

"Did you tell her about my separation?"

"I might've mentioned it. She's always asking about you and when we can go out for sushi again and stuff. Sorry, I didn't know your . . . deal was supposed to be confidential."

"Not a problem. It isn't," Allenby said. "But there's something else you didn't know."

"What's that?"

Allenby reached into his coat pocket and handed his extraction to Wade. Thong panties. Purple lace. Jasmine-scented.

Wade studied his clutch. "Thanks, but I don't think these are my size."

"She wants to marry *me,* too."

"Oh."

"Don't worry: nothing happened. The world is full of women.

I don't need to fuck my best friend's lover."

"Ex-lover, I think we can safely say. She's filing a harassment suit against me, remember? Don't be surprised if she tries something like that with you."

"I think you can forget about the harassment suit. I had a little talk with her."

"Was this before or after she took her panties off? What'd she do, offer to show you hers if you showed her yours?"

"She thinks all black men are out of control. I had to set her straight on that. And I was able to get her to understand that if she persists in trying to blackmail you, I'll use my connections to start deportation proceedings."

"Jesus. Can you really do that?"

Allenby shrugged. "Not sure. Probably not. But I sure as hell sounded convincing."

"What did she say?"

"That's when she asked if *I* wanted to get married."

Wade walked into the kitchen, opened the cabinet under the sink, pulled out the garbage container, held the panties up over it.

"I don't suppose these have any sentimental value to you?"

Allenby shrugged again. "Not a bad look. Nora spends a fortune on underwear I never see."

Wade nodded. *Present tense*, he couldn't help noticing. Did that mean Allenby was keeping his options open? Some things were better off left firmly in the past. "Brenda used to buy hers from Army Surplus."

He studied the panties once more, twirled them on his index finger, then tossed them ceremoniously into the trash, turned on the faucet to wash his hands. "I just met a girl who could have used those, actually. Thereby hangs a tale."

CHAPTER 15

Winter is icomen in
Lhude sing Goddamm,
Raineth drop and staineth slop,
And how the wind doth ramm!
— Ezra Pound, "Ancient Music"

When he has nothing else to do, he can
always contemplate his own greatness. It is a
considerable advantage to a man to have so
inexhaustible a subject.
— of Sir Leceister Dedlock in
Charles Dickens' *Bleak House*

The epochally splendid Indian summer had abruptly died, fall had blown by in the blink of an eye, and an early winter had suddenly, soddenly settled in. Wade hated winter. Even the mild, attenuated, candy-ass version that passed for the dismal season in California was enough to send him into virtual hibernation for weeks on end. At school he would hear students or staff gabbing rapturously about trekking to the mountains for winter sports— downhill, cross country, sledding, snowboarding, or even just "going to the snow"—and he would shudder and hug himself for warmth. The closest Wade ever wanted to get to snow was watching some chest-painted idiot on ESPN lose his nipples to frostbite at Lambeau Field. Swaddled in multiple sweatsuits, thermal underwear, three pairs of socks, with a blanket over his lap, a steaming mug of coffee laced with rum in his clutches, and the thermometer irresponsibly set at 73 degrees, Wade was still cold and miserable and aching for spring.

Matt Lytle was presumably not feeling on top of the world either, wherever in it he was taking refuge now. After receiving a brief phone call from Allenby the morning following Wade's final report on his investigation, Lytle had quietly rescinded his request to reapply for the CSU job. Two days later the local and national media had with considerably more fanfare reported various versions of his activities at and after the fraternity party. Wade didn't know, and frankly didn't care, if Jenna Jones had repeated the pattern of her dealings with the "hands-on" minister and cashed in again in spite of the payoff she'd received, or if reporters had put the pieces together independently; he was glad, in any case, that Larashawndria Lewis's name had not surfaced in the media accounts, either because she was still a minor or because the dirt-diggers hadn't found it, and he confirmed with Coach Porter that the freshman had returned to practice and was still on scholarship. Wade had sent Jenna his personal check for $183, electing not to tap Allenby's committee for the funds in case of future complications. He'd also enclosed an application for a CSU reader position, in case her other enterprises ran dry. She'd sent him back an email acknowledging receipt of the check and the information that she was using it for seed money for her next project, which she described as a combination porno/horror flick. She was scripting and producing it herself. She'd promised to send a draft of the screenplay soon and told him that there would be a small part in the film for him if he was "up for it." Wade hadn't replied to the email, but he hadn't trashed it either.

Sherman Slate had been offered the head coach job on an interim basis, with his long range fate to be reevaluated after the bowl game with USC. The committee had settled on the arrangement quickly to put the Lytle fiasco behind them. It was hardly, Wade had thought when the deal was struck, the ideal scenario for success, but those were the terms Slate had proposed, and he had been taken at his word. Allenby seemed undaunted by the pressure he was placing on his new hire and confident that the foundation for extending CSU's football success had been laid. The first problem facing Slate, exacerbated considerably by the media frenzy, was identifying and disciplining the players involved in the abuses at the frat party. Allenby expected him to announce soon a decision that would set the tone for the program's new administration. Wade was guessing that the two ex-military men were of like mind on the subject. He assumed that Dupree and Marston would likely be suspended from the bowl game, if not dismissed from the program, and wondered if Louis Blodgett might face a portion of the same fate.

"Beautiful day out there," Allenby said now as he burst through the door, shook off the sleet or hail or whatever the hell element he had just navigated, and deposited two large bags of groceries on the kitchen table. "Really bracing. You ought to quit sitting around, get out and get some exercise."

Wade held up his index finger and without removing his eyes from the television screen did a vigorous set of digital jumping jacks for his friend's benefit.

"I found some great steaks. Tonight we splurge!"

"As opposed to last night, when we cleansed our arteries with your Alfredo sauce, you mean?"

"You worry too much. I'll steam you some broccoli to go with your steak."

Wade, who was lucky to open a can of tuna without wounding himself, was grateful and in no way resentful to have his kitchen commandeered at a moment's notice and a repast once only imaginable turned out and placed before him. Whenever, out of a sense of fairness, Wade offered to call in an order for take-out, Allenby would shake him off, disappear into the galley, and whip up something delicious. Wade was beginning to wonder if this is what consumption of victuals was supposed to be like in domestic life, if you weren't stupid enough to . . . bind yourself up with someone like Brenda. Recalling his ex-wife's many attempts to poison him with half-cooked poultry or carbonized meat loaf, he vowed to pay attention and learn something from the master chef who was his guest—when spring came anyway, and it wasn't too damn cold to get out of his chair and go into the kitchen to observe the preparations.

Wade washed the dishes after another inspired meal. He came into the living room to find Allenby in an easy chair, apparently nearing the end of Wade's dissertation.

"I've read a lot of these stories and books you're writing about. I was a lit major, you know, before I went to law school."

"Good preparation for the nonsense you encountered there, I imagine."

Allenby grunted. "*The Faerie Queene* didn't exactly rock my world. Business or Economics would've made a lot more sense. One of my profs suggested Philosophy, if you can imagine that. I lasted about two class periods in there. All that *Ich und Du* crap from Buber? Hemingway was a kick in the pants compared to that shit."

"You might want to skip the chapter on *The Old Man and the Sea*. I had to smoke a lot of dope to get through that part myself."

"'Man can be destroyed, but not defeated,'" Allenby intoned somberly.

"Easy to write when you root for Joe DiMaggio," Wade said. "Try it when you're stuck with Joe Barry Carroll and Andris Biedrins."

"Did you ever send this out to academic presses, try to get it published?"

"I was so tired of it by the time Berkeley finally signed off that I just put it to bed. It doesn't have any of the trendy theoretical mumbo jumbo in it, so I figured—"

"That's exactly why it's readable."

"Thanks. I wish you had been on my thesis committee. I'd have had my PhD ten years earlier, before my hair started to fall out."

"There's a guy I met at a publishing convention who runs a pretty successful little press, does some academic stuff once in a while. I know he likes Hemingway a lot; he's always looking for stuff about him. Maybe I'll send this to him, ask him to take a look. I could publish it myself, but it's more up his alley."

"You think he would want to publish *that*?"

"It's no slam dunk. He says he gets about a hundred submissions a week, so five thousand or so in a year, publishes maybe ten or twelve, so it's long odds."

"Sounds like another 'Hail Mary' to me," Wade said.

Allenby shrugged. "Couldn't hurt to find out. It's just sittin' on your shelf."

The next day Wade arrived at work in a pounding rain to find a voicemail commanding him to meet Delia Herman in her office as soon as he came in. When he got there, she waved him brusquely into a chair. Another platter of pastry sat on her desk, none of which she once again offered to share.

"I guess you're happy now that you've helped to drive Coach Lytle out of our community. I just wanted to tell you that that your actions in committee contributed to the loss of a very successful employee and to a good man's embarrassment."

"I think it's fair to say he took care of the embarrassment all by himself. I just did what you asked, found out about the party."

"In any case, I just thought I would offer *you* the opportunity to withdraw from reapplying for *your* position in order to spare you the embarrassment of . . . not winning reappointment."

"Not winning is what I do best," Wade said. "But I can always use a little more practice."

"You're staying in then?"

He nodded. "I don't suppose you can tell me if there's a Japanese teacher here at CSU who has applied?"

"That's officially confidential, of course, as you very well know. But . . . I suppose it doesn't hurt to tell you that, while she was under serious consideration for a while, and would certainly have been likely to beat *you* out, there's a new candidate with some truly remarkable qualifications."

Herman reached across her desk, picked up a file folder, fanned it in front of Wade's sour gaze.

"Diversity-wise, you mean?"

"Exactly. I suppose I could leave this file on my desk for a moment while I powder my nose if you'd like to see what you're up against."

"No thanks. I can see that I'm up against you, and that's all I really need to know, isn't it?"

"There's no reason to take this *personally*, Dr. Wade. It's just that there are *so many* other candidates whose qualifications *far* exceed your own." She paused to let the naked malice linger in the air, then found a way to accessorize it: "I'm sure your old friend Gordon Brooks will be interested in giving you back your old job. Part-time, wasn't it?"

She turned to her platter, studied the options painstakingly, selected a sugar-coated jelly donut. Wade headed for the door.

"By the way," she told his back, a half-chewed chunk informing her diction, "Campus Security informs me you've been looking at pornography on your CSU computer. That's a violation of—"

He spun and blurted, "That was in connection with my research into the investigation of"—*your boytoy Matt Lytle oh shit I'm screwed again.*

"People like you always have your excuses." She licked her fingers, powdering her nose after all with confectioner's sugar, also her chin, and adding to the natural growth occurring there a little goatee of purple goop. "Perhaps you should explain them to Dr. Brooks when you—"

Perhaps **you** *should dial 911, have them send a team of surgeons to sew your stomach shut.*

"—see him to—"

Have them stitch your piehole while they're at it.

"—discuss your future here, whatever that might be."

What the hell, stitch the peehole, too.

With a shudder at the thought of whom he was allowing to direct the progress of his life, Wade forced his feet once again onto the dolorous path to the English Department, where he'd find out how much further he was willing to debase himself in order to secure the prospect of future employment. Having discarded as undependable his previous reliance upon apocalyptic intervention, part of him still held hope to learn upon arrival there that Brooks had been hit by that swine flu bug that was going around (or by the flesh-eating bacterial virus, if that was still going around, too). Alas, Wade found the homunculus in, wart and all, and available for consultation. Clara Shelby rolled her eyes and waved Wade in, then mimed the swing of a baseball bat, presumably intended for a spinal tap. Her boss was at his desk, though nearly obscured behind it by huge stacks of haphazardly piled books, binders, folders, and obviously unsorted papers. On a corner of the desk, angled out to assault the eye of visitors, was a picture of a rat chewing off one of Brooks's ears. For some reason Brooks was smiling in the photo.

"There's my baby girl," he said, beaming, when he saw where Wade's focus had unavoidably been drawn.

On closer inspection Wade realized it was the infamous Chihuahua, maybe just sticking its tongue in there, having a waxy snack. He thought it was quite possibly the ugliest mammal he had ever seen, even counting present company.

"Cute as a button, isn't she? That's my little Suzy-Q."

Wade thought of offering up "FUBAR" as a more fitting appellation, kept it to himself.

"My wife says she's smarter than me."

Wade remembered his purpose, spit on the gopher ball again.

"Glad you stopped by. Just about to give you a shout myself. We finally got the scam what am about Professor Hopkins."

"Professor *Hotchkiss*. You finally heard from him then?"

"We heard *about* him."

"That doesn't sound promising."

"We finally reached his granddaughter. I'm sorry to tell you that our good friend Aldo had a—"

"Al*den*."

"— major stroke in September, and—"

"In *September*? How the hell has he—"

"—passed away in October."

"Passed away," Wade repeated.

Brooks nodded sadly. "He died. In October."

"In October," Wade repeated again. He felt like a parrot. So he had spoken truth unwittingly to Erica. "Then his classes were continuing all this time without any—"

"Apparently his reader did a bang up job of keeping the old ball rolling."

His reader. Of course. Who needs a professor when mighty Dixon is on the job? Wade could hardly wait to break the news, see the look on that impossibly stoical young face when he told him.

"With, of course, the perhaps unfortunate complication that this individual . . . filling in may have been grading a tad too harshly for our . . . diverse student population. As you know, we're not quite Harvard or Yale around here, although I like to think we're pretty damn close."

Wade didn't offer his opinion of what the intellectual standard at CSU was pretty damn close to, but a middle-of-the-pack 1960s junior high school came to mind. What Brooks was pretty damn close to was a lawsuit from Dixon demanding back pay for the semester at a full professor's wage. Let alone a phalanx of accompanying litigation from students demanding a reassessment of their grades by an evaluator who was not concurrently enrolled in their very own class. He wondered if Brooks had even a remote idea of the implications, ethical and otherwise, of the dead man's tale and the field day the media would have when they told it.

"Of course we'd like to keep this as quiet as we can, you understand. We don't want to cause a big . . . . conflaparation."

"I've never seen one of those," Wade said, "and I'd just as soon keep it that way." Then he reminded himself again of the motive for his visit, bit his lip, and offered, "How can I help?"

It was not a sentence he had ever expected to utter in Gordon Brooks's presence, unless he somehow someday fortuitously found himself in position to pull the plug on a life support machine, but Wade was able to follow it successfully now with two suggestions: first, an enhanced compensation package for Dixon James for his work up to now and in the spring; next, a plan to turn this semester's classes over to a couple of graduate students Wade knew who were computer literate, desperate for income, and far more capable than Hotchkiss, even when he was among the living, of helping students to improve their writing. Hell, even in his heyday fifty years gone Hotchkiss had been no match in that regard for the fifteen-year-old he'd hired.

"Glad you support my thinking on this," Brooks said of their settlement.

Okay, *now or never*. "About next semester."

"I was just about to bring that up," Brooks said with a smile that might have been almost beneficent if it hadn't been so smarmy. "Mrs. Shelby was just reminding me that you might be available to help us out again. How's this sound? We'll give you back your three sections of comp like you used to do for us, *and* we'll throw in a couple of extra sections online, long as you understand as a part-time hand we'll have to defer the compensation for those bonus babies until the summer." He winked. "Gotta keep the dang bean counters happy, don't we?"

Wade did the math, swallowed hard, restrained himself from springing out of his chair to choke the life out of the mucksucker who'd offered this insane load. "Five sections of composition. That's a lot of papers to—"

"*Plus*," Brooks interrupted, fairly bursting now with magnaminity, "there's *another* perk for you that comes with this package. There's a big pow-wow on online teaching coming up next month. Dovetails perfectly with what we were just discussing. Hope you got that brochure I sent you in the campus mail."

Wade nodded. "I got it. I sent it back to you. I thought you mailed it to me by mistake. It says the conference is for deans and department heads. Maybe your boss should go."

Brooks frowned. "*He* sent it to *me*. *I* have to find someone who wants to go. I assumed you would be glad to help out your old department, especially in view of your . . . situation for next semester."

"But it's not *for* teachers," Wade pointed out. "It's all about"—*scams to raise enrollment and tricks to pretend you know who's doing the work in the classes*—"administrative procedures."

"Oh. I guess I didn't read that part."

The part in English, you mean? Maybe I can have it translated into moronese for you.

"Do you still have the brochure?"

"Oh, I'm sure it's around here somewhere. We'll find it." Brooks glanced around his office. Wade followed his desultory gaze. It wasn't just the desk that was overloaded. Heaps of crap were everywhere, papers piled on top of every flat surface and crowding the shelves full of books Brooks had never read but would tell you all about anyway. The prospects of finding anything in here were about as promising as Wade's chances surviving this conversation without a wart-mutilation fantasy. Brooks began shuffling through a few of the stacks.

Wade had never given much credence to the concept of karma, but he found himself beginning to wonder if there was something to it after all. First Brooks had knocked him on his ass—well, *back* onto his ass anyway—in his office, to pay him back for last year's lick. And now Wade couldn't help reflecting on the plot he and Angela had once concocted, regrettably aborted when she chickened out, to dispatch Brooks to an imaginary convention; the plan would have left him stranded on the infamously twisted two-lane road to August-humid Hana, quite possibly culminating in a fatal crash in his trashy rental car when he tried to overtake a tour bus on a blind curve. Maybe this conference nonsense was more cosmic payback.

Brooks gave up on his search. "Can't seem to lay my mitts on that puppy now. That's not important. I'm just glad you've decided to go."

Wade blinked. "Here's a thought: maybe they should have the conference ONLINE!"

Brooks's chuckle dismissed this preposterous notion. "It's in Ohio. Should be some great skiing out there this time of year. Twelve feet of snow on the ground out there already last I saw on the news. Be even more in January. You a winter sportsman?"

"It's in *Iowa*, Dr. Brooks."

"Oh. Well, same difference. Practically the same state. Plenty of snow out there too. Downhill your thing?"

"I try to stay in bed in winter."

Brooks, as usual, missed his drift. "I used to chase those ski bunnies down the slopes myself, believe me. Caught up with more than a few of them, too, if you know what I mean." Brooks leered conspiratorially, two cocksmen swapping tales of conquest. Wade pictured a Playmate of the Month dandling on Brooks's inert lap, sucking on his wart. "Matter of fact, if I weren't up to my eyeballs in paperwork around here right now, I'd probably bump you out of the deal and take a run at this sucker myself."

sounds like an excellent idea," Wade said, standing is exit. "And I'll be more than happy to help you out e of this paperwork"—*it all looks flammable to me*— ·sυ ɟ can"—*freeze to death in the municipal airport of your choice*—"go."

"Wish it were that easy, bucko. Hours of work ahead of me to sort all this out." Brooks waved his hands around the crammed room again. "Takes a lot of specialized training, years of it really, to learn how to—"

Unzip and pee without snagging your willy.

"—run a division of this size, you know."

Division? Wasn't it only a department that he was running into the ground? Wade told himself to let it go, tried to tote up in his head the pay for five adjunct sections at the criminal current hourly rate, turned toward the door, couldn't quite make it. "But you're the chairman, not the—"

"Dean? Don't quote me on this, of course, but let's face it, Dedalus has been phoning it in these last few years. Good thing he's finally punching out. You know what they call him, don't you?"

Wade feigned ignorance as the NCAA's undisputed all-time suck-up champion snickered and then shattered simultaneously his own season and career records for back-stabbing and hypocrisy.

"Anyway, everybody around here knows that I'm the one who—"

Can't find his ass without a map.

"—gets the work done on this campus. Fact is, I wouldn't be surprised if they ask me to step into that slot for a few years, if these new candidates they're lining up to interview don't come up to scratch."

"Well, in that case," Wade said, "I hope you'll enjoy the respite when you go to this great conference. Thanks again for thinking of me, though. Dress warm." Then, taking a cue from Jenna Jones, he leaned in to close the deal. "Rest assured that I'll make it a point *not* to quote you when I meet with the dean later today. I think a paraphrase should suffice, don't you? What was that nickname you gave him again?"

Wade walked away despising himself for resorting to fabrication and blackmail, but not as much as he despised Gordon Brooks, and not nearly as much as he despised the idea of going to Iowa in January. Or, indeed, the idea of going anywhere at any time to learn anything about online education. He already knew far more than he cared to about that epidemic. He had recently seen a posting by a college math instructor who boasted that he could easily teach forty-five units per semester using the online format. Wade thought about the engineers of the future building the roads and bridges he would be driving on and hoped fervently that they weren't taking their calculus classes from this grifter or his klatch. There was even one associate professor he knew of at CSU who had drawn a full-time paycheck teaching online from a local community college at the same time she was drawing her full salary doing the same at the university. The arrangement had lasted for several lucrative years, until a dismayed student had blown the whistle on her after transferring from one school to the other and receiving in each place when seeking assistance an identical automated message that said, "DO NOT ATTEMPT TO CONTACT YOUR INSTRUCTOR. Follow the directions in your software program for the course."

Wade called Dixon as soon as he got back to his office.

"He's *dead*?"

"Two months ago. You'll get a check with a little something extra for your labors."

"Fuck that. I'm selling this story to *The National Inquirer*."

"You have friends who still have to work here, you know. And remember, you might be getting a degree someday from this place yourself."

"Are you telling me to hush this up?"

"I'm telling you I promise to go through proper channels in the university to make sure this crap doesn't happen again. I might get my friend Allenby involved. In the meantime, I've arranged for you to continue tutoring the football team in the spring, at an improved rate of pay. Brooks is going to fund it from his reader budget. You won't have to grade all those horrible papers."

Dixon went silent for a moment, pondered the offer. Then, "You really know how to hit a guy in his weak spot, don't you? I hate that shit."

"You figured that out a lot faster than I did, kid."

"I still might have to let this cat out of the bag someday. This is too big to—"

"Take a creative writing class next semester," Wade suggested. "Put it in a novel."

After he hung up with Dixon, Wade checked his email and found a message from Erica Wiley. She had gleaned from the grapevine, or perhaps from Delia Herman herself, information about the "super candidate" whose application the A.D. had taunted Wade with. Apparently his own prospects were every bit as hopeless as Herman had led him to believe. When he went home, Wade found a message from Angela and called her back to report upon his status. He told her briefly about Hotchkiss's demise, his conversation with Dixon, and Brooks's offers.

"Iowa in January, eh? Sounds like just your lift ticket, Wade."

"I don't care if it's on the Champs-Élysées in the middle of May; I'm not going to any fucking online education conference."

"What are the chances of hanging onto the job that you have?"

"This is probably too late to save you the trouble, knowing how compulsively proactive you are, but if you haven't already sent that letter I asked you for, don't bother. They found a biracial Stanford PhD who's trans*gendered*. And trilingual."

Angela whistled. "That's got to be tough to beat."

"Pretty fucking diverse, all right."

"That raises a question, Wade. Would you chop your dick off to keep your job?"

"Might as well. I could squat to pee, and I'm not using it for much else these days anyway."

"Probably worth considering. Beats teaching five sections of composition."

"Thanks for the suggestion. I don't think I can learn Hmong, though."

"I hear that's a tough lingo for us palefaces to pick up."

"He—or she—whatever the fuck it is, also speaks—"

"Swahili. I know."

"Wait a minute. You *know* this person, Angie?"

"You could say that."

What the fuck? Then the shoe dropped. "Are you telling me—"

"That letter you wanted?"

"You already sent it, didn't you?"

"Mais oui. Je n'existe que pour te servir."

"So *you* sent the application to—"

"C'était moi, encore une fois, mon capitaine. I also wrote the letters of recommendation for him/her from several very distinguished professors/colleagues who are by remarkable coincidence all on sabbatical right now in the Congo or in Laos."

"Still putting that Stanford letterhead to good use, I see."

"Not to mention I finally got to use my MFA. Your Dixon's not the only one with some creative writing chops, you know. I also got to do my tranny voice—Herman called me up to check me, I mean *her*, I mean *it*, out. I gave me a glowing recommendation."

"I'll bet you did."

"And get *this,* Wade: I think the old bat hit on me. Over the *phone.* She suggested 'dinner and whatever, if you know what I mean.'"

"Wow. And how are you going to get yourself, and/or him/her/it, and more importantly *me,* out of—"

"Simple. I'll send another letter this week to withdraw the application. A better opportunity unexpectedly arose in . . . oh, I don't know . . . Appalachia."

"Someplace where the languages will really come in handy."

"Exactly. Then *next* week Herman gets *another* letter warning her of the hoax that's going around about this ridiculously overqualified candidate—the very one she's been raving about all over campus. She's so afraid of being pilloried for getting taken in that she quietly ends the screening process, notifies the other candidates, reinstates you, and the whole thing goes away. So . . . give it a week or so, and, the job, such as it is, as you love to say, should once again belong to only you."

"You've been a busy girl," Wade said. "I suppose I owe you big time again."

"Sure looks that way to me."

"If you make the cut for the dean interview out here, I'll take you to Manny's for a burger."

"Deal. One more thing, Wade."

"Okay, fries and a milkshake, too. Anything else?"

"Don't be in too much of a rush to chop off your dick, okay? You might get a chance to use it again someday."

CHAPTER 16

He's our teammate. We should try to help him.
—John Unitas, on casting the lone
vote among the Baltimore Colts
against expulsion of Johnny
Samples for locker-room theft

Isn't there something perverse about a nation
completely engrossed in football while
the drums of war, a deadlier game, beat
persistently yet quietly in the background?
—Robert Scheer

Wade woke to find that Allenby had left for campus early. He looked out the window into a steady dismal drizzle, turned on the news, saw the forecast of yet another storm. He felt like climbing back into bed, pulling the covers over his head, popping out again to take a peek in maybe mid-April. Allenby phoned before he could execute the plan.

"Slate invited us to watch practice this afternoon. You up for it?"

"Only if we get to stand in the rain for a couple of hours."

"Wuss. Don't ever join the Army."

"I may have to. Looks like it's either that or go back to work for Gordon Brooks. Hunting for al Qaeda in the Hindu Kush sounds like a pretty good deal by comparison."

Hunting for al Qaeda. Maybe there *was* a way out in the idea. Build on the buzz from the Bin Laden kill and sell the concept to Hollywood as a reality show: round up a death squad of ex-military or CIA mercenaries and fortune hunters, quadruple that pissante twenty-five million dollar bounty they'd put on Osama, throw in a few high profile convicted felons with the offer of a pardon—up for some real action, O.J.?—and film the gang of merry pranksters going after al-Zawahiri, or whoever the hell was calling the shots now, in his lair. Who knows, maybe catch the fucker with his pants down jerking off over some porn in a Pakistani port-a-potty, blast the be-jism out of him on live TV; imagine the ratings bonanza!

"I doubt if the weather over there would agree with you," Allenby said.

Wade parted blinds, peered outside again, saw that drizzle had turned to downpour. "I may just send my TV crew."

Hat, raincoat, umbrella, and galoshes notwithstanding, Wade was drenched when he reached his office. He was surprised to find Marcus Foster waiting there for him, in shorts and a T-shirt, studying the office hours posted on the door.

"Sorry. I guess I'm a little late. The storm delayed me."

Marcus smiled, shook it off, no biggie, then looked at Wade more closely. "That's a lot of gear you got goin'. You don't like the rain?"

"Just training for Afghanistan," Wade said. "Come on in."

Marcus sat down, waited as Wade removed his paraphernalia, before announcing his business: "I want to talk to you about the suspensions Coach Slate is going to hand down today."

"Okay." That made some kind of sense, Wade supposed, since he had done the internal investigation, but Slate had shown no intent to consult him on the decision, so it seemed unlikely there would be an opportunity for input. He could see Marcus was wrestling with what to say next.

"You ever play any football?"

So polite he had to ask. Wade laughed, shook his head, flexed a nominal bicep, mimed the click of a remote control. "Couch potato. They also serve who only sit and watch."

Marcus nodded. "You seem to know the game, but . . . people who never played got no idea what it's like out there. Crazy shit goes on all the time. One team we played against in high school—I played in a decent league, but this one team really sucked, went like 1-9, 0-10 my junior, senior years—they were just out there trying to hurt people. They knew they couldn't beat us. Their offense couldn't move the ball against our D at all, but they had some mean dogs on their own defense. They had this competition to see who could put our guys out of the game. That's how they kept score. And if they could knock a guy out for the season, that was like a big bonus to them. They'd go for knees, roll under you from behind, blindside you after the whistle, anything to try to hurt you as bad as they could."

"That doesn't sound like much . . . fun."

"When you get the teams like theirs where there's lots of rednecks going against lots of brothers, like mine, it's pretty bad."

Wade thought of Bludge, sitting in the same chair where Marcus sat now, disclaiming the "skinhead" designation.

"Rednecks like Louis Blodgett, you mean?"

"I won't use that word about him," Marcus said slowly, "but I can see why you'd make that connection. Anyway, we got into this big fight with that team my senior year when we played them at their place, our last regular season game. Eight of our guys got kicked out, suspended, too, which killed us in our playoff game, and everybody said how stupid they were. But they were just pissed off about all those cheap shots and defending themselves because the refs didn't do anything to keep it under control."

"But doesn't it just escalate when you retaliate?"

"Guy swings his helmet at you, you're gonna swing back with something, whatever you got. Like I said, if you haven't been there, you don't know what it's like."

"I can understand that."

"Gettin' back to the thing with Bludge, he told Coach the return guy kneed him in the balls after he pulled him down. We couldn't see it on the film, but a lot of times you only see the second shot, the one that gets caught."

Wade recalled Monte Stickles from John Brodie's 49er teams sneakily starting fights with a cheap shot that demanded a response, then crying to the refs for the unsportsmanlike conduct flag on his opponent. Probably gained more yardage over the years that way than he ever did trying to catch JB's passes with those stone hands of his.

"So what is it that you wanted me to . . . help you with?"

"Coach Slate is going to announce the punishments at the

team meeting tonight. Most of the guys think he's gonna kick A.J. and Mars out of the bowl game, maybe even off the team, for what they did at that party, and I think he's gonna kick Bludge out of the game, too, for . . . provoking them and for pulling that San Diego State guy's hair. I want you to help me convince Coach Slate to let Bludge play. We're gonna need every man we've got to have a shot to beat SC."

"Even the slow white guys?" Wade remembered Marcus's earlier assessment of Bludge's limitations.

Marcus shrugged. "He plays hard. Coach Slate is real smart. He could find a way to use him. I'll offer to talk to Bludge myself about . . . cleaning up his act."

"That should be an interesting conversation."

"It's worth a try. Whatever else he is, he's not stupid."

"Are you a Christian by any chance, Marcus?"

Marcus frowned, obviously taken aback by the question. "Why do you ask that?"

"Well, Bludge professes to be one, although I'm not sure what branch that would be, maybe NeoNazis of the Nazarene. Anyway, I just thought that might be a way to approach him, if you two . . . happen to have that in common."

"I'm not really a religious person," Marcus said. "I mean, I was raised in the church and everything. I believe that a man named Jesus lived, that he had some good ideas that most of us—all of us, I guess—can learn from, and that some fools nailed him to a cross, but I just never needed to dress it up with all that . . . fairy tale stuff about the immaculate conception and the resurrection, stuff like that. If other people want to believe it, that's okay with me, as long as they don't try to put me down for *not* believing it—like Coach Lytle used to do sometimes. That really offends me. I mean, in my Civ class we learned that the Sumerians had the same myths five thousand years ago, and—"

Marcus stopped abruptly, perhaps wondering if he'd gone too far. "I hope I didn't offend *you*."

Wade shook his head.

"How about you, Dr. Wade? What's your . . . religious affiliation?"

"Forty-Niner Faithful," Wade said. "And I haven't given up

entirely on the resurrection. As for the rest . . . devout heathen, I guess. I think maybe you and I are kindred spirits there."

Now Marcus nodded thoughtfully. "I will say this, though: the other side of the coin is that I know lots of guys who do need that stuff. I'm talking about guys I grew up with who would probably be dead now or in prison if someone hadn't dragged them to church, made them go, got them out of the gang life they were in or headed to. So I guess the church does have its place. A guy like A.J., maybe he could learn a few things that would calm him down if he spent his Sundays in church instead of . . . wherever else he's runnin' around to."

"Could be," Wade said, although his first reaction to the idea was to picture Dupree helping himself to the collection plate. "What do you plan to say to the coach about him and Marston?"

"Honest truth, I got no problem letting those two go. Bringing a gun to a party is pretty stupid. But like I said, we need every man for this game. I doubt we can get Coach to back off on them, but I'd be okay with that, too. A.J. can play, when he wants to; Mars not so much, mostly just mouth. But we could use A.J. on the D-line to slow down those tailbacks. It's gonna be a war out there."

Wade mulled it, tried to see how Slate would receive his participation.

"I'll talk to the coach, too," Marcus said. "I just thought it would help if you backed me up, since you're on the committee that's going to make the permanent hire. The thing is, we've got to talk to him before the meeting, because if he announces the suspensions, he won't back down. He's under a lot of pressure to clean up the mess that Coach Lytle left."

Wade wondered what Allenby would think of all this, doubted that he'd be supportive of Marcus's petition but didn't entirely rule it out. He told Marcus briefly about Allenby and mentioned his intervention as an option to explore.

Marcus shook his head. "I kind of think it would be better if it's just you and me talking to the coach. Put those two together, they might go all old school on us, don't you think?"

Wade wasn't at all sure he didn't prefer the old school

approach on this one himself, but he decided to let Marcus play it out. He phoned Slate's secretary and made an urgent appointment after practice and before the team meeting that would follow it.

"It'll have to be a real quickie, sweetie," the secretary said. "He's working like twenty-four/seven on this bowl game. We're playing USC—can you believe it?"

"Oh," Wade said. "I didn't know they had a football team."

Befuddling the forecasters, the rain let up in the afternoon, though the day was still blustery and cold. Wade put his gear back on and slogged out to watch the last hour of practice with Allenby, who handed him a thermos of hot coffee. Wade drained it, stamped his feet, flapped his arms, clapped his hands, hopped in circles, knew he must look like a complete raving maniac, didn't care, still couldn't feel his fingers or his toes or find his pulse when he tried to take it. Hypothermia was setting in, he could tell. He was going to be the first person in recorded history to freeze in forty degrees fully clothed on a California football field.

Allenby noted with approval that Marcus had enough arm to get the ball through the wind accurately to his receivers. He nudged Wade. "Maybe you ought to get out there on the turf and run under some of those passes, warm yourself up."

"Marcus already tried to recruit me. I told him I used up all my eligibility channel-surfing."

Allenby called Wade's attention to the various sophisticated attack schemes that Slate and his defensive coaches were working on. "It's not enough just to commit to the blitz. You've got to have a plan. You can't just send everybody on every play for the whole game."

Wade recalled a game when Buddy Ryan's Philadephia Eagles had blitzed all-out against Joe Montana, beaten the crap out of him for the first three quarters—and then in the fourth quarter Joe had thrown four touchdown passes. "Montana said he *wanted* the defense to blitz. He knew he could beat it."

Allenby nodded. "He knew he'd get one-on-one coverage somewhere. All he had to do is find it, then be willing to take the hit. The trick on defense is to hide it as long as you can. That's what they're working on out there."

On the last play of practice, they watched Marcus fake a handoff to the man in motion, then pull the ball down, juke the defensive end, and break into the clear.

"See that wiggle? That's what our Jackson's lacking. You can't teach that."

Several women had attempted to teach Wade how to dance. He did not have to be persuaded that one did not learn how to wiggle.

Allenby mentioned going home to start cooking. Wade, feeling the need for full disclosure, told him he was meeting Marcus and Slate briefly, would be home soon.

"Maybe I'll tag along then."

Oops.

"Don't worry, I won't interfere. I'll let you do the talking."

When he saw them together approaching the coach's office, Marcus gave them the puzzled look Wade knew would be coming.

Allenby put a hand on Marcus's shoulder, nodded toward Wade. "I invited myself. Don't be mad at him."

"I'm not mad at anybody," Marcus said quietly.

Sherman Slate, on the other hand, appeared to have pretty good reason to be mad at just about everybody: his secretary for scheduling a meeting he didn't have time for, his QB for questioning his judgment, and Wade for lending his support to the insurrection. How Slate felt about Allenby's presence Wade couldn't divine, but he had to admit, it would be interesting to see how the two of them interacted. Under the circumstances, Marcus's forecast of a tory approach seemed warranted. Slate's opening salvo certainly set that tone.

"As far as Dupree and Marston are concerned, they broke all kinds of team rules just being at that party where liquor was served. Some of their other behavior is even more repellent. There's no place for young men like that on CSU's football team.

"As for Louis Blodgett, it's as simple as this. I saw what he did, and I don't want him to do it ever again. He needs to learn that lesson, and missing this bowl game seems like the right way to teach him. It has nothing to do with his color or with his talent as a player, and it has nothing to do with the color of the other player. It has to do only with this: setting a standard of behavior for the young men on our team. I also don't approve of the language that he uses, although perhaps that by itself wouldn't warrant suspension since so many of our other players unfortunately use the same language. That's something else I'm trying to put a stop to."

Everything Slate said made perfect sense to Wade. He wondered how the guy appointed to defend Goering at Nuremburg had felt.

Marcus cleared his throat. Wade had thought Marcus might ask him to go first, found out different now: "I'd like to say something, Coach."

Slate nodded curtly: permission granted.

"When you moved me to quarterback, you talked to me about stepping up to become a team leader, not just let my play do the talking. You've also been talking to us a lot about not being enemies on the same team, about black and white coming together as we get ready for the challenge of this game against a great team like USC. I figured we could get the white guys on the team to trust us a little more, maybe play a little harder, too, if we show them that we've got their back."

Not bad, Wade thought. This kid, so quiet when they'd met, might make a lawyer yet.

"I'll talk to Bludge," Marcus continued. "I'll tell him that we don't ever want to see that shit he did again or hear him use the 'n' word like he likes to do. I think he could help us in this game, and maybe help himself, too, if you'll give him a chance to . . . redeem himself."

"Why do you think he deserves that?"

"He's our teammate. We've all done stuff we're not proud of. I can see giving him one more chance."

"I see," Slate said. He seemed unmoved. "Did you have something to add to that, Dr. Wade?"

Wade wasn't sure if he did or not. He couldn't think of

anything he wanted to add to Marcus's concise case for Bludge, and after his talk with Larashawndria he was far from comfortable defending Dupree and Marston. He decided, though, that it was his turn to play defense attorney, make the best case possible even for clients of dubious merit.

"As you know, it was never conclusively established that the gun belonged to either Dupree or Marston or that either of them brought it to the party. Blodgett says he knows for sure neither of them fired the gun. That means somebody else must have, quite possibly somebody else on the team, so if you suspend Dupree and Marston, it's likely that you'll be punishing the lesser of the offenders at that event."

Slate nodded, absorbed it, again didn't exactly appear thunderstruck.

Wade sighed, sensing shaky ground ahead, but went on anyway: "Also, the girl who was taken from the party was drunk, by her own admission, and it isn't at all clear that it was Dupree and Marston who got her that way. There's also no evidence that they . . . took advantage of her in other ways. There were plenty of other people encouraging her to drink, including, again, many who are on the team, so unless you're prepared to suspend quite a few of your players before you face USC, I'd encourage you to slow down and look at this again. If you start suspending guys who were . . . misbehaving at that party, I don't know where you'll be able to stop."

Slate looked at Allenby. "I have a daughter, as I know you do." Allenby nodded, held up two fingers. Wade, daughterless, sonless, looked away, but thought of Larashawndria again. Slate continued, "I want to send a message to the young men on this team—on *my* team—that we will not treat women in this way. I hope you understand that."

Allenby nodded again. "I agree with almost everything you've said, Coach. There's one thing I'd like you to reconsider here. The whole situation the young men on this team have been in is a reflection upon the coach you replaced. He set the standard—or lack thereof—for this team by ignoring the team rules he established, and even violating them himself, as we've all learned more about lately than we ever cared to."

"That's exactly why I'm trying to set a different standard here."

"I *do* understand that, and I appreciate it, as I know Marcus and Wade do as well," Allenby continued. "That's why we hired you for this job. But what I want you to reconsider is this: the position that Dupree and Marston were placed in by the coach."

"I hope you can see that I want these young men to aspire to a higher aim in life than pimping."

"Of course," Allenby said. "And I hope *you* can see that a man in total control over of their immediate future as football players was telling them to do something, giving them an order, as it were. They weren't smart enough, or sophisticated enough, or moral enough, if you want to put it that way, to rise above the culture we've permitted to grow here and figure out a better way to handle it. They didn't have much of a role model on this team, did they?"

Allenby stopped. "That's all I'm going to say. I'm not trying to tell you what to do. I just ask you to think about what I've said, and what these two have said, before you make your final decision. Thanks for hearing us out. Whatever decision you make, you will have my full support." Allenby shook hands with Slate, nodded to Wade and Marcus and left. A real old school exit, Wade thought, but the text that preceded it had caught him by surprise.

The others watched Allenby depart, waited to see who would fill the silence. Marcus stepped up again.

"How about if we put this to a vote of the team, Coach?"

"A football team is not a democracy, Marcus. *I* have to make a decision here."

"I have a suggestion, too," Wade said. "Dupree and Marston really hate community service, but I think it's good for them. And I can think of some ways of serving his community that would be good for Blodgett, too. How about giving them the option of a couple hundred hours—or more, you pick the number—as their punishment this time, with the provision that this is a final warning for all of them?"

Slate still seemed unpersuaded. "Anything else?"

Wade shrugged. "Marcus tells me you're going to need every man you've got to win this war with USC."

Slate frowned, then nodded, thanked them, shook hands with each, told Marcus he'd see him at the meeting, asked Wade to stay for a moment.

As soon as Marcus was out of earshot, Slate said, softly but directly, "I'd appreciate it if you didn't use that comparison—football and war—around my players or encourage them to."

Wade recoiled, then nodded abruptly, remembering the flap that Bill Parcells had got himself into with his "Jap attack" reference to a surprise play, as well as some of the other media frenzies over the inappropriateness of the comparison by other coaches or players. "Sorry," he said.

"I just don't want my players to have any confusion about the difference between the two."

Wade nodded again.

Slate smiled, for the first time in the meeting, then put out his hand again. "And thanks for bringing your concerns—and your information—to my attention. I appreciate your input. Are you coming to the game?"

"Of course," Wade said. Allenby had booked the tickets in San Antonio for them as soon as CSU's selection for the bowl had been announced.

"We'll do our best to put on a good show for you."

Marcus was waiting for Wade outside Slate's office, not to pump him as it turned out, but simply to say thanks.

"Sorry if I surprised you when Allenby came along," Wade said.

"That's okay. I think he helped us."

"I hope *I* did, too," Wade said, still not sure what his true feeling about the right way for Slate to proceed would be. "You were great in there yourself. Thanks for trusting me to try to help."

"I do trust you, Dr. Wade."

Wade heard his mother: **Trust the world; most people want to help**.

"I don't envy your coach having to make this decision. I

guess you'll find out in a few minutes if you'll have those guys with you against USC."

"He might give himself a little more time to think it over now," Marcus speculated, then added quietly, "This is about more than just a football game, don't you think?"

Wade nodded. "Good luck with Bludge."

Back at the condo, after scrumptious chicken scallopini, Wade told Allenby about the end of his conversation with Slate. Wade had been so taken aback at the time that he hadn't thought to explain himself, probably wouldn't have chosen to in those circumstances anyway, but afterwards he'd had a few second thoughts. Marcus had talked about high school players trying to maim each other, and Wade remembered reading in Jim Brown's autobiography about the New York Giants trying to poke his eyes in the pile-ups; they couldn't stop him, so they tried to blind him. How much different from war was that? Even though media wonks routinely chastised, even ridiculed, players or coaches for making that comparison with their sport, maybe it wasn't so far-fetched after all. He told Allenby about being startled by Slate's rebuke.

Allenby was unsympathetic. "Sounds to me like he handled that just right. He's seen the real deal, and he knows the difference. He could've ripped you a new asshole there."

"But what about the injuries to—"

"He's right," Allenby interrupted. "There's no comparison. Football, it's over in three hours and you go home. War's not like that."

"Tell that to Darryl Stingley," Wade said, "or rather to his widow now. Tell it to Kevin Everett."

"Those injuries are rare, so rare that they're newsworthy— in football. In war they're every day. They're the norm. Trust me, there's no fucking comparison. You want to throw names around, ask Pat Tillman's folks if football is the same as war."

Wade had to admit, that was a tough argument to beat down. Allenby wasn't finished.

"Look, football is a violent sport, no doubt about it. There's a reason Teddy Roosevelt banned it for a time. There are high speed collisions on every snap. Covering or running back kicks is mayhem. Guys get clotheslined, horse-collared. People get hurt badly, knees destroyed, concussions, even paralysis once in a while. A handful of high school kids get killed every year, and once in a great while a college or pro player drops, usually when his asinine coach has him running without water in 110 degrees. Those are tragedies, every one of them. But those are exceptions to the rule. In war, the exceptional *is* the rule. You know this: you've read the books, seen the films that got it halfway right. You know what the Nazis did, how the Japanese literally ate their POWs alive. Christ, those fuckers in Bosnia that made the fathers and sons kneel and chew each other's nuts off."

Wade nodded, saw that more was coming.

"In war, eighteen year old boys get their balls blown off before they've even had a chance to use them. Arms, legs, eyes, brains, faces get blown to bits or burned up. Medical technology puts some of these guys—and women, now—back together somehow, keeps them breathing, and then they have to figure out how to live with what's left. I'm not saying a football player who blows out a knee is completely the same guy again afterwards, but it's a hell of a lot different from a guy having to learn to walk on sticks. Hell, you saw the pictures a few years ago of George W. jogging with the Iraq vets on their dual prosthetics, right? How did that make you feel?"

Wade had seen the photos several times, with mixed reactions. There was, of course, the stunning, stirring resilience of the veterans, but . . . . "Every time I saw those shots, I thought about asking Bush when he was going to send his twins over there to help out with the house-to-house searches in Fallujah."

Allenby nodded. "You've asked me several times about Vietnam, and I've mostly put you off. I'll talk to you about it just this once; then we'll not speak of it again. Agreed?"

"Of course."

"First thing to say is this: you carry around all this guilt for not going over there, and I'm telling you that you need to let that go. I'll admit, there's a part of me that's proud I served, put my ass on the line. Almost any veteran will tell you that, even the ones that came home in pieces. But there are other ways to put your ass on the line. If I had to do it over again, believe me, I'd have joined the Civil Rights Movement and taken on Jim Crow instead of the Viet Cong. I'd have been with the peace marchers, too. There are times when you've got to kill the bad guys to survive; that wasn't one of them."

Wade tried to put up a fight. "Hemingway said the freedom fighters in Spain helped to save the world with their holding action against the fascists before World War II. You could say the same about what you guys did against the communists in—"

"*You* could say that; I wouldn't."

"—Vietnam. I just think you guys deserve a lot of credit for—"

Allenby held up a hand, blew out a sigh. "Did you ever hear the expression LOTI?"

Wade shook his head.

"Most people haven't." Allenby poured himself a slug, then poured another into the glass, knocked half of the double back, looked at Wade. "You sure you don't want some of this?"

Wade shook his head again. Allenby nodded. "LOTI," he repeated.

Wade leaned forward.

"LOTI means 'Leave Only the Insects.' Kill every man, woman, child, and animal that you see. Those were our orders when we went into Viet Cong villages, or villages that someone in intel thought were Cong, and—"

Allenby paused, swirled his glass, then lifted it to his lips again. Wade flashed to the way the War on Terror was being fought, how he'd feel when he read in the newspaper or saw on CNN a story about the "hot pursuits" in Afghanistan or Pakistan where U.S. forces or a drone would blow up a house or a village because there was intelligence that said a terrorist or two might be holing up there—and then we'd wind up killing people who had nothing to do with terrorism, who couldn't get out of the Taliban's or al Qaeda's way or out of ours when we came after them. Even if we "took out" the target, how did we justify taking out those innocents with them? What were we expecting from the next generation of survivors in those villages when they saw us casually wipe out their families?

"—and that is exactly what we did." Allenby set his glass down, poured another shot, studied it for a moment, then turned his eyes back to Wade. "Let me be clearer. That is exactly what *I* did. I killed children, Wade. I killed babies. I killed fucking puppies. Shot them, stabbed them, burned them up. Someone somewhere up the chain of command ordered it, and so we did it. *I* did it."

On some level Wade had known from the day he'd met Allenby that this was possible, but somehow he hadn't integrated this reality into his appraisal of his friend. "It was . . . *war*," Wade breathed now. "You *had* to—"

Allenby shook him off. "Please don't tell me what I had to do. I did what I did. And I think about it every single fucking day."

Wade wondered how many others had done the same in Vietnam. How different was what Allenby had done from dropping napalm from a plane, burning up a village that way? Or, from his father's day, dropping bombs on women and children who had nothing to do with the making of a world war? How did you rationalize your individual behavior as a soldier when your government decided that an action was necessary in order to expedite the end of a war whose ultimate result would be greater carnage if you *didn't* take these unspeakable actions?

Allenby started to stand up, then sank back into his chair. "I guess it's good that we had this conversation. I know you've been wanting it. I hope you understand why I don't ever want to have it again. I know you won't judge me for what I've said here or what I've done because I know that you understand that you can't know what *you* would have done yourself in my situation."

Wade nodded. *Probably shot my toe off and cried wee-wee-wee all the way home.*

"You can know what you hope you would do, what you believe would be the right thing to do, but you can't know for sure until you've been there and done it like I have." Allenby paused, polished off the Scotch, stood up with a trace of a wobble that Wade had never seen from him before. "I played a little football, too, as I've told you. So please don't try to tell me it's the same as war, okay?"

"Okay," Wade said softly. "I won't say that any—"

"I'm going to bed." Allenby set his glass down with a thunk, steadied himself, headed for the bedroom, reached the door.

"Thanks for . . . talking to me," Wade said, just to say something. "And thanks for your help at the meeting today."

Hand on the knob, Allenby turned, nodded, gave Wade a tired smile. "You know I don't approve of what those boys did. But if Coach Slate decides not to keep them out of a football game because they brought a pistol to a party or . . . pulled somebody's hair, I hope you understand why I won't object to his decision. It won't be the worst thing I've seen."

CHAPTER 17

You all can go to hell, and I will go to Texas.
—Davy Crockett

Drink the first drink, sip the second, skip the
third.
—Knute Rockne

I like nonsense. It wakes up the brain cells.
Fantasy is a necessary ingredient in living.
—Theodor Seuss Geisel

"Now *this* is what a city should look like," Wade said, welcoming the sweet warm winter sunshine on his face and the sparkling current at his feet.

He and Allenby had checked into their hotel in San Antonio and were taking a stroll on the River Walk. Wade had always admired cities built around a central river or lake and wondered why more urban planners didn't incorporate this principle instead of centering modern civilization around shopping malls. In the city where CSU sat, the consecration of getting and spending had annihilated all vestiges of common sense, aesthetics, or concern for the environment, setting off an immitigable asphalt tsunami that was burying forever in all directions some of the most fertile and productive soil the world had ever seen.

Allenby nodded vaguely. "It's one of the two or three habitable towns in Texas."

"You make it sound like they still hang brothers for spitting on the sidewalk."

"Let's just say I'm glad it's not my blonde wife, soon to be *ex*-wife, I'm walking with."

"Come on. Tim Duncan's got to be a god around here. His

wife's a blonde. Plus the Admiral played here too."

"And the ratings for the NBA Finals were the lowest in history. A relative handful of affluent locals go to those games; a few more watch on TV. That leaves a lot of Texas peckerwoods just itchin' to pick a fight with the boys on our team—or even with a grown man in a business suit if I look at 'em crosswise or they think I did."

"There must be some history here you haven't told me about."

Allenby sighed. "There is. Might spoil the walk if we talk about it."

"Go ahead if you want to," Wade said.

"It's nothing next to 'Nam, of course, but . . . I got into a fight here, spent a night in jail. Only time in my life. Almost kept me out of law school. Took me ten years to get the record cleared."

"You were attacked?"

"Some jackasses in a bar, 1966. I was stationed in Corpus Christi, about to ship out for my first tour. A few of us were watching the NCAA finals on TV. That was the year—"

"Texas Western versus Kentucky," Wade said. "I saw that game on TV, too."

"You probably saw more of it than I did. My friend and I got a little excited when Texas Western took the lead, and the local patrons didn't like it, decided it was their job to shut us up. We should've just walked away, of course. But we were young and full of piss. Plus we wanted to see the rest of that game."

"But . . . it didn't work out that way?"

"They didn't have a TV on in the jail." He paused, sighed. "The Texans came at us with beer bottles. Bartender pulled out a baseball bat and coldcocked my buddy, broke his jaw, swung at me and just missed. The cops got there in time to keep them from killing both of us. Our sergeant got us out the next day."

"Jesus."

"We were on our way to Vietnam to fight the enemy, keep the world safe for democracy, all that shit you bought into when you were young and stupid. But this was in my own country, in the *uniform* of my country, and those fuckers in the bar weren't even rooting for the team from their own state. All they saw was five black guys against five white guys, and the black guys were winning, so they decided to get even. That's my memory of Texas."

Wade tried to put it into perspective. "When I talk to students now about sports history, they're always astounded when they find out the Longhorns won the national championship in football in 1969 with an all-white team. They can't believe it could have happened in their parents' lifetime. They see the game now, and the whole defense, all the skill positions on offense, they're all black. That's the world they know."

"Progress," Allenby acknowledged.

"Signs of it everywhere," Wade said. He decided this was a good time to tell Allenby about the phone call he'd had from Bludge on the day after the meeting with Slate. He still had the conversation in his head.

"I guess I'm supposed to thank you."

"I guess you're welcome. What for?"

"Our new quarterback says you kept the coach from kicking me off the team."

"That's quite a statement."

"He full of shit?"

"Someone might be, but I don't think it's Marcus."

"What's that supposed to mean?"

"He's the one who made a case for you. I mostly kept my mouth shut, tried not to screw it up."

"Why would he stand up for me?"

"Beats the hell out of me. Let me know if you ever figure it out."

It was from this call that Wade had learned how Slate had elected to proceed. The coach had called Thaddeus Marston in before the team meeting, told him he wasn't getting any playing time in the game anyway, and interrogated him again about the party. Marston had confessed to bringing the gun, and Slate had suspended him and made the decision to let Bludge and A.J. play.

"Maybe in this next generation, kids like Marcus will make

a difference," Wade said now to Allenby after the recap. "If he can make a dent in Bludge, who knows what else he might be capable of pulling off?"

"I hope he's not wasting his time there." Allenby slowed down, looked around, his turn now to put matters in perspective. "For the handful of gifted ones like Marcus that make it out of the ghetto or the projects, maybe the world will be different. But black kids are still killing each other every day in Oakland and Stockton and L.A. And they're still *fryin'* brothers and draggin' 'em behind pick-ups in this state. We got a long way to go."

When they returned to the hotel, Allenby excused himself to meet with some of his software clients from L.A. "They're USC alums, came out for the game, thought they'd kill two birds. You want to guess what odds they're offering on the game?"

"The spread is 41 points now, isn't it?"

"Vegas pulled it off the board. These guys can't find anybody to take a bet. They're offering—get this—50 to 1."

"That's crazy!"

Allenby shrugged. "The last time USC played a team from our conference, they scored five touchdowns in the first ten minutes."

Wade took out his wallet, peered in, pulled a lonesome twenty. "What the hell. Let's live dangerously. Throw this in the pot for me."

Allenby laughed, pocketed the bill. "Got enough left in there for a haircut?"

"I need one, huh?"

"Wouldn't hurt."

Wade reached up, patted himself self-consciously. "Not much left up there to—"

"Why don't you just shave it then? You'll take ten years off."

"The Bruce Willis look?"

"I was thinking more like Don Rickles."

"Who could resist that?"

"I had a bottle sent up to your room in case you want to take a break from suds."

"Always trying to improve me, aren't you?"

Allenby grinned cryptically. "Enjoy." Wade wondered if he was still picturing the tonsure.

Wade decided to wait on the barbering, find a spot cheaper than the hotel shop was likely to be. Better to conserve after throwing away that twenty. He headed for the elevator, then lingered before stepping in. The River Walk had brought to mind a distant Christmas program filmed in this city, with his mother's favorite singer, Perry Como, mid-seventies by then, the pipes really starting to go, but reaching down deep at the close and nailing her favorite hymn, "Ave Maria," one last memorable time. They'd saved the tape, watched it . . . religiously every season. Now Wade realized it was *his* all-time favorite holiday recording that was playing in the lobby, "I'll Be Home for Christmas," the lyrics prosaic but Sinatra's diction and phrasing perfect, the poignance palpable, almost unbearable. *Mom is gone*, Wade thought. *I'll never be home for Christmas again.*

Wade waited for the song to finish, then wiped his eyes and went up to his room, fumbled with the key card, put it in the door, didn't get it open. He had turned to take a look at the surrounding room numbers, make sure he was in the right place, when the door was suddenly yanked open from within and an assailant jumped out on top of him, knocked him to the floor.

Christ! Allenby was right. I'm going to die in Texas. He tried to scream, but nothing came out. *I'm going to—*

"Kiss me, you fool!"

What the FUCK? *Angela.*

Wade rolled over, sat up, took inventory. No evident fractures of the skull or limbs, no sucking chest wound, maybe a chipped tooth or two, not to mention the HEART ATTACK I JUST ALMOST HAD.

Angela was in a blouse and panties, nothing else, grinning ear-to-ear.

"What the hell are you—"

"Aren't you glad to see me?" She leaned in, puckered theatrically. "Give us a kiss."

Wade smooched her, inhaled Scotch fumes, tried again for information.

"What are you doing here?"

"Allenby flew me in. He got me a rental car, too. He wanted to surprise you for Christmas. So . . . are you surprised?"

"Allenby?"

"Still quick as ever on the uptake, aren't you? Same old wizard Wade. Kiss me again."

"Don't you want to get out of the hallway and—"

"Kiss me again first."

"—put some clothes on?"

"Okey dokey—on the hallway part, anyway."

Wade stood up, picked up the key card, which she'd knocked from his grip. The door had closed behind her when Angela had attacked. She grinned, tried to jump on him again. A sedate couple of seniors stepped out of the elevator, then averted their eyes.

Angela smiled and waved their way. "I'm a surprise." They appeared to debate for a moment stepping back into the elevator, then put their heads down and hurried past to their room. "Your neighbors aren't very friendly. Good thing you're not that way." Angela reached around from behind to feel him up as Wade fumbled with the plastic again.

"Can't you get that—"

She tried to grab the card away from him, but Wade swatted her away.

"—in? I think you're putting it in backwards."

Wade glared at her, persisted, and on his third try threw the door open.

"My hero," she said. "Do you want to carry me inside?"

Wade rolled his eyes. She laughed, hopped on his back, and settled for a piggyback ride, all hundred and five pounds of her, across the threshold. He staggered in, plopped her onto the bed, thinking shit, that was *hard*, good thing it wasn't Brenda he was packing; he'd have had the rest of that heart attack, croaked in Texas after all.

Angela sat up, hoisted a bottle from the bedside table. "Allenby had this really good Scotch sent to the room. I . . . started without you."

"So I see. But you left some for me?"

"A little. Maybe we should get another bottle." She put the bottle into her mouth, tipped her head back, swallowed, grinned again. "Allenby got me a ticket to the bowl game so I can go with you guys, too."

"*You*'re coming to a *football* game?"

"Don't worry, I'll bring a book. I won't get—"

"This is Texas, remember? Do you want to get—"

"—bored."

"—shot? You can't bring a book to a football game here."

"Okay, then. Let's go eat. I'm starving."

Wade realized he was hungry, too. "Okay, then, put your drawers on, and we'll—"

"Oh." She looked herself over, then around the room. "I had some . . . slacks around here somewhere." She grinned again, gave up the search, took another swig. "I guess I took them off. Send out for room service. I'm horny, too."

She extended her arms toward him, tried to pull him down onto the bed alongside her.

"I read your screenplay. It sort of got me in the mood."

"What are you talking about? What screenplay?"

"On your computer."

"What computer? I don't have a computer here with—"

"The one in your office, stupid. I hacked into it with my Notebook." She waved a hand at the coffee table where her indispensable laptop sat. "You never change your password."

This was true. Wade's had been UNITAS19 ever since he'd been at CSU.

"Do you have any idea how dangerous that is?"

"I'm beginning to," Wade said. "What fucking screenplay?" There might be a few ideas he'd jotted down, maybe some emails he'd sent to Erica, about his decapitation plans for Yoshi and Delia Herman, but—

"*Six Ways from Sunday*," Angela said. "Some student sent it to you as an attachment." She folded her arms over her chest, cross-examined sternly: "Do you even know how to open one of those?"

"Yes, Angela, I know how to open a fucking—"

"It's stupid, of course, but I have to admit the script is sort of edgy, sort of a cross between—"

"Hornography," Wade said. "I know. I read *that* in her email. But—"

"It's about this minister who fucks a bunch of girls in his congregation and in the end he gets castrated."

"Oh."

"Remember when you tried to make me watch the bathtub scene in *I Spit on Your Grave?*"

Wade remembered, reflexively covered his sac. One of the kooks in his film club had raved about the flick, persuaded the group to show it, but left out the part about the . . . cutting edge. Wade had invited Angela to the screening, hoping to improve the mood for inducing aquasex afterward.

"She says there's a part in it for you. I wonder if she wants you for the minister. Last time we talked, you were thinking of cutting your dick off anyway."

"I think she has someone else in mind."

"There's another wrinkle in the script. After they hack the guy's schlong off, they nail him to a cross."

"I see," Wade said. "So it's a religious spectacle, too. Maybe Mel Gibson will want to direct, put some butts in the seats."

"Maybe," Angela said. "As long as they're genre-bending, they should make it a snuff film, too, actually crucify the guy on camera."

"In that case, let's see if we can cast Gordon Brooks."

"Can you imagine how many people would pay to see *that?*" Angela picked up the bottle again, stared at it for a moment. "Did you call room service yet?"

"Not yet."

"Do you think we should get drunk together and see what happens first?"

"I think you're already there." He put a finger on the bottle to mark her inroads.

"Better catch up."

She handed it over. Wade took a sip. Wow. Good stuff,

indeed. He took another. Maybe he could become a Scotch drinker after all.

"So, what did you guys talk about?"

"Allenby said I should shave my head."

"You should grow a mustache too."

"I tried that. I looked like Señor Wences."

She patted the bed, lay back, beckoned him near. "I shaved for you, too. Want to see?"

"Sure." Wade's loins stirred. Then his heart started thumping, too, reminded him to take a look before leaping, after passion, into the abyss. "As long as I'm not going to read Ronnie's initials or anything down there somewhere."

"He's gone, Wade. How can I prove it to you?"

Wade took another sip, swirled, gave it some thought, swallowed, tried to be fair. "Putting a bullet in him would probably be best."

"I've got a better idea."

She unbuttoned her blouse, unhooked her bra, tossed them aside, pulled him close, kissed him hard—then suddenly pushed off harder.

"Oh, shit, Wade, I think I'm gonna be—"

"CHRIST, Angela. You could at least let me get out the way."

Scotch and assorted other half-digested matter had spattered his shirt and pants as well as the bedspread. A particularly nasty little gob had hit the bullseye on his nose. Wade sped into the bathroom, found towels, brought one back for her, tried to wipe himself dry.

"Sorry."

"I should hope so."

"Are you okay?"

"I don't know. I've never had a woman throw up on me before."

Wade grabbed his pajamas from his suitcase, went back into the bathroom, took off his clothes, cleaned up more thoroughly, put the PJs on, picked up more towels, wetted one of them and a washcloth, brought them back to the bed, found Angela tippling again.

"I decided to have a little more."

"Good idea. You needed something to wash that vomit off your lips anyway." Wade took the bottle from her, wiped it clean with his pajama top, had another sip himself, then dabbed the wet towel at damp spots on the bedspread.

"I can't believe a woman never hurled on you before. You mean all those years you were married to—"

"Brenda usually made it to the toilet. I believe that's the standard place to make a deposit."

"I said I was sorry. Do you ever . . . miss her?"

"Only when another woman . . . uses me for target practice."

"You weren't my *target*. It was just—"

"Collateral barf damage?"

"—an *accident*." Angela peered into the relevant gap of Wade's PJs. "Isn't your dick supposed to be hard by now?"

"Not sure. I'll have to check the manual. I don't know what the standard refractory time is after being hit by projectile vomiting. How did it work with you and Ronnie?"

"Don't be stupid, Wade. I never threw up on Ronnie."

"Oh. Thanks for saving yourself for me."

"Why do you always have to bring *him* up? Isn't there something more important to talk about?"

"Like what?"

"Like how are we going to sleep with all this vomit in the bed?"

"Maybe someone should've thought of that before she started—"

"Don't be a nag. How come you still don't have a hard-on? Have you gone gay on me?"

"I think maybe I have. That's what Jenna Jones wanted to know, too."

"Who's Jenna Jones?"

"The girl who wrote the screenplay that you read."

"Are you in love with her?"

"I don't think so," Wade said. "Just another girl I didn't get a hard-on for," he lied.

"There must be millions of them."

"Billions," Wade said. He took another swig from the bottle. "All the girls in China, for example. And India."

"But not Japan. We made an exception for Japan, didn't we?"

Wade shrugged. "It's only fair. We bombed the shit out of them, after all."

"That was a long time ago."

"Still. Did you know we dropped napalm on them, too?"

"Duh."

"Oh. Well, some people don't know that."

"Some people don't know shit. Tell me something I don't already—"

"I'll bet you didn't know this: new research by a team of scholars at CSU reveals that it was Ronald Reagan who dropped the atomic bomb on—"

"I knew he *wanted* to, but—"

"—Panama. That's how he *started* World War II. You look like you're going to—"

"OOPS. There goes some more."

"I think I'm getting the hang of this. I almost got out of the way that time."

"This is way easier than having multiple orgasms with you, Wade."

"Are you finished now?"

"I think so."

"Maybe you should try to get some rest."

"I had *way* too much Scotch." She closed her eyes, opened them, studied Wade. "So did you. Don't you at least have to pee?"

"Now that you mention it, I think I do. Maybe I should . . . pee on you. Even things up a little."

"What, did you see that in one of your disgusting porno movies?"

Wade had another slug, shook his head. "I learned it at school."

"Oh, sure."

"Really. The football players pee on each other at parties. It's how they impress girls."

"Trust me, I won't be impressed. Just run along now and use the toilet."

"Next time, try following your own game plan."

Wade set the bottle down, stood, tried to brush off fresh puke, succeeded mainly in transferring it from his pajamas to his palms, turned to go back into the bathroom.

"If you find some aspirin in there, bring it back with you."

"We're in a hotel, Angela. There's not going to be any aspirin in the bathroom. You have to pay for everything around here."

"Shit. You may have to cut my head off then."

"Fine. You'll make a nice addition to my collection. I don't have a true blonde in there yet."

"Pervert."

"Barfbreath."

"Fuckwit."

Angela, almost out, opened her eyes when Wade, down to tomorrow's undies now, came back from his latest round of ablutions. She was clutching the Scotch again.

"It was nice of your friend Allenby to send us this bottle."

Wade nodded.

She pulled it to her chest. "He wants us to be happy."

Wade nodded again, reached for the bottle. "That sounds sort of . . . sappy."

Angela giggled. "Nobody rhymes any more. Did you really tell Gordon Brooks that Dr. Suess was a better poet than T.S. Eliot?"

"Don't be ridiculous," Wade said. "I told him Dr. Suess *was* T.S. Eliot."

"Oh. What did he say?"

"He already knew."

"Oh. Maybe you should try not to drink so much next time you want to fuck me, Wade."

"Maybe next time you should try not to throw up on me so much, too."

"See, we're learning to compromise. We should write a book about relationships."

"We should get some sleep first."

"I bet it would be a best-seller. You could write the part about what *not* to do."

"I think you could contribute to that part, too."

"I'm sorry I hurt you, Wade. I'm sorry I threw up on you, too."

"I accept your—"

"That's nice. But you still didn't get a hard-on, did you?"

"—apology." Wade followed her gaze, confirmed the diagnosis. "I guess I didn't."

"We won't put that part in the book."

"Okay by me." Wade dabbed with the wet towel at another pool of recycled Scotch.

"Maybe Allenby can find someone to publish it. He told me he might be able to get your stupid Hemingway book published."

"I thought you *liked* my—"

"I sort of *had* to say that, didn't I? Come on, Wade, Hemingway's a—"

"Choose your words carefully, woman. It's a long hike back to Connecticut in your G-string."

"I don't want to fight, Wade. I think I need to sleep now."

Angela closed her eyes. Within seconds she was snoring. Wade went over to her laptop, found the script she'd read still up on the screen, running down the battery. He started to shut it down, then decided to flip through, see if he could find the part Jenna had in mind for him—and there it *was*: MAN WITH A HARD-ON. The writing wasn't as awful as he'd expected, some talent there; maybe hook her up with Dixon, get some editing help, clean up . . . the grammar, anyway.

He shut down the computer and clicked the TV on, muted, searched for football, couldn't find any. It was bowl season; there had to be a game going on somewhere. He had no idea what else might be on. What an alteration *that* was: Wade had spent his childhood and adolescence so thoroughly programmed by the networks that he'd known by rote what ABC, NBC, and CBS were airing at virtually any time of the day, week-round. Now that there were a million channels to choose from, he almost never watched anything except sports, news, or movies.

He bumped into a *Seinfeld* rerun, wondered if the show was still on ten times a day in Texas, too. It was the only program in many years that he had watched regularly to the end of its original run, long gone now, of course. The finale the same night Sinatra died, he remembered, FS in the spotlight again, as ever, *usque ad finem*, stealing the scene on the national stage even with his dying gasp. In a life full of double whammies, there was yet another for Wade: his only show and the only singer that mattered, gone in one night (in "one foul swoop" as one of his students had lamented).

Angela half-opened a bloodshot eye, blinked at the screen. "What's Georgie doing?"

"He's having his ultimate fantasy episode."

"Oh. What is he—"

"He's trying to combine sex and watching TV."

"Oh. What's *your* ultimate fantasy, Wade?"

"Easy." Wade closed his eyes, smiled, pictured it again, perfect as always: "Mid-air collision between the team planes carrying the Yankees and the Dodgers."

"Great. Here I am, a beautiful, intelligent—"

"Inebriated, snoring—"

"—*slightly* indisposed woman, lying nearly naked in bed right next to you, and you fantasize about—"

"Football's probably more appropriate this time of year," Wade conceded, picking up the remote. "Let me try again to see if I can find—"

"Don't you *dare* change that channel. I'm *watching* this. I *hate* it when you do that." Angela closed her eye. "I can't believe you'd want to watch football while you're fucking me."

"Don't worry about it. I can't find any football on."

"You're not fucking me either."

"I knew there was something missing from this—"

"Fantasies are better when you actually make them happen, Wade." She opened both eyes now, looked at him, tried to focus, caught the screen behind him again as a giant hoagie slipped between the sheets. "What's Georgie doing *now*?"

"He's adding to the fantasy. He's bringing food to bed."

"Oh. Does that turn you on?"

"Not really." Ever since Brenda, Wade hadn't been too keen on food in bed. "You can get cockroaches in your pillow case that way." Also in your asscrack, he seemed to recall.

"What would *you* add then?"

"Don't you think I have enough trouble doing one thing at a time?"

"Come *on.*"

"Okay. Add to the football and the fucking, you mean?"

"If you must. Or you could start over, and—"

"I'd probably put Sinatra on."

"That's right, you turn off the sound on the football, don't you? That's *so* annoying. Why do—"

"Do you think I want to hear some John Madden wannabe going 'Boom! Boom! Boom!' while you're shrieking with ecstasy when you come?"

She blinked in surprise, seemed glad to hear it, proud of herself: "*Do* I shriek with ecstasy when I come?"

"It's a fantasy, remember?"

"Oh. Ronnie always used to say I was—"

Too much information. Wade wanted to clap his hands over his ears, bury his head under the mattress.

"—too inhibited in bed."

"*What?*" Christ, if Angela was *inhibited*, what did that make Brenda in bed? Comatose? Dead? And what kind of fucking freaks had Ronnie been sharing his sheets with to elicit the complaint? "Jenna has a frisky monkey we can fix him up with if you think he's game for some interspecies action."

"Okay. Aren't you even going to ask me what *my* ultimate fantasy is?"

Wade looked around the room, at the TV, gone to commercial now, the almost-empty bottle, the puke-spattered bedspread. "This isn't it?"

"I want to make love in the Lincoln Bedroom."

"Oh." Wade worked on it for a minute. "Are you saying you want to be president?"

"No, stupid."

"Oh. Well, surely you don't want *me* to be—"

"I want to fuck President O—"

"Oh. *Him.*"

"Does that hurt your feelings?"

Wade shrugged. "Better him than going back to Ronnie again, I guess."

"I *told* you, I'm—"

"Maybe I can hook up with Michelle if you're going to be busy with—"

"She's way out of your league, Wade."

"Who isn't? I still don't think you're quite clear on how this *Fantasy* League works."

Actually, it wasn't a bad idea, now that he thought about it. Maybe another kickass TV concept in there. *Ultimate Fantasy: Wife Swapping at the White House.* Think of the fundraising implications. The Hollywood power couples would be all over it. Imagine how much Babs and her hubby would pony up to join the fun. The Republicans would go postal, of course. O'Reilly would have an apoplectic fit, burst a jugular in mid-rant, die right on the air—*his* ultimate fantasy comes true, too! A win-win all the way around. Wade tried it out on Angie.

"It wouldn't be *wife* swapping, stupid. We're not married."

"Oh. I suppose that could hang up the negotiations. I'll talk to Allenby. He actually *knows* him. Maybe he can help us out."

"Allenby's nice." Angela drained almost the last of the Scotch, set the bottle at her crotch.

"And generous," Wade pointed out.

"Good-looking, too."

"I suppose."

"If I can't fuck the president, maybe I could fuck him. I'll bet *he* could get a hard-on if he was here." She looked around. "He's not here, is he?"

Wade nodded at the bottle. "Only in spirit."

"Which room is he in?"

"The one without the vomit all over the bedspread."

"Maybe I should call him. Do you think he wants to fuck me?"

Wade sighed, reached for the bottle, took it out of Angela's grasp, tipped the last drops into his mouth, then soothed her brow and pushed her head back on the pillow. She closed her eyes. He wondered if she was finally going back to sleep, down for the count, or if this was the onset of an alcoholic coma. He gently wiped the last vestige of vomit from her lips.

"He can't," Wade said, shaking his head sadly. "He's gay, and—"

Her eyes popped back open. "No way."

Gravely now: "*And* he has AIDS."

"No fucking *way*."

And, tragically at last, Wade nodded. "I gave it to him."

CHAPTER 18

Il faut de l'audace, encore de l'audace,
toujours de l'audace.
—Georges-Jacques Danton

If he can't score, don't give him the ball.
—William Mack Brown

The game began with an onside kick.

As the scramble to recover it and then to sort out who had done so unfolded, Wade tried to remember the last time he had seen a bowl game start that way. Of the hundreds he had watched in a lifetime, had he actually ever seen this before? Maybe Stanford in a distant Rose Bowl? He looked at Allenby.

"Can't remember the last time I saw it either. Look, we got the ball!"

For Wade onside kicks had held heretofore a special place in hell. The memory of the 49ers' fumble at the end of the playoff game against the Cowboys in 1972 to complete the squandering of a three-score fourth-quarter lead was among the lowest points of his spectating life. If there had ever been a glimmer of hope for Wade to become a man of faith, it had begun to vanish in the aftermath when the insufferable Roger Staubach had attributed the miraculous Dallas victory to divine intervention. Wade had shattered the chair he was sitting in and kicked a hole in the wall of his parents' house. Eight days later, determined to thwart the avarice of Anastasio Somoza by personally delivering relief supplies to the victims of the Merry Christmas earthquake in Managua, Roberto Clemente had died when his plane plunged, upon take-off, into the sea, and Wade had given up on God forever.

"Great idea to use that kick at the beginning of the game,"

Allenby said now. "It never works at the end when the other team's expecting it."

Wade foreswore begging to differ, closed his eyes, banished until its next unbidden apparition the unspeakable image of Preston Riley. CSU came to the line of scrimmage, spread the formation wide across the field, the former QB Bonner stationed almost at the USC sideline as a wideout, Marcus in the shotgun to take the snap. USC called timeout.

"Well, I guess the word didn't get out. Slate's two for two— made 'em burn an early timeout."

Wade nodded. "Too bad they don't keep score that way instead of touchdowns. We might be able to beat them at timeouts."

"We just might beat them anyway," Allenby said. "I like our chances with this coach."

Time back in. On the first play from scrimmage, Marcus took a low snap. Three linemen from USC burst in and buried him for an eight-yard loss.

"So how do you like our chances with this line?"

"Not a great start," Allenby conceded. "Let's see what he does this time."

The second play yielded a significant improvement. Marcus took a truer snap, faked to a man in motion, surveyed receivers briefly, dodged the first lineman to break through, dodged another, then pulled the ball down and set sail down the field. Receivers peeled back and, if not exactly throwing textbook blocks, at least got annoyingly in the way of defenders. When he reached the USC twenty, Marcus made a sudden swivel move that Paula Abdul would have killed for. The last two USC DBs skidded by, collided with each other, and Marcus raced into the end zone.

Allenby looked at Wade, who was wide-eyed in disbelief. "Not bad for his first NCAA carry, wouldn't you say?"

Wade surveyed the field for penalty flags, saw none. Could this be true?

"Look! They're going for two!"

Slate had sent what appeared to be the kicking team out, but at the last moment the holder stood to take the snap. The receiver on the right ran to the post, clearing the corner. The kicker flared to the right, uncovered, and the holder threw him the ball. A massive USC defender flattened him vengefully as he reached the goal line. Too late. Two points. Another defender nailed the passer, also too late. Way too late. Fifteen yard penalty assessed on the kickoff. USC was going backwards.

"Is this a dream?" Wade said. "Wouldn't it be something if that two-point conversion turned out to be the difference in—"

"Fifty-nine minutes to go," Allenby said. "Don't start the party yet."

"I can't believe Angela didn't see that," Wade said. Nursing the mother of all hangovers, she had begged off when Wade tried to rouse her, said she would try to make it for the second half. Unless she decided to slit her throat instead.

"Think he'll try another onside kick?"

"No one's *that* crazy."

"Maybe even our wimp kicker can get it out of the end zone from there."

Aided by the penalty, CSU was kicking off this time from midfield. USC had returned four kickoffs for touchdowns during the season, and CSU had led the nation by yielding five, so booting the ball beyond the reach of the third string Trojan tailback with the 4.3 speed in the forty seemed like a very good idea.

Instead Slate ordered the ball kicked low and hard. It smacked a startled USC lineman in the crotch as he tried to lurch out of the way.

"*Dodgeball!*" Wade cried. "You're *it.*"

The ball richoted toward the onrushing CSU squad. Bludge dove on it, and his teammates piled on top to protect against forcible repossession. The CSU offense raced onto the field, took up a new formation. USC's defense looked confused, appeared to debate calling another timeout. Before they could decide, Marcus took the shotgun snap, this time handed it to the man in motion, Frank "Flash" Jackson, then took off down the sideline in the opposite direction. Jackson faked a reverse to the other wideout, rolled to the hashmark, then suddenly stopped and lofted crossfield back toward Marcus a flutterball that looked like something Wade or his ninety year-old auntie might have authored. All alone at the fifteen, Marcus churned impatiently in place, waiting for the ball. At last he reached up to snag it, dodged a pursuing safety, juked another at the five, then scampered into the end zone again.

"Beautiful," Allenby breathed.

"How far do you think this 'trickeration' can take us, though?" Wade wanted to know.

Allenby shrugged. "Tricks are how Boise State beat Oklahoma. A pass by a running back or a wideout is almost always good for one free touchdown if you have the balls to call it."

Wade remembered that Unitas had made just such a brazen call, at the Giants' goal line no less, on the penultimate play of the most famous game in history: Ameche had missed the call— and the tight end wide open in the end zone—before plunging into history himself on the ensuing snap.

This time CSU kicked the extra point. Fifteen-zero.

"Taking it easy on them now," Wade said.

Allenby grinned. "Wouldn't want to be accused of running up the score on these pansies, now would we?"

The next three possessions changed the tone of the game and the spirits of the CSU contingent considerably, if predictably. USC mounted consecutive touchdown drives of sixty-five and seventy yards without reaching third down. In between CSU suffered a three-and-out, Marcus getting sacked on two of the three plays and his receiver viciously separated from the ball before limping off the field on the third. Following the second USC touchdown and extra point, Marcus went onto the field with the kickoff return team to try to pad CSU's one-point advantage.

Wade wasn't sure he liked that idea. "I hope he doesn't get killed back there. They don't call those the suicide squads for nothing."

"Slate just wants to get the ball into his hands any way he can."

"I can't believe he's coming out of the end zone!"

Marcus had fielded the long kickoff and sprinted toward the sideline where a horde of USC tacklers awaited him. Just before they reached him, he suddenly stopped, whirled, and threw a hard lateral pass back to a teammate at the opposite sideline. It was the old chestnut that the Titans had hauled out with next to no time left on the clock in Nashville to shock Ronnie's Bills out of a chance to lose yet another Super Bowl.

There the pleasing parallel broke down: Marcus's receiver had positioned himself too close to the sideline and stepped barely out of bounds as he caught the ball. CSU would start at its own eight yard line.

"Clear sailing ahead if he'd stayed in bounds," Allenby noted in response to Wade's spasm. "Another good call."

"Could've worked," Wade had to agree. "How many more tricks do you think Slate has up his sleeve? Nothing too fancy down there against the goal line, I'm guessing."

"I hope he stays aggressive. That's what he said he'd do."

CSU lined up in the T, Jake Bonner in at QB, Marcus a decoy at slot receiver. Bonner handed off twice to Jackson, back at tailback, who was stuffed and driven back two yards each time.

Wade tried to look on the bright side. "Even taking a safety wouldn't be the end of the world here."

Allenby still wasn't buying the conservative approach. "Just the end of our lead."

"Might taste better than a blocked punt in our own end zone."

On third and forget it, Marcus took the snap in the pistol formation and appeared to hand off again, apparently conceding the series, but at the last split-second he pulled the ball away from Jackson, leaving him to be devoured by half of the swarming Trojan defense, as Marcus sprinted for the sideline. A wideout brushed the cornerback who was closing on the play, and suddenly Marcus was alone on the edge, a step ahead, then sprinting down the field to the end zone, a school and bowl record run of ninety-six yards.

"What a fake," Allenby raved.

Wade was dazed. It was a play on a par with the interception return Marcus had made in the San Diego State game, only this time he'd taken it all the way for a touchdown.

CSU kicked the extra point to go up 22-14. In the second quarter, infuriated USC began to try to assert its might by throwing the ball, as Slate had predicted, and a series of well-disguised blitzes along with a pair of passes dropped by lackadaisical receivers enabled the CSU defense to survive the next few possessions. In the meantime, the USC defensive line utterly dominated CSU's offense, and Marcus scrambled merely to get rid of the ball or get back to the line of scrimmage. Nearing halftime, USC ran a play that demonstrated the disparity in the level of talent on the field. On a simple sweep, the old Student Body Right from John McKay's concise playbook, several pancake blocks were executed to perfection by the various All-Americans on the offensive line. The tailback turned the corner, and no one was there to tackle him. Sixty untouched yards later he somersaulted flamboyantly into the end zone.

"At least his own guys are beating him up," Wade said, after the tailback's teammates lumbered down to maul him in celebration.

The love-fest went on too long, and a referee threw his flag.

Allenby shook his head, his disgust evident. "You know who started all this self-congratulation crap don't you?"

"Is there any way we can blame it on Bill Clinton?"

"You need to get over that oral fixation of yours, Wade. Blowjob envy is warping your sense of historical perspective. It was in Nixon's first term. Remember that home run Reggie Jackson hit in the All-Star Game?"

Wade remembered. "Tiger Stadium. Off Dock Ellis. Blasted the ball off the light tower and stood there at home plate playing with himself for half an hour, then slow-danced around the bases."

Allenby nodded. "Back before he 'stirred the drink' in pinstripes. Fucking hot dog. Too bad he didn't have to face Bob Gibson in his next at bat."

Wade, ardent NL fan, a Mays-Aaron-Clemente man all the way, had his own version of the appropriate revenge, never shared until now. "Or . . . someone in the dugout sends out for a bazooka—"

"I can see it: Detroit, that'd be no problem. Be there—"

"—right around the time Reggie's finally rounding third, and then just when he's about to cross the plate, BLAMMO! Blast his showboatin' ass to smithereens."

"Not bad," Allenby conceded. "Even Gibson could've appreciated that."

"Of course, they probably still would have counted the run, but—"

"At least it might've spared us the nonsense it begat, these clowns humping each other in the end zone in the first half when they're still behind."

Down on the field the USC tailback had not moved from the spot where his teammates had pummeled him. Now it appeared that he was injured.

"Serves him right," Wade said. "Looks like he did himself in with that double gainer off the high board."

"Either that or his own guys knocked him out of the game." Allenby shook his head. "Idiots, all of them. When they get to the end zone, why can't they act like they've been there before?"

The lamed tailback was helped off the field. USC kicked off. This time CSU managed to drive the ball for several minutes, Marcus converting three third downs into firsts with a quarterback draw, a bootleg, and a scramble.

Allenby nodded with approval as Marcus slowed the pace, ran the play clock all the way down before every snap. "Slate's trying to milk the clock, keep his defense off the field until halftime."

"Smart move, after their last dazzling appearance."

"I haven't seen any dumb ones yet."

With only a few seconds remaining in the half, CSU tried from midfield a variation of the play that had netted their second touchdown, this time bringing Bonner in motion to take the hand off from Marcus for the longer heave to the end zone. Now, though, three USC defenders stayed with Marcus all the way down the field. Another receiver came free down the middle, but Bonner didn't take his eyes off his primary target. He stayed locked on Marcus and threw the ball into the triple coverage. Marcus gathered, leaped, got a hand on the ball, then was smashed by two of the defenders; the third dove to the turf in vain for what would have been a meaningless interception as the clock ran out. Marcus had prevented any of the DBs from catching the ball in a position to return it to the opposite end zone, preserving CSU's lead, 22-21.

"Hell of a move just to make a play on that ball," Allenby said. "I hope he didn't get killed on that hit. It looked like one of those DBs tried to take his head off."

Marcus slowly got to his feet, then jogged with his teammates toward the locker room. Wade exhaled. "Looks like he's okay. But did you see the guy wide open in the middle?"

"Of course I did. Everyone saw him—except the guy who threw it. And to think we spent just about the whole season with that shit-for-brains at quarterback."

"Great call, though, if they'd just executed."

Allenby nodded. "I'd rather see that than sit on the ball at the end of the half. I've seen too many coaches take a damn knee there."

Allenby went to the Men's. Angela, shrouded in dark glasses and turban, clutching her constant companion, made her entrance moments after he left.

"So, did I miss anything?"

"I can't *believe* you brought your laptop."

"*I* can't believe I'm at a fucking football game on Christmas Eve."

Wade was still shaking his head at the computer. "How far do you think that thing would fly if I flipped it like a Frisbee?"

Angela pressed it to her chest like the precious child she would apparently never have. "I didn't want to be bored if this was a blow-out."

Wade pointed at the scoreboard. "Do you have any idea what an accomplishment it is for us to just be *in* the game with USC at halftime, let alone—"

"Do *you* have any idea what an accomplishment it was for me just to get out of bed with this exploding head? What do you mean *us* anyway? I don't see any shoulder pads on you."

"Don't forget, this is the coach *we* hired." Allenby had returned. He smiled at Angela, gestured toward his coat. "I have a flask in case you'd like a nip or two to get you through the second half."

Angela groaned histrionically, put her fists up as if to pound him. "Is there any possible way you could cancel this obscene halftime show and get this game over with? I need to go home and throw up."

On the field USC's marching band was flaunting its comically vast superiority to CSU's underfunded ragtag crew, whose uniforms looked like they hadn't been replaced since they were purchased at a deep discount from Professor Harold Hill. After half an hour or so of timeless pageantry that seemed like three, the teams came out for the second half. CSU lined up to receive the kickoff this time.

"Now we'll see how pissed off the USC defense is," Wade warned, recalling the hit on Marcus that had ended the first half and expecting more of the same.

Allenby didn't seem worried. "Slate's had time to make some adjustments, too. We'll see what he comes up with."

"I like your attitude," Angela told Allenby. "Mr. Optimism over there is usually ready to crap in his hat before the game even begins."

"You know what they say," Wade said. "Unlucky in love, fucked in football."

"We'll put it on your tombstone."

The third quarter passed unremarkably except for the fact that the outmanned, fatigued, and increasingly debilitated CSU team somehow stayed on top. Its players hopped, hobbled, or crawled to the sidelines repeatedly after tackling or being tackled by the stouter Trojans, but refused to surrender the lead. USC cooperated by continuing to ignore the easy route of running to daylight, instead launching pass after pass even when Slate's all-out attacking schemes disrupted the rhythm of the passer. Three drives ended when the Trojans' quarterback was brought down behind the line of scrimmage or had the ball batted down by a blitzer. Noting that Bludge was in on a couple of the sacks, Wade shared with Allenby what Marcus had told him.

Allenby nodded. "Slate figured out the right way to use him. He's got enough straight-ahead speed to pressure the quarterback, but he'd be lost trying to guard those running backs downfield. Makes sense to blitz him, play to his strength."

At the beginning of the fourth quarter Marcus evaded a sack at midfield, pump-faked the containment defender onto a prayer mat, and raced down the sideline to the USC twenty yard line. Flash Jackson trailed the play all the way across the field to screen off two pursuers. Just as they evaded his block and converged to make the tackle, Marcus pitched the ball back to his startled teammate, who bobbled it, then clutched it, and ran uncontested the rest of the way into the end zone.

"*That's* what you missed in the first half," an exultant Wade told Angela.

Allenby said to Wade, "You realize how special what you're seeing is?"

Wade nodded, his heart still racing. "I saw Gale Sayers score six touchdowns in one game against the 49ers when I was a kid. This is the best running I've seen since then."

"The end of the play is what I loved," Allenby said. "Pure genius. The downfield lateral is the most underutilized play in the game today. All the coaches are so focused on avoiding turnovers that they've killed the dynamics of the game. Remember early in Deion Sanders' career when his teammates would try to pitch him the ball after a pick? All the announcers and reporters would go apeshit because it was supposedly so stupid? It was actually the smartest thing they could do. Think about it: your own offense stinks, you're out there with the ball now against the other guys' offense, five linemen and a quarterback—that only leaves five athletes to make the tackle—so get the ball to your fastest man, however you can. Of course, you don't try it when you're protecting a lead at the end of a game—"

Wade flashed to Eric Wright, better known as "Airhead" Wright for weeks afterward in the Greater Bay Area (and by a far more envenomed epithet for*ever* after in Wade's household) for risking a pitch to Ronnie Lott at the end of the 49ers' first

Super Bowl, when all he needed to do was fall on the ground to let his team run out the clock.

"—but when you're in a game like this against a physically far superior team, plays like that are what give you a chance to win."

The Trojans answered the improvisation with a mostly smash-mouth drive, then closed the deal with a fade pattern to their ace receiver, who got away with a flagrant push off in the end zone, then shook the ball and his ass tauntingly over the supine defender.

"That's not *fair*," Angela shouted.

"You're right," Wade said. "Should've been offensive pass interference."

"He's been doing that all year," Allenby pointed out. "You're not going to get that call against USC in a bowl game."

The referee allowed the score but threw another flag for unsportsmanlike conduct. The receiver bounced angrily away from his chastising position coach, then shifted into his "What took you so long to throw it to me?" routine, patterned after the works of the noted contemporary philosopher Terrell Owens. Apparently energized rather than dismayed by the display, USC overcame the penalty on the kickoff after the extra point and promptly forced a punt. With six minutes remaining and CSU clinging to a one-point lead, 29-28, Slate adjusted again as the USC offense came back out onto the field to face his exhausted defenders.

"Look! Marcus is coming in on defense. He's going to cover that stud wideout."

Angela followed Wade's extended finger. "Does that mean we're going to win?"

"It means we're getting desperate."

As if deliberately taking up the challenge, USC called another pass to the receiver who had just scored and celebrated. Marcus stayed with him stride for stride, knocked the ball down. USC tried it again; this time Marcus jumped the route, almost intercepted the pass.

Allenby flinched at the near miss. "He's in the end zone if he picks that off. Game over. We win."

"He isn't Superman," Wade said. "Pretty damn close, though."

On third down the Trojans flipped a screen pass to their back-up tailback. He turned it into a fifteen yard gain that was nearly much more except for a saving tackle by Bludge, who never gave up on the play, chasing the runner down from behind when he cut back to change directions. As the ballcarrier was going down, Bludge swung a fist and punched the ball loose. A.J. Dupree fell on it, and his teammates began to celebrate. The CSU offense ran out onto the field, but the referee waved them off, signaled that the runner had been down before the fumble occurred. Slate challenged the call, and a review ensued. The officials conferred, deliberated, and apparently debated the inequities in the Treaty of Versailles. Replays on the giant screen in the stadium appeared to show that the ball had come loose just before the tailback's knee hit the ground, but it was hard to be sure. After a lengthy delay the verdict was announced: down by contact, USC to retain possession.

Wade muttered, "What a surprise. USC gets another call."

Allenby shrugged. "That one could've gone either way."

"Yes, but God hates me, so there was never really any doubt."

"The whole world revolves around Wade," Angela explained. "The God he doesn't believe in punishes him by making his football teams lose."

"Not just my *football* teams," Wade protested. "There's also—"

"The Warriors will never make the playoffs again in your lifetime, Wade," Angela said. "Accept it, move on, get a life."

A deflated CSU defense lined up again. Bludge had almost been the hero, Wade thought. And A.J. Dupree had made the almost-recovery. What a boost it would have been for *him* after all the classrooms and courtrooms he had passed through to reach this point: he had come within perhaps a quarter of an inch and a referee's discretion of making the play that could have sealed a bowl game victory against mighty USC.

The reprieved Trojans went back to the ground game, and

six plays later tailback number three sauntered into the end zone, giving them their first lead of the day. The extra point made the score 35-29, with less than two minutes remaining.

"Okay, here we go." Allenby hadn't given up. "Winning time. A touchdown and a conversion now and we go home happy."

Unitas time, Wade thought. *Joe Montana time.* "Marcus must be exhausted," he said, as the quarterback/cornerback came out again with the kickoff return team. "What else can they ask him to do?"

"It was worth a shot to shut down that wideout," Allenby said. "At least Slate didn't try to have him go both ways for the whole game. He let Marcus spend his energy on offense for most of the game. Now he needs one score to win. Who would have thought USC-CSU would come down to whichever team has the ball last?"

USC kicked away from Marcus, tackled the returner inside the twenty, then set up its defense to take away deep routes and sidelines. Short passes over the middle secured a couple of CSU first downs and moved the ball to midfield but burned a timeout. On the third series two passes fell incomplete, and on third down, under heavy pressure, Marcus had to scramble out of bounds with only a two-yard gain. Fourth down and extinction awaited. Slate sent in the play. Three receivers lined up wide right; Marcus looked at them as he took the shotgun snap, then pivoted and threw the ball immediately to the left, where the tight end had run a quick hitch. As the cornerback came up to tackle him, the receiver pitched the ball back to Jackson, who had trailed the play. He hurdled the downed corner and took off. He wasn't brought down until he was knocked out of bounds at the USC fifteen yard line.

"The old hook and lateral," Allenby gloated. "Still works like a charm. Just like on the playground."

Tinker Owens, Wade was thinking. "But we still need fifteen yards."

"That should be pretty easy, shouldn't it?" Angela wanted to know.

Wade and Allenby looked at her, then at each other. Wade

shuddered. Allenby smiled. Two plays went nowhere. Marcus scraped himself off the turf and called the second timeout after being flattened by a blitzing linebacker. On third down Slate called a play he had mentioned in his interview, sending Jackson straight down the field. Slate had talked about using it early in the game; obviously he had changed his mind and saved it for the end instead. Jackson beat the cornerback with a burst of sheer speed and then broke his pattern off toward the post. Marcus juked the same blitzer who had blasted him on the previous play and barely got the pass away. Just as Jackson put his hands up to pull the ball in, the free safety jarred it out of his grasp. It appeared that the hit had come early and that he had pinned one of Jackson's arms. The back judge studied the play right in front of him, moved his hand toward his hanky, twitched above it tantalizingly, then left it in his pocket.

"Pass interference!" Wade jumped out of his seat, nearly splattering Angela's laptop on the concrete at their feet. "How the hell can they not call that?"

"Are we getting screwed again?" Angela asked.

"Jackson didn't come back for the ball," Allenby pointed out. "He's just learning to play that spot. You can't turn a guy into a receiver in three weeks. Maybe that's why they didn't try to throw it to him before."

Wade nodded glumly. "Marcus was lucky just to get that off. Anybody else back there and it would have been another sack."

Allenby agreed. "Bonner would've been flat on his ass, sniffing smelling salts again and trying to guess how many fingers."

With another fourth down coming up and six seconds remaining in the game, Slate called his last timeout. Time for one more play, one last chance to save the day.

"What's he got left?" Allenby wondered. "Statue of fucking Liberty?"

"Only if Marcus can hand it to himself."

Bludge came in along with another substitute for the final play. He had lined up at end on the extra point kicks, but Wade had not seen him in the game on offense otherwise. Marcus took the snap in the shotgun, faked first a hand off and then a throw to Jackson coming in motion behind him, then pulled the ball down and sprinted toward the other sideline. Most of the defense followed the fakes to the wrong side of the field. It appeared that Marcus had an angle to the end zone and was going to run for it; the ubiquitous linebacker, however, read the play and bore straight for him. Just before reaching the line of scrimmage, Marcus jerked to a stop, stepped back, and surveyed the field. Standing alone in the corner of the end zone twenty-five yards away was Bludge.

He had lined up as a tackle-eligible on the play and then dragged across the field to the opposite side, unattended. Marcus juked again to try to get the linebacker to alter course, but this time the fake didn't work, and the Trojan hit him fiercely just after Marcus brought the ball back up and let it fly. He was driven face-first into the turf, unable to watch what happened next.

Wade, Allenby, and Angela jumped to their toe-tops amid the thousands straining to witness the end-game miracle. Bludge eyed the prize spiraling toward him, held up his hands, reached for victory, caught a toe in the turf, stumbled, staggered, tried to recover, grasped desperately for the pass as he fell to the ground—and dropped the ball.

CHAPTER 19

Defeat is worse than death, because you have
to live with defeat.
                                    —Bill Musselman

La gloire est éphémère, mais l'obscurité est
éternelle.
                                    —Napoleon Bonaparte

You don't know what one word of encouragement
or respect or love might do, what repercussions it
might have in someone's life.
                                    —Luis Alberto Urrea

Wade, Allenby, and Angela watched the players and coaches,
winners and losers almost equally stunned, leave the sidelines
and converge on the field.

"No bucket of Gatorade for USC," Wade pointed out.

"We don't need to see that played-out, tired-ass routine,"
Allenby said.

"Ever, ever again," Angela agreed.

"But especially not now, not from USC. They know they
lucked out."

The head coaches enacted the customary formalities, shaking
hands and speaking briefly, and then USC's controversial leader
made a point of finding Marcus Foster, around whom more than
a dozen opposing players were also crowding. It appeared that
the entire starting defense, among others, had gathered to pay
tribute to this nobody from nowhere who had nearly beaten them
in their bowl game.

"That team is showing some class," Allenby acknowledged.

Wade nodded grudgingly. It was hard to make nice with USC.
He found the coach, like his gum-chumping predecessor, unduly

cocky, sitting on that vast trove of talent in L.A., wondered how he'd fare if today's rosters were reversed. And the players weren't even pretending to be students. *Me and Matt made history*, Reggie Bush had proclaimed from the Heisman podium, midway through his third year of college, after following his ballroom-dancing teammate Leinart in winning the award. No wonder Larashawndria started sentences that way. "I guess you don't have to *go* to class to show it."

A small contingent of CSU fans, who had been massed along the sidelines poised to storm the field and tear down the goalposts to celebrate an epic upset, now milled about in purposeless confusion, as Angela noted with a nod in their direction.

"So much for deconstruction."

"I never understood that nonsense anyway," Wade said. "I just hope our gang doesn't turn into a lynch mob." He pointed toward the corner of the end zone where Bludge had dropped the pass. He was still kneeling there, forehead to the turf, as if awaiting not a noose but a ritual beheading.

"How can you *stand* this?" Angela said. "This is like getting your heart broken."

"Welcome aboard. Now you know what it's like for the rest of us." Wade suddenly remembered the bet he had made, looked at Allenby. "I just realized that drop cost me a thousand bucks. How much did you lose?"

Allenby gave Wade a puzzled look, as if he didn't know what Wade was talking about. Oh well, Wade thought. That's chump change for him. Maybe it was the wrong moment to worry about that stuff.

"Let's go down and wait outside the locker room," Allenby said. "I want to congratulate Slate on a great coaching job."

Angela took a pass, decided to head back to the hotel. Wade tagged along with Allenby to the locker room, where the players were filing in. Slate was shaking hands with each player as he came through the door. When the last one had passed through, Slate turned to his visitors.

"Please come in."

Allenby held up a hand. "We don't want to intrude on your

privacy. We know you need some time to talk to your team."

"That's okay. We feel like you two are a part of this team, too. Please join us."

Allenby glanced at Wade, making sure, Wade intuited, that he understood the high honor that was being conferred upon them. It also occurred to Wade that Slate was still auditioning for the permanent coaching position and was prepared to reinforce his candidacy with his demeanor now. More power to him.

Before dispersing them to the showers, Slate called the team together, stepped into their midst. Wade could see the raw emotion in his eyes. What could anyone say in this situation?

"We just had a very long game, so I'm going to keep this short. I just want to tell all of you how proud I am of the game you played, of the effort you made. We came up a little short against a great team, but no one here—no one"—Wade followed Slate's eyes as the coach tried to meet Bludge's, but the linebacker/ never again tight end, slumped on a bench at the perimeter, did not look up—"has any reason to hang his head."

"I know there were a lot of tough calls out there, but that happens in every game, and we all know that's not the reason we didn't win. I hope I don't hear one word from any of you blaming the referees for this loss."

"Let's not tarnish the fact that we played in a great game, against a great team, and gave them a battle for sixty minutes that they won't forget. They know who CSU is now, and so does America. I'm proud of all of you, and proud I got the chance to coach you in this game."

A few players began to clap, then a few more, and then suddenly the entire room was filled with applause. Slate nodded acknowledgment, obviously moved.

Wade looked at Allenby. "Gettin' a little misty yourself?"

"I've never seen this after a loss."

Wade looked at Bludge, who still had his head down.

"I'm going to talk to the man with the hands."

Allenby grunted. "Tell him he set back the cause of Aryan Supremacy by a century or so."

Wade approached Bludge warily. A couple of his teammates

moved away to give them space, but Marcus caught Wade's eye, came over to join him and spoke up before Wade could think of what to say.

"I should've made a better throw. It was a little high."

Bludge looked up in obvious surprise, then back down. "Bullshit. It was perfect. I fuckin' dropped it."

"Don't beat yourself up. I could've run it in. There was just one guy to beat."

"Right. And the one guy was a first team All-American who's going to be a first round draft pick in the NFL. He led the Pac-12 in tackles, and he already tackled your ass twenty times today. You did the right thing. All I had to do was fuckin' catch the ball."

"You did a great job getting open. Receiver isn't really your position."

"You think?"

Bludge spread his arms and inspected his hands as if he wanted to fire up a chainsaw and lop them off on the spot.

Marcus tried again. "We played in a great game, man. We almost beat USC."

"*Almost* ain't worth shit and you know it."

"You were a big part of it. You recovered that kick, caused a fumble, made a couple of sacks and a bunch of tackles. You were all over the field."

Bludge was still studying the floor. Marcus paused, looked at Wade, gave a small shrug, tried another tack. "I didn't know a white man could move like that."

Bludge looked up at the jest, spoke slowly. "In the biggest game of my life, I dropped the fucking ball to lose it. End of fucking story." His head went back down.

"I dropped a pick that would've won it for us, too," Marcus said. "No one wins or loses a game by himself."

Bludge's head stayed down. Marcus reached out, put a hand on his shoulder. Wade gaped in spite of himself, felt as if suddenly transported to Yoknapatawpha County: *let flesh touch with flesh and watch the fall of all the eggshell shibboleth of caste and color too.* After a moment, Marcus pulled his hand off the shoulder and put it out for a shake. "I'm glad we got to play together. You're a good teammate."

Bludge lifted his head, stared at the extended hand for a moment, then put his own out to meet it. "I know I only got to play in this game because of you. Maybe I didn't deserve that, or maybe I deserved what happened at the end. Either way, I know I should thank you."

"You don't have to thank me for shit. Just work hard this spring, this summer, come back stronger, we'll do better next year."

"Yeah, maybe we will. Now that we've got a quarterback."

Wade watched Marcus walk away, pausing to accept hugs or backpats from other teammates as he headed to his locker before hitting the shower. Wade turned to Bludge.

"You think we ought to let him in our club?"

"Fuck the club. Fuck you. Fuck me."

"That about covers it, I should think." There was also the matter of the thousand bucks Bludge had cost him, but Wade decided to let that go for now.

"You think I'm an asshole, don't you?"

"I think you played a hell of a game and dropped one ball at the end. And I think you made a friend, if you'll just let that happen."

"Him?" Bludge jerked his head after Marcus. "He'll be on top of the world if he plays like that next season. He won't need a friend like me."

"I'm guessing he'll be the same guy he is right now. And you might be surprised how friendships are formed and survive."

"Are you talking about you and your rich black buddy? He still want to kick me off the team?"

"I think he'd rather string you up by the balls, let you see how the other side lives, but if you could give up the 'n' word, start with that, I believe in time he could take a different view of you."

"I don't really need that word."

"Good."

Bludge looked Wade in the eye. "Are you gonna make

everybody else give it up, too?"

"How about if we just agree to work on what's in our own control first?"

Bludge considered it, appeared to assent. Then said, "Can we at least keep the spics and gooks out of our group, though?"

Wade grinned in spite of himself. "I guess you're going to live after all."

"Is that a good thing?"

Wade shrugged. "Too close to call."

Bludge trudged to the showers. Wade found Allenby pocketing his cell phone, talking with Slate.

"I just offered Sherman the permanent position as our head coach. I thought you'd like to be the first to congratulate him."

Wade shook hands with the coach and then said to Allenby, "So, did you tell him yet about scheduling USC again for the opener next year?"

Allenby laughed. "I thought we'd save them for homecoming. We'll start with a creampuff like Ohio State."

"I suppose Tennessee-Chattanooga wasn't available?" Slate deadpanned. Then added, "I always liked Pat Hill's philosophy at Fresno State: go anywhere to play anyone at anytime. That's the way to build a football program. No pushovers to inflate your record. That's the approach I hope we'll take."

Allenby nodded his approval, and Slate continued: "I know the schedules are made several years out, but if you can get another game with USC anytime down the road, that's fine with me. I just hope I'll be around to coach it."

Allenby smiled. "I hope so, too. And I hope we'll be around to see it."

Wade and Allenby went back to their hotel, stopped in the bar for a drink. Angela came down to join them but settled for coffee.

"Losing sucks," she said. "The game's been over for two hours, and I'm still depressed. How do you deal with it?"

Allenby shrugged, hoisted his Scotch. "Libation helps."

"In moderation," Wade said.

Angela shot him her *Drink piss and die* look.

"How do you celebrate victory then?"

"Libation's good for that, too," Allenby said.

"Physical intimacy is a great way to celebrate *or* commiserate," Wade offered.

She gave him the look again. "Grown men hugging and kissing and patting each other on the butt, you mean?"

"That wasn't exactly what I had in mind."

Allenby stood. "I'll leave you two to"—he paused, looked at Wade, then smiled at Angela—"celebrate or commiserate in the fashion of your choice."

"You're not joining us for dinner?"

"Flying out in an hour. Business to clean up in L.A."

"Is he going through with the divorce?" Angela asked after Allenby picked up their tab and left.

"As far as I know," Wade said. "I introduced him to Erica Wiley."

"That's one foxy lady. I always thought you had your eye on her yourself."

Wade took a beat, soaked in the ambiance of the saloon, became Sinatra: "'I only have eyes for . . . *you*.'"

Angela batted her baby blues. "I hope that's not all you've got for me. Eyes." She punctuated with a meaningful glance.

"Ready to try again?"

She finished her coffee. "Can't be any worse than last night."

"You're a fine one to talk."

Angela decided she was hungry after all, so they decided to take it slow, have dinner first in the hotel. Afterwards, when they went up to their room, she went in to take a bath, get further into the mood. After a few minutes she whistled Wade to come in and scrub her back, admire the view.

"That feels so good."

"Any other vital parts need attending to in here?"

"I hope you're feeling extra frisky, big boy. We're gonna make up for last night."

How about making up for last year?

"I never went to a football game with Ronnie, you know. Even though he'd *played*. I hope you understand what it means that I went to a game with you."

"Half a game," Wade said. "And you brought your fucking—"

"Quit nitpicking. Why don't you go in and warm the bed up for us?"

Well-fed, well-lubricated, yesterday's disaster and today's defeat behind them, delight just ahead, Wade sat down happily on the edge of the bed, shucked his shoes, switched on the TV. Expecting *Seinfeld* again, he bumped instead into the end of an old movie. *Sleepless in Seattle*, he remembered. Not quite as relevant tonight as *Horny in San Antonio*, but you had to pay extra for those. Besides, maybe it was an omen: Angela could have doubled for a pre-collagen Meg Ryan any time, and, back when he had more hair, a few people—well, one or two anyway—had in fact told Wade he looked a bit like Tom Hanks on a bad day. There were even some parallels in the plots: after all the twists and turns their paths had taken, he was finally going to make love again to the girl of his dreams. Tom and Meg strolled off arm-in-arm to happy-ever-after land; credits rolled, quickly replaced by the blast of a commercial. Wade lowered the volume, heard Angela start to drain the tub, glanced at the bathroom, clicked onto ESPN. Still time for a quick peek at the highlights before creating some of their own. Even though CSU had lost, some of those runs Marcus had made would be playing in Wade's head forever, and he wouldn't mind another look right now.

The news he turned onto knocked him right off the bedspread and onto his knees. Angela heard the clump as he hit the floor, came dripping out of the bathroom draped in a towel.

"What are you doing, Wade, praying for—"

"Marcus Foster," Wade croaked, as he gestured unsteadily at the TV, his eyes brimming with sudden tears. Angela's towel fell to the floor.

Wade raised the volume with the remote. The announcer said again the words that couldn't possibly be true: "Earlier this evening, after nearly leading his team to a spectacular upset victory over highly favored USC, CSU quarterback Marcus Foster was shot and killed at a San Antonio night spot."

CHAPTER 20

That's the thing with the young these days,
isn't it? They watch too many happy endings.
Everything has to be wrapped up with a
smile and a tear and a wave. Everyone has
learned, found love, seen the error of their
ways, discovered the joys of monogamy or
fatherhood, or filial duty, or life itself. In
my day, people got shot at the end of films,
after learning only that life is hollow, dismal,
brutish, and short.
> —Martin Sharp, in Nick Hornby's
> *A Long Way Down*

As a culture, as a country, we've got to start
respecting life.
> —John Lynch, at the funeral of
> Denver Broncos' teammate
> Darrent Williams

Allenby sat next to Wade at the memorial. He had been in the
air when Wade reached him with a text message from Angela's
phone. As soon as he hit the ground, he had taken a flight back
to San Antonio to help with the arrangements. "I told you bad
things happen in Texas," he'd said when an ashen Wade met him
at the airport. "We ought to give this goddam shithole back to
Mexico."

The details of the killing had emerged quickly and clearly,
confirmed by many witnesses. There was no mystery to unravel.
Marcus had been at curbside leaving The Thirsty Horse Saloon
with his teammates when a trio of drunk or drugged up local
gangbangers in Trojan regalia had pulled up in a car and begun
taunting a group of players that included A.J. Dupree over their
loss. Dupree had dragged one of the kids out of the car, laid him

out, and got his hands on the second when the third produced a pistol and started firing. Marcus, rushing to try to pull Dupree away from the fight, had caught a bullet in the temple and died almost instantly. A.J. hadn't suffered a scratch. Later he had submitted to his thirteenth arrest.

The service was held in the campus chapel right after Christmas, before the team would disperse for the rest of the semester break. Sherman Slate was asked to deliver the eulogy. He spoke quietly and calmly, telling the story of Marcus's life, touching briefly on his heroics during the season and his final game, but emphasizing more the leadership he'd shown. At the end he turned to his team, sitting in a unit, and asked the African-American players to pay special attention to his next words.

"It's not white people any more that are our problem. I'm not sure I ever thought I'd live to see the day when I'd say that. I come from people with family members who were lynched in Mississippi. I've been called *boy* and *nigger* to my face. I took crap in the Army, took crap in my first few jobs—but things are changing, things are getting better. And *we've* got to change and get better, too. We've got to stop this senselessness. We've got to stop killing each other. This was a black boy who, without a father in his life to show him the way, somehow learned how to be a man. This was a young black man who valued his education, prized it, who had great athletic talent but who was planning on doing much more with his life than just play ball. And now he won't get that chance—because another young black man denied it to him."

"I know that most of you sitting here in front of me today have heard this statistic before, but I'm going to say it to you again, and ask you to remember it and take it to heart: the number one cause of death among young African-American males in this country is murder at the hands of other young African-American males."

"I want every one of you to make a pledge today to live your lives in the right way, to honor Marcus Foster. Don't let his death, or his life, have been in vain. Learn from him, learn from this."

Then Slate looked again at the larger audience, put a hand upon his chest. "I know I need to learn something from this too, and take some responsibility for what happened. I made a decision not to suspend a player"—he turned briefly back to the team—"your teammate, to give him another chance. Maybe we all need to look at that again. How many chances do we get before we get it right? How many innocent lives do we jeopardize before we say enough is enough? Where do we draw the line? I'm here to tell you today that hereafter I'll be drawing the line in memory of Marcus Foster and trying to keep the future Marcus Fosters, of whom I hope there'll be many, alive and thriving and achieving all that they can achieve—but that he won't get the chance to. Let's *all* pledge now to keep his memory alive by the way we live *our* lives."

After Slate stepped away from the lectern, many of Marcus's teammates came forward to speak. Some were tongue-tied, some teary, some funny, others eloquent, all emotional. It turned into a very long day, but Wade didn't get tired of hearing the tributes. Nothing seemed trite. He wondered, if he himself were gunned down tomorrow, how many people would line up at his send-off to say these words of appreciation for the life he had lived? How would *his* time on earth measure up? He pictured his ex-brother-in-law, drunk or stoned, cutting in at the head of the line of mourners, mouth full of funeral baked meats, to tell his famous story of how Wade had tried to help him potty train his pit bull and been bitten in the ass for his trouble.

Finally, when it appeared the last word about Marcus had been said, Bludge rose from his seat alone at the back of the team's section and came slowly forward. Wade held his breath, hoped for the best.

Bludge began by gesturing dramatically at the casket. "A lot of people here today probably wish it was me in there instead of Marcus," he said, then paused for the harsh truth to settle and for a few murmurs, perhaps of assent. "Especially after I dropped that pass against USC." A few nervous laughs now bubbled up. "I might even be one of them," he continued, to more uncertain laughter. Wade allowed himself to breathe. Maybe it was going to be all right.

"I didn't know this guy well, and I'm not going to pretend that I did. I don't have any funny stories about horsing around together or any"—he paused, found the word he wanted—"heartwarming tales about our experiences growing up together, or getting to know each other, because we didn't have any. To be honest with you, until a few weeks ago, I hated his guts."

That silenced everyone.

"Believe me, I know how stupid that sounds now. I *was* stupid. I didn't even know him, but I hated him." Steady up until now, Bludge began to lose his bearings a bit. "I just want to say that I'm sorry for the stuff I've said, stuff I've done." He paused, drew a deep breath. "Marcus was a friend to me even though I didn't deserve a friend like him. I won't forget what he did in that game or what he did for me, for all of us, in his life."

Bludge looked into the crowd, found Wade. "There's some words I've said that I promise not to say again. I'll try to be . . . a better man."

Bludge's voice broke on the last phrase, and Sherman Slate stepped up to comfort him. Wade had wondered if he would ever see a black man hug a white man without thinking of Sammy Davis, Jr. and Richard Nixon; at least he had lived long enough to see the balance of power reversed. He looked at Allenby, who shrugged. "Words are easy. Bear Bryant *talked* about wanting to be the one to integrate the SEC. We'll see."

In the crowd milling about afterwards Wade spotted Larashawndria, standing out even in a circle of other athletes. He started to move toward her, then saw that two football players had beaten him to it. He scanned the body language, figured out what was going on: they were hitting on her. *At a memorial service.* Some guys could block out anything. He hoped they wouldn't try too hard to impress her, resort in this setting to their frat party repertoire.

"She's beautiful, isn't she?"

Wade turned toward the soft voice and found himself face to face with Marcus's fiancée.

"Aren't you Dr. Wade?"

Wade flinched. He knew, of course, that scholars had held the title before physicians, and he would admit to an initial thrill the first few times he'd heard it coupled with his own name or seen the combination in print after all the years of struggling to finish his dissertation at Berkeley. On the whole, though, he had always found its usage among academics an affectation, never more so than on the lips of this woman, who was going to be a medical doctor, someone who could save your life. It was the sort of thing that oafs like Gordon Brooks insisted on. Wade was amused by colleagues who signed their names with the title or put it on their voicemail messages. He even knew community college teachers who insisted on "professor."

"I'm Wade, yes. I'm so sorry for—"

"I thought you might say something . . . at the . . . ."

Her voice trailed off. Taken aback, Wade stammered a response. "I'm sorry. I just . . . didn't . . . I couldn't—"

"No, wait, *I'm* sorry. That didn't come out right. I'm not blaming you. I couldn't talk up there either. I would've fallen apart."

Wade nodded, recalling his silence at his mother's funeral. The grief was just too deep. Words had seemed . . . not just useless, but . . . impossible.

"I just wanted to let you know that Marcus told me about you. He was really grateful for your help. He said you were really . . . a friend to him."

Wade nodded again. "Thank you for telling me that. I . . . thought the world of him, too."

She started to cry, adding fresh tears to the volumes that had obviously poured out before. Wade was reminded of Kurtz's Intended, looking at the rest of her life ahead now without the one she'd planned to spend it with. How did anyone ever fill that void?

"Marcus told me you're going to be a doctor. He was very proud of you."

She nodded, thanked him again, kissed his cheek, hugged him, and then she was gone.

Wade was surprised to find Dixon James waiting for him to

exit the embrace.

"I talked to A.J. on the phone yesterday. He feels like shit about this. That was pretty cold what the coach said about him."

"That was pretty cold what happened to Marcus, too."

"A.J. didn't kill him!"

"A.J. got him killed. What's the difference? I thought you said A.J. was an idiot, anyway."

"He *is* an idiot, but—"

"It's not his fault?"

"Something like that. Did you ever hear about what his own mother did to him?"

Wade shook his head, not sure if he wanted to hear it now.

Dixon persisted. "He wrote a paper about it for his Soc class. It's a lot better than that crap he tried to write about World War II."

"That's not too hard to believe."

"I mean it. You should read it. His mother used to get high and put out her cigarettes on his *face*. That's how he got some of those scars. When she gave him a bath, she would hold his head under the water until he thought he was going to drown."

Wade thought, for maybe the millionth time, how incalculably fortunate he had been to have parents who had made their children's fulfillment the center of their own. How did you even begin to understand the world from the standpoint of someone whose own mother waterboarded him or used him for an ashtray?

"I'm not saying it justifies what he did, just . . . ." Dixon let the sentence trail off, nowhere to go. He looked over in the direction of the casket where others were still gathered to pay their last respects. "I guess Marcus was a pretty special dude, huh? Not just on the football field, I mean."

"I wish you could've met him. He would've liked you. He's someone your age you could have talked to who would've understood that SAT vocabulary of yours."

"I did talk to him once."

Wade was surprised again. "I didn't know that."

"Just on the phone. He called me to find out how A.J. and

Mars were doing with their classes. I told him I was doing everything I could. He thanked me, offered to study with them if I thought it would help. He . . . sounded like a really nice guy." Dixon looked over at the casket again, a trace of bewilderment or perhaps bitterness in his eyes now. "I guess it's true what they say about what happens to nice guys."

"Yeah, well, let's not forget what happens to idiots either."

"What do you think *will* happen to A.J.?"

"Well, for one thing, I don't think he's playing any more football for Sherman Slate. Or for anybody else, for that matter. Maybe if you've helped him learn how to read and write a little bit this semester he can find some kind of a job, if he doesn't get convicted."

"Mars said his family might put up some money to help A.J. hire a lawyer. I might ask my dad, too. He's pretty tight, though."

"I can think of more prudent investments. Besides, the university will provide an attorney, up to a point anyway. How's Mars doing?"

"He's pretty upset, of course, but . . . he talked his teachers into giving him Incompletes in a couple of his classes. I think he might try to finish them. He asked if I could help him. With A.J. . . . away, he'll actually have more time to study. You know what he's really pissed off about, though?"

"More than Marcus's death, you mean?" Marston had quit the team after his suspension from the bowl game. Invited to attend the memorial anyway, he hadn't shown up.

Dixon looked away, then met Wade's gaze again. "Well, aside from that, of course."

"What?"

"He says he would have caught that ball that Bludge dropped. He one hundred percent guarantees it. He says if the coach would've just put him in for the last play, we would've won the game. We would've beat USC. He would've been the . . . hero."

"I see." It was harder, of course, to be the hero when you didn't make the travel squad in the first place and then got your ass kicked off the team entirely before the game was ever played. *And now please meet our next contestant for the Ultimate*

Fantasy Challenge.

"He thinks Slate might be sort of a . . . reverse racist."

Wade laughed. "That sounds like something Mars would say. Now I've heard everything. Like Ward Connerly, you mean?"

"Well, I'm not sure he knows who—"

"Don't kid yourself. Mars wouldn't know Ward Connerly from Ward Cleaver."

Dixon frowned, stumped for once. "Who's Ward Cleaver?"

Wade realized he had taken another small step in his own steady progress toward irrelevance. Could senility and death be far behind? *Hotchkiss country, here I come.* "Never mind. You can live without that information. And so can Mars. I hope you can help him finish those classes."

Wade paused, remembered where he was. "Marcus would want that, too."

Wade went home, sank into a chair, suddenly was racked with sobs. He'd made it dry-eyed through the service, his first since his mother's, but now felt his grief come gushing out at the terrible thought of all the years Marcus had lost. Wade's mother had made eighty, and her death had still torn him apart; Marcus had barely passed twenty. All that talent, all that promise, all that hope he had to put into the world—gone.

The phone rang. Wade tried to compose himself, picked up, expecting Allenby with plans for a dinner neither had the stomach for.

"Are you crying?"

Angela. She'd flown home in the middle of an abysmal Christmas Day.

"No."

"Bullshit."

"All right, you win. I just . . . lost it for a minute there."

"That's okay, Wade. You . . . loved him, didn't you?"

"I don't know that I'm entitled to use that word. I . . . hardly knew him. I just met him this—"

"That word won't kill you, Wade. You *loved* him."

"If you say so."

"I was with you the night he was killed, remember?"

"Of course I re—"

"I saw your face. I saw . . . what happened to your heart."

"My dick, too-oo," Wade tried to point out, but stuttered on another sob.

"No dick jokes now, Wade. Just let it all out."

"Okay."

"I've been wanting to tell you that you've got something special going on with those kids you're working with. I can see that you really know how to . . . connect. I envy that, actually. I mean, my students know I'm smart and all, but they don't . . . *get* me like yours do."

"Thanks for saying that."

"I'm not just saying it, Wade. It's true. I saw it before with Marvin, of course, but—"

"Look how well that turned out. He lasted one semester."

"You were honest with him, Wade. You're probably the only adult in his life that ever was."

"His grandmother kicked his ass every day."

"His grandmother was in New York, Wade. You took care of him here. And you reached out to these football kids in the same way. That was no small thing, what happened with that wacko linebacker."

"Bludge? You're right. He came through big time at the service today."

"I'm glad to hear it," Angela said. "I just wanted to tell you that . . . you're doing a great job."

"Now you sound like my mom. Compared to the way I used to fuck up my composition classes, you mean?"

"As I recall, your chief contribution from those days was falling asleep at department meetings and getting a boner."

"The good old days," Wade remembered. "I used to get a hard-on every time I thought about you."

"Don't try to sweet-talk me, buster. Half of your hard-ons were for Erica Wiley or the D-cups in your classes."

"I thought we weren't supposed to be talking about my dick."

"Are you going ahead with your plan to establish a scholarship fund in Marcus's name?"

"Allenby already put in fifty thousand."

"Put me down for a thousand, too."

"You don't have to—"

"I don't have to do shit, Wade. Put me down."

"Okay."

"I'll take it out of the lingerie fund. You might have to settle for *au naturel* the next time you get lucky."

"When's that going to be?"

"MLA's in San Francisco. My interview with Berkeley is on Thursday. I'm trying to set something up at CSU for Friday. Who knows, maybe I can . . . squeeze you in."

"New Year's Eve day? Should I order up another bottle of Scotch to celebrate in case you—"

"Cram it, Wade."

"Okay."

"Gotta go now."

"Ronnie waiting up?"

"Ronnie's ass is out of here. He's sleeping in his car for all I care, if it hasn't been repossessed again."

Wade didn't care where Ronnie slept either, as long as it wasn't with Angela. He pictured Christmas in Connecticut, his old rival homeless, carless, trying to get comfy on the crest of a ridge of stalagmites at the bottom of a frozen pothole. Sometimes it was hard to top the consolations of schadenfreude. "Okay. I feel . . . better now. Thanks for calling."

"Glad I could help. But you still have that phone from 1982, don't you?"

"I guess. Why?"

"Join the Industrial Revolution, Wade. You need to get Caller ID. I could've been . . . anyone . . . you were . . . blubbering to."

Instead of the only one. Wade tried to fight the feeling. "I'd hate to miss any of Yoshi's death threats or extortions. She's almost as creative on the phone as she is in . . . you know."

"No, I *don't*, but thanks for sharing, asshole."

"Why do I always feel more like myself after I talk with you?"

CHAPTER 21

The administrators seem to see the CSU as an
institution where they can get rich rather than
an institution of higher learning.
—California State Senator
Leland Yee, Jan. 22, 2007

The assumption is that you cannot find a
qualified man or woman to lead the university
unless paid twice [the salary] of the Chief
Justice of the United States.
—California Governor Jerry
Brown, letter to the CSU Board
of Trustees, July 12, 2011

Marriage is, indeed, a maneuvering business.
—Mary Crawford, in Jane
Austen's *Mansfield Park*

"What can you tell me about the university president?"

Allenby had made lasagna, enough for a couple of leftover
meals. He and Wade were having an early supper before Allenby
headed home for the celebrations/divorce wars awaiting him in
the remainder of the holiday season.

"Not much," Wade said, off the top of his head, then paused
to give the question more thought. "You'll need some heavy
artillery if you plan to shoot him in his office. That's about all
I—"

"I've got a meeting with him tomorrow in L.A. Have you
ever met him?"

"I've never even *seen* him. Most faculty haven't. He's been
here two years, and he's spent the whole time looking for a better
job. That's probably what he's doing in L.A."

"Maybe not. He just renegotiated a new deal for himself here."

For weeks Wade had heard rumors of ongoing high-level contract negotiations, but he hadn't closely followed the newspaper accounts or more than glanced at the proliferative trail of email messages from irate faculty, many of whom appeared to be devoting the better part of their waking hours to sounding the alarum.

"Let me guess: he's annexing the athletic fields for his private golf course and spending the bond money for a vacation home in Baja."

"Close. CSU is becoming a real institution of higher earning. He's getting an eighty thousand dollar annual raise, a hundred thousand extra to his pension fund, a quarter of a million in guaranteed severance pay, plus he gets a paid sabbatical for a year at another quarter mil with no strings attached whenever he steps down, and a guarantee of a full professorship if he decides to come back."

"Full professor of *what*? He's never taught a class."

"I'm sure they'll think of something," Allenby said. "The Board of Trustees takes care of its own. He's the one who gave them that free full medical benefits for life package, remember?"

"I remember. At the same time he was raising required contributions from faculty and staff by thirty percent and stiffing us on COLA."

"Faculty and staff don't vote on his salary. Or on his golden parachute."

"The faculty did give him a vote of no confidence," Wade pointed out.

"That was last year, right? The Board gave him a raise, then, too, remember? A vote of no confidence from the faculty is practically a badge of honor these days. I heard he spent that last bump on a Bentley."

Wade grinned. "*That* I have seen. He made the mistake of parking it on campus one time, you know, with his CSUPREZ vanity plates?"

"Yeah?"

"The pledges from Kappa Chi swiped it, painted it pink, and plopped it in the fishpond. Upside down."

"Well at least that's one positive contribution a fraternity on this campus has made."

"Rumor has it they've still got the license plates in their strongbox. Use 'em for some kind of a hazing ritual now. Cockspanking I think they call it."

Allenby made a prune face. "What ever happened to squirt guns and water balloon bombs from the balcony?"

"Good clean fun, you mean?"

"Well, of course, sometimes what those balloons were filled with wasn't exactly *clean*, if you know what I mean."

"Nothing's really changed, then, has it?" Wade said. "What's your meeting with his nibs about?"

"Not sure what his agenda is. Maybe he wants to sound me out about making Delia Herman a vice president."

"Swell. That should pave the way for my future around here."

Allenby shrugged. "I'll put in a good word for you. Maybe I'll tell him to make you vice president instead."

"Put me up for vice pope while you're at it."

Angela was coming in tonight. Wade had offered to coordinate the local arrival and departure, provide the transportation to and from the airport, but Allenby decided to drive, and Angela had her Berkeley interview first, so each wound up renting a car. Wade had the evening free until Angela's arrival. He turned on a bowl game, the first he'd tried to watch since Marcus had died, but found his concentration wandering inevitably back to San Antonio. Eventually he grew drowsy, closed his eyes.

He woke with a start to a rap on the door, realized, Jesus, he'd fallen asleep during a football game. A first. He opened the door. Yoshi rushed in past him, burning leather all the way.

"Very fucking cold out there! I knock long time! How come you no answer? You have other girl in here?" She darted her eyes suspiciously at the bedroom.

Wade nodded. "J.Lo and Lady Gaga came by again. They wouldn't take 'no' for an—"

"I think you just watch fucking football again." Yoshi shifted her eyes to the TV. "Too busy answer fucking door when I knock."

"I think the game is over," Wade said. "Too bad you missed it. Rice University was kicking ass. You don't see that every—"

"I have to ask you favor."

"—millennium." *The gall,* Wade thought. *The sheer, unmitigated gall of the female of the species.* "Sure," he said. "Anything. Name it."

"I need get marry right away."

"Good luck with that."

"I serious." Yoshi's face showed that she was. "I need *you* marry me."

"Are you fucking nuts? Why would I marry you? I *hate* you."

"Most marriage end that way, you say so yourself. We just have . . . starthead."

"*Headstart.* But *why* do you think *I* would want to—"

"I pay you. How much you charge me?"

"Four billion dollars. Plus a pre-nup. I get to keep it all, even if I disembowel you on our wedding night."

"You don't want marry me?"

"I think you're getting the picture."

"I give you one thousand share of Cisco."

"Pass."

There was another knock on the door. Wade started, then slumped his shoulders, sighed, tried to frame in his mind the introductions he was about to perform if this was who he thought it was going to be. He gave up and opened the door. Angela walked in beaming, then saw Yoshi and did a double-take. Yoshi glared at her, scurried by, then hissed to Wade from the doorway, "Lot of money. You think about, call me."

Wade helped Angela out of her coat, hung it up, accepted a greeting peck. "And that, in case you hadn't guessed, was the sweet and lovely Yoshi."

"Gosh, Wade. She's beautiful!"

"So was Tokyo Rose."

"Careful, there. The PC police won't like that. Hasn't she been forgiven and exonerated?"

"I wouldn't be surprised if the prime minister puts flowers on her grave," Wade said. "What you really mean is 'How did a dip like you get with a babe like that?'"

"Let me guess: she wants to be a citizen, and she thought you were her ticket?"

"You're too smart for your own fucking good, aren't you? Why couldn't we just leave it at she fell for my irresistible charms and my enormous organ?"

"I've seen the organ. The charms must have improved considerably."

"How was Berkeley?"

"San Francisco. What can I tell you, Wade? The UC job is mine if I want it. They *love* me there. They love me everywhere."

"Get over yourself," Wade said. "They shitcanned you at Stanford."

"As I can always count on you to remind me at every conceivable opportunity. Why is that, do you think?"

Wade shrugged. "Kind of a strain . . . keeping company with a superhero. Brings you down to earth a bit."

"*Keeping company*? Who did you turn into, Jane Austen? Can we turn the fucking TV off?"

"Be my guest."

Angela picked up the remote, snuffed *SportsCenter,* turned abruptly back to Wade.

"Do you remember when you proposed to me?"

"I think we decided it was just a dream."

"Pipe dream, you mean?"

"I might have had a little too much to smoke that night," Wade conceded.

"You weren't stoned. You were, however, married to somebody else."

Wade nodded. "It . . . put a crimp in the proceedings."

"Right."

"They didn't . . . proceed."

"Right again. You're divorced now, Wade. Maybe you should try again."

"Maybe I should just stay divorced. Allenby's on his third divorce, and he's the smartest person I've ever met."

"I thought you said *I* was the smartest person you've ever met."

"That could've been pre-coital blandishment."

"I see. Your version of foreplay?"

Wade nodded. "Saves wear and tear on the fingertips. How smart could you be, anyway? You went to UConn with Ronnie."

"That's not true! He followed me there, and—"

"You opened the door when he knocked. *After* he hit you. *And* tried to screw Marvin Walker out of millions of dollars."

"Only because you wouldn't have Christmas with me last year." Now yet another Christmas missed had come between them, though this one through no fault of their own. "I couldn't go through another Christmas alone."

"Try going through one with Brenda sometime. You might change your mind."

"I left him, Wade. It's over."

Wade sang, "'It seems to me I've heard that song before.'"

"Sinatra again?"

"Of course."

"What's TOSTM, anyway?"

"The only singer that matters."

"Oh. *He* got married again, didn't he?"

"And again and again. Another 0-for-4."

"What do you mean? I thought the last one was—"

"Out with another guy the night he died."

"Oh. Well, serves him right for all the screwing around he did before. Are you ever going to ask me again to marry you, Wade? Or should I let you try to . . . hammer out a deal with Yoshi?"

Pow! Getting right to it tonight. Christ, she hadn't sat down yet. Not even a prolegomenous sip this time. Wade swallowed air, rubbed his forehead. "And you'll do what? Commute from Berkeley, or—"

"We'll work it out. Are you going to ask me, or—"

It wasn't as if he hadn't been thinking about it. He held up a hand to slow her down. "You know that part in the wedding ceremony where the preacher or whoever is officiating—"

"You make him sound like a referee. Does he have a whistle?"

"—always pauses and says if there's anyone in attendance

who knows a good reason why these two idiots shouldn't try this, speak up now or forever hold your—"

"I don't think that's exactly the King James version, but, yeah, I know what you're talking about. What about it?"

"I had another dream last night."

"Oh, God, here we go."

"Just as I'm reaching for the ring to put it on your finger, the preacher says that bit—and Ronnie pops out of the audience, bops up to the stage, smacks you, backhands the preacher, and—"

"What are *you* doing while all this is going on?"

"—tells me he's gonna kick my ass if I ever talk to you again."

"And?"

"I rush up to him, get right in his face, and"—Wade balled his fists, demonstrated his form—"and . . . he kicks my ass. You run off with him, tripping over your train, while I lie there and bleed."

"Christ, Wade. Even in your *dreams* you get your ass kicked?"

Wade nodded. "*And* lose the girl."

Angela shook her head. "You need therapy, Wade."

"Actually, Jenna says I just need a good blowjob."

"Of course. Which she no doubt offered to supply. Oral herpes come with the deal?"

"Maybe. I just couldn't see myself . . . going down a trail that Matt Lytle blazed for me."

Angela wrinkled her nose. "I can see why you wouldn't want to dwell on that."

"Yeah, well, that's not the only thing I don't want to dwell on."

"What do you mean?"

"It's going to be really hard for me to forget about you and Ronnie . . . together."

"Try, okay? I've forgotten him. If I can, *you* should be able to."

"Right."

"Look, would it help if I told you we—Ronnie and I, I mean—didn't . . . do that much *extra* stuff?"

"It would help if it were true, but I know you way too well. You *love* the extra stuff." He laid it out there, gave her the chance

to deny it, which she didn't. *Too inhibited*, Wade thought. *Christ.*
"I think the only thing that would really help would be if you
could tell me he's . . . completely impotent and you loved him
only for his beautiful mind."

"Okay, he was *completely*—"

"Fuck you, Angela."

"All right, I deserved that. There's a new year coming. Let's
start over, Wade."

"How the hell do we do that?"

Almost before the question was out of his mouth, Wade
started to review the dreadful litany he was invoking: go to
counseling, learn to communicate, volunteer together, collaborate
on projects, have a baby. *Eat shit for the rest of your life.*

He looked at Angela, wondered if she was going over the
same list, which obscenity she would pick. Then she smiled
demurely, patted his shoulder, cocked her head and said, "Maybe
that blowjob you need would be a good place to start."

CHAPTER 22

To shun the Heaven that leads men to this Hell.
                                                    —Sonnet 129

How Could Hell Be Any Worse?
                                                    —Bad Religion

Angela shoved Wade with both hands onto the sofa, plunked herself down almost on top of him, snaked a hand toward his fly, made a little "Doo Wop" mew and move as she started to jiggle the zipper.

Wade closed his eyes with a beatific smile, sank his head back luxuriantly on the cushion, awaited at long last deliverance sublime. It just couldn't get any better than—

BOOM! BOOM! BOOM! The sudden, sharp pounding came from outside somewhere nearby. *Shit!* Another fucking after-party at the condo next door, or—what the FUCK? It was Wade's door being pounded upon.

Wade couldn't believe it. Not *again.* If that was who it ALWAYS used to be, his idiot ex-brother-in-law, hit a pedestrian and jumped bail again or knocked up another fifteen year-old, and "just needed a place to crash, man," then this was it, the last time it would ever happen: Tommy was getting an icepick through the eyeball into whatever peanut-sized portion of his cortex remained from all those years of LSD and PCP. *No jury in the world.* Wade was sure of it, given the circumstances.

Angela unhanded him, sank back into the sofa. "Maybe you'd better see who that is."

"I guess you're right. Be right back. Don't lose your place."

Wade rezipped, hopped toward the door. The knocking came again, louder now. CHRIST, what if it was BRENDA herself out there pounding on the portal, another triumphant return to hearth and home? Maybe she'd gone back on the upchuck diet, dropped a quick fifty again, down to a slinky two-forty-five, wanted them to give it one more try, her timing impeccable, as always. *You're divorced*, Wade reminded himself firmly.

"Aren't you going to answer the door, Wade?"

Pick your poison. Or, GOD, if it was both of them again, forget it, he was going to kiss Angela goodbye and climb straight into the oven, no Sinatra miracle comeback for him. He pulled the door open, thinking, *Don't panic. Maybe it's nothing. Maybe it's—*

Two burly, bullet-headed police officers, one Nordic, one Hispanic, stared him down.

Wade was okay with cops. Quite a few of them over the years had passed through his classes. He'd never been one to ridicule or fear them, generally trusted them to try to be helpful, certainly respected them for the risks they took every day, especially in an era where potshots at cops were the norm and more than one local gang had been known to initiate members by requiring them to kill one. Wade had no criminal history to speak of, a few parking tickets here and there and a couple of freeway speeding citations, quite a feat in the shitty Tercel he'd been driving at the time, nothing more serious than that. There *had* been a few parties over the years, well more than a few, that he had attended and . . . partaken in, when cops had stopped by to calm things down or carry off some evidence, but those days were far behind him. Maybe it was the condo next door these guys were looking for.

The white cop now glanced at a notepad, moved his lips in apparent practice, and then said: "Are you . . . Wade Malcolm?"

Or maybe not. Maybe they were looking for that identical twin Wade had out there that students were always telling him about, the one he'd never met, the guy they always saw on campus who looked *exactly* like him only with a little more hair and not quite such terrible clothes. What an irony if his double's name was the exact reverse of—

"Malcolm Wade," he told them. "What's this—"

"Oh, yeah. I guess this is last name first. Do you teach at CSU?"

"I used to," Wade said. "I'm a counselor there now. What's this all—"

"We have a warrant for your arrest."

"*What*?"

"What's happening out there, Wade?"

Then it dawned on him: Angela! Of course! It was another of her kooky, harebrained schemes. She'd gone over the top this time: set him up for a BJ and then yanked it away! She'd hired these clowns to pose as cops, scare the shit out of him. Pretty fucking funny, wasn't it? And talk about perfect timing! How the hell had she pulled that off? *Right* when her parted lips were poised above his rising flesh. Oh, there would have to be some *massive* retaliation for this one.

"My partner's going to read you your rights in a minute."

They were doing it just right, just like on TV. The uniforms looked perfect, too. Maybe she'd recruited real cops to get in on the act. This was not a girl who did things halfway.

"I'll have to ask you to put your hands behind your back, please."

Wade complied, decided to play along, get in on the fun, put an antic disposition on. "Sure." He grinned. "I understand that's the best position to receive fellatio. Ready when you are." He winked, a little fey, but what the hey, all in the spirit. "Guess I didn't need to zip up after all, eh?"

The white cop narrowed his eyes; the Hispanic cop put his hand on his club. Wade suddenly pictured his brains being splattered onto the welcome mat in a display of Border Patrol justice; he wondered if these guys weren't quite all the way in on the joke.

"What the hell is going on?" Angela had come up behind him.

"Good one, Angie. Now tell your friends here to—"

"What are you talking about?" She glared at the officers. "I don't know these guys from Adam 12."

"Please tell me that you're kidding."

"I'm not fucking kidding, Wade."

"Oh." Wade turned to the officer who had cuffed him. How

did you retract a wink? "Sorry for that crack about—"

"Do you have a computer in your dwelling, sir?"

"Yes, of course, but—"

"Where is it?"

Wade nodded at the corner in the living room where he'd moved his desk when Allenby took over the second bedroom. *Allenby!* If only he were here now to—

"You'd better call Allenby," Angela said. "Unless you think *he* set this up as a prank."

"We'll have to take that, too. It's no prank, ma'am."

"What's the charge?" Wade sputtered. "Why are you taking my computer? What the hell are you—"

"You can't barge in here and arrest him like this. He hasn't done anything." Angela swatted at the air around them as if to fight off an invasion. Wade pictured the cops' clubs descending in sync, symmetrically crushing that perfect face of hers, before she fell heroically into his arms to draw her final breath. Except it would be hard to comfort her, as she bled out, with his hands clasped behind his ass.

"I'm afraid we can, ma'am." The white cop turned to his partner. "Better grab up that laptop, too."

"That's mine!" Angela screamed. "Keep your fucking hands off my—"

"You might want to rethink your own position here unless you want to get arrested, too, ma'am. Trust me, this pervert ain't worth it. Please try to calm down."

"Don't tell me to calm down, you fucking stormtroopers. What the hell are you saying he—"

Wade jumped back in. "*Pervert*? What the hell are you saying I—"

Mrs. Partridge from two doors down now came trotting onto the scene in her ancient bathrobe, a posse of Christ and all of the Apostles quite possibly in tow. "It's about time you got here, officers!"

Before the cops could respond to her greeting, the door next to Wade's opened and squinty-eyed Simon emerged in his underpants, which looked a lot like Yoshi's. It looked like he shaved his legs, too, although those, it was safe to say, did not in any other form or fashion remotely resemble any woman's Wade had ever seen or even imagined. Maybe Delia Herman's if she'd remembered her razor or a hacksaw.

"Hey, man, you want to keep it down out there? Some of us have to go to work in the morning, you know?" Simon said.

You hypocritical prick, Wade thought. *Go back inside and stick it in—*

Julio poked his head and unclothed torso out to join in the rebuke. "You got us out of bed, Wade-o. You're a bad, bad boy!" Then he reached for Simon. "And *you're* letting *cold* air in, *gatito.*"

"*They're* the ones you should be arresting, officers!" Mrs. P. pointed dramatically at iniquity's den. Wade wouldn't have been too surprised to see flames bursting from her fingertip, though her rhetoric was slightly undercut when her bathrobe fell open and fully revealed her breasts, which Wade could not say whether custom had staled but age had certainly withered.

"Fuck you, you stupid dried up old bitch."

"Yeah, fuck you, *abuela.* Go to—"

Hell will probably be just like this, Wade decided. Perpetual rounds of *coitus interruptus* surrounded by a crowd of self-righteous/half-naked kibitzers.

Julio yanked Simon inside and slammed the door. The Hispanic cop escorted Mrs. P. homeward. Wade heard her squawking all the way. Maybe she was inviting *him* to this week's babble-fest and Wade was getting the better end of the deal after all. Could prison be any worse than sunrise service with the Pentecostals?

"Some neighborhood you've got here." The white cop looked like he was thinking about kicking in Simon and Julio's door and taking them for a ride, too. He eyed Wade now with increased contempt. "You've probably heard all about what happens to chickenhawks like you in the slam, haven't you?"

"*Chickenhawks?* What are you talking a—"

"You have a computer at CSU, too, don't you?"

"Yes, of course I do, but what the—"

"Of course he does," Angela confirmed. "But what—"

"Guess what we found on it."

Shit! Wade turned to Angela. "*Six Ways from—*"

"Shit!" She slapped her forehead.

"—*Sunday.* But that's not *mine*, that's—"

"*Child* pornography," the officer said.

CHAPTER 23

I don't have to talk about whether or not I got
raped in jail.
—Tupac Shakur

What a falling-off was there!
— *Hamlet*, I.v.

Things always have a way of working out for the best.
*Not quite, Mom. You got just about everything else important
right, but you kind of missed the mark on that one: dad left, you
got sick, Marcus got shot, and I'M IN FUCKING JAIL.*

Wade stared in horror at the human flotsam surrounding him
in the holding tank. He did his best to keep his back up against a
flat surface, tried not to breathe through his nose. The B.O. was
unbelievable, a Weapon of Mass Destruction merely waiting to
be harnessed. Why spend billions on biohazards research when
all we really needed was to tap the illimitable killing power of
human stink? Wade had hit the diversity jackpot. The whole vast
California melting pot was here: whites, blacks, Mexicans, a few
Asians, maybe even a Native American or two. How the hell was
he going to pee in here with all these . . . cellmates—God, who
ever thought he'd say that word?—watching his every move?
He'd neglected to ask the cops to let him visit the toilet before
they jerked him out of the condo, and his bladder was sending
increasingly urgent signals now. If he didn't relieve himself
soon, he was going to explode or wet his pants again; imagine
how *that* would play to this crowd.

Wade's horror increased exponentially as a filthy, hulking,
wild-eyed, scramble-haired biker/methhead/swamp creature
missing all of the teeth between his incisors looked his way
repeatedly and then bore down on him. Wade closed his eyes,

stepped away, bumped into a snarling *Norteño* with a tattoo on his forehead. Wade's Spanish was primitive, but he translated the cursive roughly as I KILL WHITE PUNKS AND EAT THEIR BRAINS. He edged back to his former spot, saw the creature still bearing down, closed his eyes again, lay a suppliant palm upon his neck. *Please don't let him be a vampire, too.*

"Hey, dude, is that *you*?"

Wade opened his eyes, faced his interlocutor, made the mistake of inhaling, caught a whiff of rotten gums and decomposing molars.

"I *know* you, dude."

Wade sucked air through his teeth, stared back as the wild face erupted in a cavernous grin. Wade noted with alarm that his new friend was also missing both of his thumbs.

"You still work at CSU?"

Wade swallowed, nodded.

"Don't you remember me?"

Wade shook his head.

"I was there like, shit, I don't know, five years ago."

Wade decided to trust his tongue, see if it would work. "I don't seem to place your . . . face."

The grin again. "Oh, yeah, I lost some choppers since then. Had me a little crystal problem. That's all behind me, though."

"I'm glad to hear it."

"Good old Wade. You still hittin' the bong, dude?"

Wade frowned. "I think maybe you have me confused with . . . Wade Malcolm."

"Don't you remember that party we had after a bunch of us passed your class? You were stoned off your—"

"You were in my *class*?"

"—*ass* on that good Mendo grass. Remember me *now*?"

Wade shook his head. "Sorry, I—"

"Buck Mason. I had you for Bonehead, dude. I was gonna play football. Before I"—the grin again—"got involved in the pharmaceutical game."

Wade tried to avert his eyes, couldn't keep them off the mangled hands.

Mason held the remnants up obligingly for closer inspection. They smelled almost as bad as his breath. Maybe it was a cesspool he had crawled out of. "Guess you're wondering what happened here. Everybody always wants to hear."

Wade felt he could live comfortably without the information but didn't have much of an option.

"Got me a little overextended financially. Picked up some raw materials on spec but didn't get my product turned around in time. Cost me both of them twiddlers."

"They . . . cut your thumbs off?"

"With pruning shears. Hurt like hell. Don't recommend it if you ever have to go in for thumb removal."

"I'll keep that in mind. Are you *sure* you were in my—"

"We read *Fear and Loathing*, dude, don't you remember? *In Las Vegas*."

"I remember the book," Wade said. "I just don't remember—"

"That's the first book I ever finished in my life. Honest truth, it's still the *only* one. I was thinkin' about bein' an English major, dude, *writin'* my own books, you had me so turned on to literature. Then you stuck me with a fuckin' C, and I changed my plans. You remember tellin' me I had more potential to be a drug addict than a writer?"

Wade shook his head. "I can't imagine I said *that*."

Mason nodded. "Wrote it in the margin of my paper."

"That must've been your peer evaluator, or"—Wade tried to remember if that could have been a semester when in desperation he was paying Brenda to grade a few papers for him, help him out in her inimitable way.

"Sure looked like your chicken scratch to me. I could show it to you. I still got that paper somewhere, 'less it burned up in that fire I had. I've moved a few times, too. Anyhoo, you had a big influence on me, Wade."

"I guess that's . . . good."

"Hey, it is what is, and it's all good."

Wade winced as verbal abuse was added to the amalgam of atrocities assaulting his senses. He wondered if this was the first time *Homo sapiens* had managed to combine those two of his very favorite locutions in one sentence. "Maybe you *did* learn something in my class."

"Been a hell of a ride since, let me tell you. Was one point where I was cookin' up the stuff and the cash was pouring in so fast I stayed up seven straight days and nights to keep up with the demand. Didn't sleep a fuckin' wink for a *week*, dude. Started seein' giant green bunnies in my backyard, snakes big as Volkswagens. Then some of them snakes turned out to be narcs, and I went away for awhile."

"Sorry to hear—"

"Hey, I got no regrets. Had to do it over again, I'd do 'er all the same way, thumbs or no thumbs."

Wade shuddered, reflexively wiggled his own opposables.

"I'm on the bounce-back now, though."

"I can see that."

"Thinkin' about comin' back to CSU next semester, once I get clear here. Them damn fees keep going up, though. Probably need some kind of a scholarship or somethin' to help me pay the bills. Think you could write me a letter of recommendation?"

Wade looked him over again, the whole package, the wild eyes, the filthy, matted heap of hair, the septic breath, the wretched unwashed mutilated mitts. "I don't see why not."

"Same old good old Wade. What the fuck are *you* doin' in here, dude?"

Wade was spared a recitation when Erica Wiley showed up to spring him.

"Your friend Arthur sent me to the rescue," she told him, after he had peed prodigiously, while they waited to retrieve his possessions. "He's flying back this afternoon, asked me to stand in until he gets here. I bailed out Angela first, drove her home to take a shower. She was *not* a happy girl."

"Christ! They arrested her, too, didn't they?" Wade was a little fuzzy on what had happened after the cops had squashed him into the squad car. "What the hell did she—"

"Apparently she said some . . . expressive words in the street while you were being . . . detained, and the cops called in a back-up car. She wasn't easily restrained, I gather."

"I'll bet she fought like a wildcat."

"They booked her and she spent the night."

"Poor Angela," Wade said.

"Not the best timing in the world, was it? She's interviewing for the dean position today."

"*Shit,* that's right! Great. Did Allenby find out why the hell *I* was arrested for—"

"That screenplay a student sent you? *Six Ways from Sunday,* I believe it's—"

"But all I did was—"

"—called. The 'little girls' mentioned in the script are ten and eleven years old, Wade. That makes it kiddie porn."

"But I didn't *write* that shit! All I did was download it, actually *Angela* downloaded it, and—"

"All you have to do is *read* that stuff or have it on your computer to raise the red flag these days, Wade. Plus there must be someone out to get you at CSU. There've got to be a couple hundred faculty peeking at naughty sites now and then; someone made a point of flagging you."

"Delia Herman is a *dead* woman," Wade said.

"I'd be careful making threats like that," the police clerk said sharply, as she handed Wade his wallet. Her parting glare told Wade all he needed to know: she'd already tried and convicted him; he was now officially in the eyes of the world a child defiler.

Erica guided him to a gleaming Lexus, clicked to unlock the doors. Wade paused at the passenger's side, sniffed his pits. "Are you sure you want me in there?"

"I can always sell it after if I have to."

"It looks like you just drove it out of the showroom," he said as he got in. "How the hell do you get it this clean?"

"It's called washing your car, Wade. Maybe I should've left you in jail." She gestured for him to buckle up, then pulled out into traffic. "I got arrested once. Did I ever tell you?"

"Are you just saying that to make me feel better?"

"Actually I was telling Arthur about it just the other night. I want to thank you for introducing me to him, by the way. He's quite the gentleman."

Wade nodded. "How come you got arrested?"

She smiled. "I was a little concerned about sharing that story with him. I was afraid we might have been on opposite sides of the fence when he came back from Vietnam."

"You were busted in a peace march?"

"A sit-in. At my alma mater, South Carolina State. We lay on the floor and held hands, and the cops tore us apart, picked us up, and took us to jail. Some of my friends were quite badly hurt. All I got was this." She took one hand off the wheel, pulled the hair away from her temple, exposed a scar.

"Christ!" Wade said. "You're lucky you didn't . . . lose an eye or something."

"You and Angela are lucky, too, I guess, that . . . peace officers are a little more subtle these days."

Wade pictured again the bullet-heads and their batons that didn't crack down upon his or Angela's noggin. "What happened to you after you were arrested?"

"It turned out that one of the cops had . . . an interest in me. He let me go after an hour or so in jail. In exchange for . . . certain promised considerations later."

Wade glanced across the seat, raised his eyebrows.

"Promised under duress, my friend—and never delivered, I assure you. I went straight to New York, took my mother's maiden name, never looked back. Pretty easy to disappear in Harlem in those days. After a few years I came out to California and . . . got into the movement again."

Wade couldn't pass on the cliché. "Were you a . . . Black Panther?"

"No," she said, thoughtfully, not dismissing the question quite as readily as he'd anticipated, "but I knew some of them. I even met a girl who was on the fringes of the Weathermen."

"Holy shit!" Wade gulped, looked at her with different eyes. "You didn't . . . blow up any buildings or anything, did you?" *Please don't tell me you killed children, too.*

"Hardly. I dated a Panther for a little while; that's about the extent of my adventures. He thought he was a poet."

"Any good?"

"He was much more proficient at . . . other things. I told Arthur that when your young man Marcus was shot, it reminded me of when I was with my Panther, and he was attacked by another in his group. He was beaten very badly. I tried to intervene and—"

Just like Angela.

"—was knocked to the floor, managed to crawl away. My friend wasn't so lucky. He was never the same after that."

"Were they fighting over who was going to lead the group, or—"

She turned, looked at him again. "They were fighting over me, Wade."

"Wow."

"Is that so hard to believe?"

"It's not hard to believe at all."

"What's still hard for *me* to believe is that they thought the way to settle the winning of a woman's heart was to beat each other senseless in her presence. You men are such primitive creatures."

"Some of us are quite refined," Wade said. "Remind me to introduce you to Buck Mason. What did Allenby have to say about your adventures?"

She smiled. "He asked me for another date. He's cooking dinner for me at my house tonight, then taking me dancing for New Year's Eve."

"I can't vouch for his two-step, but you're in for a treat when you eat."

She smiled. "I don't think it'll be a . . . wasted trip for him, either."

"You think it could be something serious?"

"Far too early to tell, my friend."

She stopped at his condo, pushed the shifter into park, let the engine idle, reached over to pat him on the cheek. "Try to stay away from those porn sites, now, okay?"

He nodded.

"You might also want to think about cleaning up the language in your campus emails."

"What are you talking about?"

"You know, like the ones you send to me. I keep getting 'OFFENSIVE' labels on them before I can open them. As you know, I'm not so easily offended, but . . . all I'm saying is it wouldn't kill you to learn how to write without using all those f-bombs." She paused, shook a playful finger at him. "What would your mother say?"

"'**Clean your plate. Do your best. Tell your father that you love him**,'" Wade said automatically. "'**Marry a girl with a good head on her shoulders.**'"

Erica softened. He'd spoken of his mother often on their walks, and she knew he was still mourning her. "About your *vocabulary*, silly man."

"Oh. I didn't send too many f-bombs to Mom, actually."

"Thank heaven for—"

"She didn't like email anyway. She still wrote letters, regular mail, right up to when she got sick at the end. She was like that her whole life. When I was in college, she knew I wasn't fitting in, was lonely as hell; she wrote to me every single day."

"I'll bet she sent you cookies, too."

Wade nodded, tasted the memory. "Oatmeal-raisin, with walnuts and coconut. Best cookies in the world."

"What were her letters like?"

"Just normal stuff. What was going on at home, stuff like that. Not a lot of what you'd call style. They're not going into anybody's library. Just full of . . . love."

"No f-bombs of her own?"

"Mom wasn't into sarcasm. She didn't need it."

Erica smiled. "Hard to imagine living in this world and not needing that."

"You didn't know her." Wade's turn to soften. "I wish you had. One of the women who helped my sister take care of her at the end told us, 'Your mom never says anything bad about anyone.'"

"Sounds just like you."

"Yeah, right."

Wade opened the door, started to get out of the car, then paused. "Good luck with your big date tonight."

"Thank you. Whither you and Angela?"

"Good question." Whether they would ever make up for last night's interruption had been at the forefront of his mind every moment since, apart from time spent inhaling putrefaction. "I *wish* I could tell you where we left off last night when the cops arrived, but I'm afraid it might be censored as OFFENSIVE," he said. "*My* lips are sealed," he added, hoping fervently that the same policy didn't apply to all parties involved.

Erica laughed. "Chivalry is not lost: another gentleman lives!"

Wade stepped onto the sidewalk.

She put the car in gear, ready to roll, then leaned across the seat to advise him through the window: "Listen to your mother, Wade."

Wade went inside, tried to call Angela, punished himself with a vicious lacerating scour in the shower, get rid of the skin at least if not the stink, then tried her again, still no answer. Maybe the cops had strip-searched her last night, and she was never going to speak to him again.

Wade picked up his mail, found a letter postmarked in Italy, then mailed to the campus before being forwarded to his home address. Marvin Walker had found a team in Milan that had cleared him to play in spite of the heart condition that had scared off the NBA. He was starting, playing pretty well, getting to know his teammates, picking up a little bit of Italian, and doing his best to accommodate the urgent needs of a multitude of female fans, all of whom, Wade was relieved to learn, were positively religious in their practice of birth control. The letter concluded with the news, a tad untimely as a result of the mail delay, that Marvin was home briefly to celebrate the season and an offer to send Wade a ticket if he wanted to come ring in the New Year in Times Square. As much as he appreciated the characteristically generous if untenable offer, Wade couldn't help shivering at the prospect: *why is everyone I know trying to fly me into the fucking snow?* Maybe next year, get the whole gang together, go to Poland for the holidays, toss Brooks out over the Arctic Circle, let him have a yuletide . . . pow-wow with the polar bears.

When the phone finally rang, Wade ran to grab it. Still no Angela, though: it was Allenby, checking in from the airport.

Wade kept it short, remembering that however long imagery of the overnighter would haunt his own dreams, it wouldn't be the worst thing Allenby had seen, and thanked him for dispatching Erica.

"Busy day all around, I'd say. Sorry I couldn't get back earlier myself. I'm working on getting all the charges dropped. Good thing there were no photos attached to that file your porn star sent, or you might be in more trouble than a few phone calls from your lawyer could get you out of. You can pick up your computers, by the way."

"How did your meeting with the president go?"

"I didn't get any face-time yet. More on that later. Did you hear the news about Delia Herman, though?"

"Please don't tell me they made her vice—"

"Guess again."

Wade heard something in his tone, went the other way: "They fired her deep-fried ass?"

"Bingo. The president called to offer me the A.D. job on an interim basis. Wants to pay me three hundred thousand a year, plus a double secret signing bonus from that famous discretionary fund of his. "

"You're kidding! What did you tell him?"

"I told him that figure would represent approximately a ten thousand percent paycut for me, and—"

"Wait a minute; let me run the numbers."

"—that I'd consider it, fuck the bonus."

Wade saw Rutger Hauer blowing up his bounty at the end of *Wanted: Dead or Alive*. "Smart move," he said. "I can see how you made your fortune. What about Herman? She's probably threatening a lawsuit, am I right?"

"That might've been Plan B."

"Oh, yeah? What was Plan—"

"She went out the office window."

"—A? *Her* office? *Fourth* floor?"

"Correct."

"Wow. What a way to go!"

"She's not exactly gone."

"What do you mean? How could anyone—"

"She landed on a janitor."

"*Shit!*"

"Must've been his thoughts precisely. He actually reached out, tried to catch her. Broke her fall—and both of his arms. She broke her back, both legs, shattered her pelvis, lots of other stuff, but she's still breathin'."

"What a fuck up. Christ, she couldn't even do *that* right. So she got the bad news and went straight out the window?"

"There's some speculation she might've been pushed."

Wade whistled. "That would take some shove."

"Where were *you* at around ten a.m. today anyway?"

"I can tell you exactly where I was. I was . . . in the police station . . . making a death threat against Delia Herman."

"You really know how to cover your ass, don't you, Wade?"

"Erica can vouch for me. I just want you to know I . . . copped a feel before I gave Herman the heave-ho."

"Good job. Next time, though, look out for custodians below."

CHAPTER 24

Then give me welcome, next my heaven the best,
Even to thy pure and most most loving breast.
—Sonnet 110

After Allenby rang off to take another call, Wade went to check his email and remembered that he had to go retrieve his hardware from the cops. He fetched his Civic, which had replaced the Toyota totaled by Tommy in Tijuana, recalled Erica's chiding and almost gave it a rinse, but decided the next rain would do the job. He picked up the computers without incident, dropped off CSU's in his office, set a date with Technical Services to hook that one up, then took his own home. After an hour or so of wrestling with wires and plugs, one near-electrocution, and the creation of several elaborate new curses for his catalog, he clicked open his inbox, found a message from Jenna: "Thanks for the free publicity, Doc. Great stunt you pulled for our flick. The offers are pouring in! Next time you get busted, though, try to flash the camera."

Christ, he thought, *what* publicity? What camera? He turned the TV on, flipped through news on several channels, didn't see anything to worry about. It couldn't have made the papers yet. What the fuck was Jenna talking about?

Allenby called back.

"That other call I got? It was from the Chairman of the BOT. Good thing I put the president off. They might have some other plans for me. They're not too happy with our feckless leader, it seems."

"How's that? I thought you said he just signed a new sweetheart deal."

"He did. But apparently at approximately the same time,

he was negotiating a deal to also hook up with a big research foundation in L.A. Four hundred thousand a year, plus another huge package of perks."

"Christ. Isn't that double—"

"Dipping? Of course it is. Actually triple-dipping if you count his 'consulting work,' which he spent more days on last year than he spent on campus."

Wade was impressed. Now *there* was leadership by example. The administration's version of feathernesting reduced the faculty's efforts in that estimable pursuit to the approximate level of a kindergarten bully's filching milk money from his fellow five-year-olds.

"How did all of this come to light?"

"Still putting that together, but it seems likely Delia Herman was involved. She may have threatened to blow the whistle, get him fired, and he retaliated by—"

"Firing her first?"

"Who knows, maybe ordering a hit, too. I'll keep you posted as I find out more. Got to go do some cooking now. Did you try my recipe for eggplant parmesano yet?"

Wade took the hint, went into the kitchen, started to assemble ingredients, most of which Allenby had stocked for him. Perhaps he could manage not to poison himself after all. Angela turned up before he had a chance to find out.

Maybe not the best hair day in the history of the world, but otherwise it would have been impossible to guess where she had spent the previous night. In a crisp new jacket and skirt ensemble, she was absolutely glowing. Even better, she came through the door with a loopy grin for Wade instead of the knee in the groin that he was half-expecting and probably more than half-deserving.

"I guess there's no need to ask how the interview went."

"Are you cooking?"

"Trying to."

"Something's burning."

"Figures."

"Turn it off. I brought home take-out." She hoisted the bag

she had carried in with her, set it on the coffee table.

Wade salivated on cue. "Manny's?"

"Where else would a girl go on New Year's Eve in this—
Look Wade! You're on TV!"

She jabbed a forearm at the screen, nearly poked his eye out
with a lacquered nail. Wade had left the set on after his earlier
search for news. He followed her extended forefinger dreadfully
now. And there he *was*, handcuffs and all, being hustled by the
brawny cops into the police station. How had he failed to see the
photographer on the scene? For the first time in his life, Wade
was glad that his parents were gone, would never have to see
this, their son, PhD and all, busted for—

"How come I'm not on there, too?"

"Are you *disappointed*?"

"We went to *jail* together, Wade. Isn't that amazing? Just like
Rosa Parks and Martin—"

"I don't think they went to jail together." *Or for child
pornography.*

Wade picked up the remote and clicked the TV off as his
fifteen seconds of infamy ended and the latest on the local gay-
bashing congressman who had been arrested for solicitation in
an SFO men's room came on.

"I gather our little . . . escapade didn't come up during your
meeting today? Allenby's taking care of—"

"Not an issue. They want me. It's just a matter of whether
they can get me."

Angela's grin turned cocky. She bounced an eyebrow, and he
stepped toward her, started to put his arms around her. Then her
cell phone rang. She pulled it out, switched it off. "Shit! I keep
forgetting to change this number."

"Our hero again?"

She nodded. "He's calling like five hundred times a day."

"Sounds like he misses you. Maybe you should—"

"Maybe you should shut up, Wade, okay?"

"Okay."

"It's fucking over with Ronnie." She jammed the phone back
into her jacket pocket.

"Okay."

"You still don't believe me, do you?"

He shrugged. "I never understood what you saw in that . . ." —Larashawndria helped him out again—"assbag in the first place."

Angela sighed, tried again. "Women like muscles. It's the way we're wired. We like to be with a guy who's big and strong and can pick us up and sweep us off our feet, and—"

"Punch your lights out, if need be?"

"You're just never going to let that go, are you?"

He shrugged again. "You couldn't see your face as well as I could. Purple isn't really your best color."

Another sigh. "Okay, look at it this way: you like big tits, right?"

"Not enough to get punched in the face for."

"Come on, be honest, for once. Answer up." She took her jacket off, laid it on the coffee table next to the food, stepped nearer, almost in his grill.

Wade had always thought that Angela's breasts were perfect, firm and perky and proportioned just right for her slender body, and he loved the way her dark nipples leapt instantly to full alert at the slightest touch of his tongue, teeth, or fingertips, but in truth an objective appraiser would probably not describe her breasts as "big." He started to equivocate: "I like tits that—"

"Don't bullshit me, Wade. I'm not going to run out and get them enlarged for you like Ronnie wanted me to do."

"Oh." Add another chapter to Buffalo Bill's autobio: *Why I'm the Biggest Assbag in America.*

"It's okay. It's not like you have the biggest dick in the world either."

"Oh. I don't?"

"I mean, I'm not going to lie to you. It would be nice if you were hung like a horse, instead of—"

"Like a pony?" Wade said, hopefully.

"—a chipmunk, I was thinking, but—"

"Oh. Do chipmunks even *have* peckers?"

"You must have been sleeping in Biology."

"Trying to peek into Debbie Dooby's cleavage, actually."

"Big tits, right?"

"Right," Wade remembered, reverently.

"I rest my case."

Angela half-patted, half-smacked his cheeks, then stepped into the bathroom to refresh herself. Wade bent to sniff the burgers, saw her phone vibrate in the pocket of her jacket, picked it up, what the hell, decided to answer it. He took the phone into the bedroom.

Angela came in after him a few moments later, wearing nothing but a smile. San Antonio, Wade thought. Let's try this again.

"Did I just hear you talking to someone?"

"I had a chat with Superbowlman."

The smile went away. "You answered my *phone*?"

"Don't get so high and mighty with me, missy. Who the hell hacked into my computer?"

"What did you tell him?"

"You're on the next flight back, can't wait to kiss his black ass again."

"Bastard."

"That isn't the plan?"

"It's the last time I'm telling you, Wade, I—"

"I didn't really tell him that. I told him you were . . . with me now."

She nodded slowly. "I guess that's good. I just don't want him to be—"

"I also told him something else to make him feel a little—"

"—bitter."

"—better."

"Oh, yeah? What else did—"

"You went in for that titlift after all, and now you look just like Dolly Parton."

She reached for the bedspread, drew it back. "You men are sick, sick, sick."

"That sounds like a cue to hop into bed if I ever heard one."

She plumped a pillow, a little more emphatically than

necessary. "Someone could wind up sleeping on the couch with his dick in a sling instead if he keeps running his mouth."

"Oh. I . . . like your outfit."

"That's more like it."

"Are we actually going to . . . try this again? Aren't we going to eat first?"

"Shut up and take your pants off, Wade."

Later they—who would've thunk it?—pulled a Brenda and ate the burgers in bed, then drifted off in each other's arms. Wade woke to the sound of Angela sawing logs, found himself needing to visit the toilet, accidentally woke her when he disengaged.

"I wasn't snoring, was I?" she asked when he got back.

"No, and I didn't have to get up to pee."

"Dickhead. Do you have any idea how annoying *that* is?"

"Consider the alternative."

He climbed back into bed, put his arms around her, kissed her gently, nuzzled her breasts.

"I'm glad you didn't get a boob job, Angie."

"What you see is what you get."

"What you've got is good enough for me."

"Thank you." She placed a hand strategically. "Same here."

"Thank *you*, too," Wade said. "Actually," he added, drawing consolation where he could as he felt himself become aroused again, "at least there's one advantage. I have it on excellent authority that a small dick is better for anal sex."

Angela twisted her lips. "And I certainly hope you never find it necessary to share *that* information with me again." She tapped him on the forehead with her free hand. "But maybe it'll come in handy when you enter your latent phase."

"Maybe you *are* too inhibited," Wade said. "You don't even want to try it?"

"How about this: I'll strap on a ten-inch dildo, and you can try it first."

"Oh. Well, maybe that wasn't such a good—"

"I thought you'd see it my way."

"Our mutual friend Erica Wiley would call that an exercise in narrative perspective."

"Tell her she's welcome to use it in her class any time."

"Okay. Well, then, I guess maybe around here we'll just stick with . . . missionary style."

"Don't exaggerate, Wade." She turned on a hip, tightened her grip, moistened her lips. "Have you ever seen a missionary do *this*?"

CHAPTER 25

The friendship of a great man is a gift from
the gods.
　　　—Cezanne, letter to Monet, 1894

This too is part of America's promise—the
promise of a democracy where we can find the
strength and grace to bridge divides and unite
in common effort.
　　　—Barack Obama, Acceptance Speech,
　　　2008 Democratic Party Convention

"The wedding's off. I just thought you'd like to know."

Allenby gestured for Wade to take a seat in the Office of
the Athletic Director, where he had at least temporarily set up
headquarters. The outer room was for some reason unattended;
no staff had been on duty at the secretary's desk or the assistant's,
so Wade had walked right in. Allenby had summoned him for
updates on "a variety of matters." Maybe he was planning on
order of ascending importance.

"What happened?"

"They tried to drive to Tahoe on New Year's Day."

"In that snowstorm that shut down the freeways?"

"The Dink didn't have chains, of course. Car got stuck; they
both almost froze to death. I guess Jennifer came to her senses,
realized what a mistake she was making. She decided to dump
The Dink, have the baby, and put it on the adoption roster."

Now *there* was a list to which Wade would not be subscribing
anytime soon. Maybe Brad and Angelina would step up again,
add a troglodyte to their collection.

"I suppose that's . . . for the best."

Allenby shrugged. "I spoke with the president about some
of your ideas."

"Oh? I thought you said he was pissed at you for declining to be his defense attorney."

"Not *him*. The other guy."

"Oh." *Christ.* "I forgot you're tight with *him*, too."

"He's on vacation in Hawaii. He called to congratulate us on our great game against USC and on hiring Sherman Slate. He's also sending a personal contribution to our Marcus Fund. We only had a few minutes, of course, but he was interested in your thoughts."

"Did you tell him my plan to trade Cuba for Israel?"

It was the centerpiece of Wade's revisionist foreign policy strategy. He'd always thought that if the Allied powers at the end of World War II had simply encouraged the world's Jewry to relinquish their relics and settle in and around Havana, many of the post-war world's most pressing problems could have been averted. The island would have been transformed into a sparkling jewel with a thriving economy, the U.S. would have had ninety miles off its coast a "stalwart ally" instead of a communist nuisance, and Castro would have stuck with his original plan of pitching for the Yankees, ideally getting bombed by Mays's Giants in the '62 Series, altering the course of that historic cause of aggrievement, not to mention the Bay of Pigs, as well. For the Arab nations, discontiguation from a feisty nuclear-armed porcupine neighbor ready to blow them all to kingdom come at the provocation of a sneeze had much to commend itself, too. It was just unfortunate that no one had thought of the idea in 1945. Wade wasn't saying it would be easy to pull off now, but with Fidel finally fading out of the picture, this was the time to try. He hadn't heard anyone propose a better solution yet to prevent Gaza from combusting into World War III.

"It didn't come up," Allenby disappointed him now with a laugh. "We stuck mainly to the domestic agenda. He liked your plan to play the college football national championship game on the Martin Luther King, Jr. holiday."

This was such a no-brainer that it was inconceivable to Wade it hadn't already happened. With the NFL regular season over and no competition for the Monday national TV audience except a meaningless mid-season NBA travesty or three, the ratings would be off the charts. The whole country would be watching, half of it snowbound, nowhere else to go, suds would flow in epic measure, and sponsors would pour their gold into the NCAA's coffers.

"He especially liked your idea about allocating a portion of the proceeds to the historically black colleges."

"I don't suppose you got to ask him about *Hunting for al Qaeda*?"

Allenby laughed again. "I told him you'll be eager to lead the team yourself as soon as you can get fitted for snowshoes."

"Sounds good."

"He sends his regrets on *Wife Swapping at the White House*, though. He's flattered by your interest, but he and the First Lady don't swing that way."

"Angela told you about that, huh?"

Allenby nodded, rolled his eyes. "He wants you to write up your King Bowl proposal, send it to him, ASAP. He's gonna throw his weight behind it."

"The President of the United States wants *me* to write—"

"Why not? You're a published author now."

"I *am*?"

"You're about to be." Allenby reached across the desk, found an envelope. "That guy I sent your dissertation to?"

"He already read it?"

"Liked it a lot. He wants to bring it out in the fall."

Best of all he loved the fall. "You've got to be kidding. That piece of—"

Allenby handed the envelope to Wade. "See for yourself. He says it's very refreshing. Ninety-nine percent of the stuff he gets from scholars in the humanities is arcane, jargon-driven nonsense that no one would ever read without a blowtorch to his balls. Put the cottage industry of academic publication out of business and how many of the fatheads who crank out that crap could earn a living wage? But your book makes sense, and it doesn't hurt that it's about a writer people still give a shit about. He says some of those quotes from Hemingway's letters had him on the floor."

Wade shared the opinion that these excerpts were easily the highlight of the tome. "Too bad I didn't put more of them in, let him write the whole thing."

"Now you sound like one of your students. Anyway, he'll have a contract offer out to you by the end of the week."

"He's going to *pay* me to publish *that*?"

"I don't think we're talking *Harry Potter* dollars here, but, yeah, he'll offer you something." Allenby reached back onto the desk, picked up another envelope, handed it to Wade as well. "In the meantime, here's some cash to tide you over. Those USC alums finally settled up."

"What are you talking about? I thought we lost that—"

"We lost the game, not the bet. I told you, Vegas pulled the straight spread bet off the books. After haggling a bit with those go-go-Trojans guys, the wager we wound up with was 50 to 1 against USC winning by seven or more. That two-point conversion came in handy after all. I put your twenty bucks in and advanced you a thousand more against your book."

Wade opened the envelope. "Are you telling me there's—"

"Fifty-one thousand, after recouping the advance. Not a bad little year-end bonus. Take Angela out to dinner someplace where they don't use plastic forks."

Wade scanned and handed back the publisher's letter, put the cash in his briefcase, tried to stop his head from spinning.

Allenby consulted a list. "I guess next up is the latest on the Delia Herman investigation." He looked up at Wade. "I see you're still walking around free, so I guess they haven't made you for the dirty deed."

"Not yet. I destroyed the novel I started about carving her up for Halloween, so I think I'm home free."

"She's . . . home free, too. She went last night."

"I thought you said her condition was stable, and—"

"There's a possibility that someone . . . expedited matters."

"Oh." Had he missed a chance to pull another plug? Wade flashed to Unitas on Don Shula, the genius who kept him on the bench too long against Joe Namath in Super Bowl III. What

w
fi
he

da
Sh
aga
me

thou

was

jump
black
head—
The t
they s
They'
"S

"She offered a big fat bribe to Delia Herman."

"So *that's* where my stock options went."

"Fuzzy thought she could squeeze more o

wonder your Angela invented. But the off

her. Looks like that deportation scheme

true after all."

Allenby returned to his list. "

whatever the hell capacity I'm

Slate's contract for two a

gave him after the gam

"Great idea," Wa

"It's the leas

about Dupree

Wade o

it. "If it

wou

"Well, for one thing, the redecorating fund. Apparently that window she went out of only cost ten thousand, and the other ten went straight into her pocket. But that was just small potatoes. She had a deal in place with Lytle for a $250,000 kickback if we reinstated him. That little arrangement should also put paid to any plans *that* lard-ass had to sue the university to collect the salary he's been saying we owe him."

"I read that he's off on some missionary project in Zaire now."

Allenby nodded. "Trying to restore his image before the next round of fires and hires."

Or still craving chocolate.

"There's more," Allenby continued. "What's the last you heard about your little Nipponese friend? Care to know how she almost got the inside track to knock you out of your job?"

"It wasn't just diversity perversity?"

ut of that surgical
er is enough to hang
I concocted may come

For my first official act in—
acting in—I've extended Sherman
additional years beyond the three we
."
de said.
I can do after steering him the wrong way
I should have . . . backed him up."
could see the pain in his friend's face, tried to ease
hadn't been Dupree, one of the other players probably
d have done about the same. None of them likes to take any
it, and those gangbangers were looking to unload."

Allenby sighed, looked away. It was nothing they hadn't thought and said a hundred times before, and it didn't do any good then or now. Marcus's fate hung between them, filling the room.

Wade broke the silence with his own brief report: "Coach Slate told me he went to see A.J., encouraged him to finish a degree in prison if he's convicted. He gave Marston a release to transfer to another school, told him to go back to the JC he came from first and take a reading class instead of another fifteen units of P.E., then try to play at a level where he might get off the bench, maybe Division II."

"Good. Slate gave Jake Bonner a release, too, told him he wants to recruit a more mobile quarterback."

Wade hadn't heard that before. "Could've used him for another year with Marcus . . . gone."

"Could have. But the kid wants to start, and it wasn't going to happen here. Slate's a straight shooter."

"I'm glad you extended him. Better to lock him up before NC State offers him a tobacco plantation or something."

Allenby nodded. "USC might be after him, too, if their guy

goes back to the NFL. They have to be wondering what our guy could do with their talent."

"I wouldn't mind seeing that myself," Wade said. "Except that would mean I'd have to root for USC" *and forfeit forever what remains of my soul.*

"I won't stand in his way if he gets a chance like that. But unlike Matt Lytle, I believe he wants to be here. And he'll tell me the truth if he decides to look at another job. We put a reasonable buyout clause into his contract. Which brings me to my second official act. I'm rewriting *your* contract, giving you a raise."

"You might be on shakier ground there. I haven't done anything to merit that yet. Although this new White Power Club looks like it could really take off."

"Sign me up."

"Actually Bludge is . . . coming around. He made a donation to our Marcus Fund, too. He said he wanted to get the ball rolling." Wade hadn't felt the need to inform Bludge of Allenby's prior contribution. "I'm going to try to get him involved in administering the fund."

"You don't give up easily on people, do you?"

Wade shrugged, his mother in his ear again: **Give everyone a chance to do the right thing.**

"We'll make the raise ten thousand, for now, put you at a hundred thousand per year. Those meetings you sat through with Delia Herman have got to be worth at least 10K. We'll call it compensation for pain and suffering. Can't give you back the years listening to her bullshit took off your life, but at least you can get rid of that dinosaur you call a TV."

Wade laughed, didn't try to defend his antiquated Emerson.

"There might be some other opportunities around here for you, too. I decided to recommend Marilyn Porter for A.D."

"Good choice," Wade said. "She should have had the job last time around."

Allenby nodded at the empty lobby outside his office. "Herman's assistant is out on her ass, too, so there's another opening if you're interested in moving up. I talked to Porter and she's comfortable with you in that job if you want it. She appreciated your help with her freshman this semester. That would put you at about one-twenty."

"Me? Assistant A.D.? Don't you think it should at least be someone who could, you know, make a free throw if he shot one?" Wade flashed to Michael Jordan shooting the freebie with his eyes closed *in a game,* the cocky motherfucker—and making it, of course. Wade was lucky if he hit the rim.

"We'll bring Marvin Walker back to tutor you."

"Hey, I had a letter from him. He's up to 51% from the line. Pretty good letter, too. Periods and everything."

"See? You're made for this job. Cal Logan is okay with you in that slot, too."

"Oh? I didn't know he'd have a voice there."

"I'm thinking of asking him to take over my slot in the Boosters Club," Allenby said.

"Burying the hatchet after all these years?"

"That last team he quarterbacked won eight games. He's got some leadership skills. Just because he's a horse's ass most of the time doesn't mean I can't learn to work with him. It's not like I'm appointing him Secretary of State or something. I give him credit for this, too: he loved the job Slate did in the USC game, admitted that we made the right move losing Lytle."

Wade nodded.

"Anyway, about your deal, just think it over. You don't have to make up your mind right away. There's another possibility as well. If the BOT is serious about wanting me to take on this presidency, I'm gonna need help, too. Someone I can trust."

"Surely you're not saying—"

"Nah, we won't put you up for vice president, too much red tape to cut there. Call it assistant to the prez. Probably goes about one-fifty." Allenby looked Wade over as the number registered. "*You,* of course, would have to spend most of it on clothes appropriate for . . . a human being."

Wade grinned, surveyed sheepishly his present sartorial outrage. "Angela's been barking about cleaning out my closet and having that bonfire again." He smoothed a frayed J.C. Penney's collar, turned back to his benefactor. "Since you're making all my problems go away, could you do something about the 49ers' offense?"

A knock on the open door announced Angela, as if prompted from the wings. She had stayed through the weekend, survived the barrage of New Year's Day bowl games, even managed to divert Wade from a few. "Are you guys talking about football again?"

Wade stood to greet her. "Actually we were talking about you. What do *you* think the 49ers should do about—"

"Fuck you, Wade."

Allenby had stood in greeting, too, now moved past Angela toward the doorway. "I'll excuse myself for a moment and let you two lovebirds—"

"Sorry," Angela told him. "I didn't mean to take it out on you. I just came by to congratulate you on your new position, whatever you decide it is. And to thank you again for rescuing us from a life behind bars"—she gestured toward Wade—"where this reprobate probably belongs." Then she pointed at the empty lobby. "I see there's been some turnover in the staff here. If you're interviewing him for the secretary's spot, I have to warn you that his public interaction skills are sadly lacking. That's why we tried to keep him in a classroom."

Allenby smiled, headed toward the Men's. Angela turned back to face Wade, let him feel the full effect of her grooming. Elegantly coiffed today, brimming with confidence, bursting with vitality, she sported beige suede over white satin, and form-fitting black slacks; accented by a sparkling string of pearls atop a hint of cleavage, the overall impact was somehow at once impeccably professional and irresistibly sexy.

"You look like shit," Wade said. "They'll never let you into Manny's dressed like—"

"I just stopped by so you could wish me luck, not that I need it. I've got my second round interview in a few minutes."

"Wow. That was fast."

"*Some* people don't want to let a good thing get away." She pageant-walked off, Sarah Palin by Tina Fey, trailing an intoxicating fragrance that made Wade want to chase after her and bury his nose in her neckline.

He licked his lips instead and called lamely in her wake, "Good luck."

She waved a hand airily, flipped him the bird, didn't bother to look back to see if he saw.

"That's some strut she's got goin'," Allenby said, as he returned to share the view of Angela's departure. "How the hell did you let a woman like that get away from you?"

Wade sighed. "Well, it didn't help any that I still had Brenda on the books while we were . . . trying to be together."

"Maybe you should've tried a little harder."

"Truer words were never spake." Therewith, the sad, familiar story of Wade's life: should've tried harder to . . . get a girlfriend (or at least a date) in high school; get along with his bosses; find a sane advisor for his dissertation; get away from his wife; incinerate his in-laws—the list was endless.

Wade thought about his encounter at the jail. It always astounded him whenever he would hear people say—and he heard it all the time—"If I had it to do over again, I wouldn't change a thing." What kind of an imagination-deprived numbskull wouldn't change *anything*? Wade could make five mistakes before breakfast. Why not get it right if you had the chance to do it over? Yet he'd met so many Buck Masons who had spent years in debt, in addiction, in abusive relationships, in *prison* for Christ's sake, but still blithely blabbered, "I'd do it all again. It made me who I am."

"One good decision could make up for a lot of bad ones," Allenby said.

"I don't know. Maybe it's too late."

"Maybe it's not. She came back to CSU. Seems like she came back for you."

Wade shrugged. "She might just be flirting with CSU to drive up Berkeley's price. Or to get a better deal back at UConn."

"That sounds more like something Matt Lytle would do."

"I hope it pays off better for her than it did for him."

"Don't sell yourself short," Allenby said. "You've got a decent job, you pull in a little extra in the summers, you're about to be a published author, you can take a joke or make one, you have no beer belly, no major debts, no degenerate children snorting up your resources—she could do worse."

It sounded like something Angela could put on a T-shirt when they were out in public together, a notch up from the *I'm with Stupid* that you used to see everywhere. Wade was no stranger to damnation by faint praise: he would go to his grave recalling his finally-approved dissertation's earning the label "No worse than the rest of this term's lot." But Christ, now it was going to be published. Imagine the astonishment of the Berkeleyites when they rediscovered Hemingway, thanks to Wade, icon of New Historicism. Even Angela would have to give him his—

"Don't fuck this up, Wade. You only get so many chances with a goddess."

"What happened to 'The world is full of women?'"

"The world is full of women like Yoshi and Brenda. And a few others I could name from my own files."

"What about you?" Wade asked. "You seem to be . . . hitting it off well with Erica."

Allenby shook his head, sighed. "I decided to give it another try with Nora. She's agreed to cut her spending in half, and I'm either taking this job or going back to work full-time at my company, so I won't be hanging around the house all day trying to get her into bed."

"So true love will out after all."

"That and a good strong pre-nup. She came to her senses, and I guess I came to mine. I don't really have the inclination to start chasing pussy again at my age."

Wade frowned. "You and Erica didn't—"

"A great lady there, no doubt," Allenby interrupted. "We could definitely enjoy each other's company. But she was honest with me when I told her about my situation. She's not sure she's ready to play grandma to my daughters' broods. She also told me the one thing she regretted most in her own life was not trying harder to make her second marriage work. She said to make sure I give it my best shot before I give up on my third. She's protecting herself, too: she's doesn't want any half-in, half-out, half-*ass* relationship."

"They always want the whole ass, don't they?" Wade said. "Look, this might be totally premature, but . . . if I decide to pop the question to Angela and she for some insane reason decides to accept, would you consider being my best man?"

"Honored."

"I figured since you lost your shot with The Dink, I should make it up to you."

Allenby smiled wryly, nodded.

Wade continued: "You know, if Angela gets this dean job, there might be a chance for me to go back to the English Department. What do you think about the idea of a man's going to work for his . . . wife?"

"Doesn't *The Inferno* put that in the ninth circle of hell?"

"I never made it that far with Dante," Wade confessed. "I've been to the eighth circle with Brenda, though."

Wade tried to figure out how he wanted to close this conversation. It wasn't going to be about Brenda. "You said once I'm your best friend. You got me a job, gave me a raise, helped me find my condo, got my book published. What did I ever do for you?"

Allenby spread his hands. "Everyone at my company is trying to push me out the door. My wives divorced me—or threatened to—my kids don't speak to me except when they want money, my dog died. Fucker was neurotic anyway. You're it. You're elected."

"Friends are hard to come by, aren't they?"

Allenby shrugged. "Our family—or families—and our work take up so much of our time."

"Watching football takes up a lot of time, too," Wade pointed out. "Not to mention the emotional toll."

"At least there's no alimony to pay." Allenby looked at his watch. "I think they want me in this interview with Angela. Anything you care to say in the candidate's behalf?"

"Don't sit too close if they're serving Scotch."

Wade had arranged to meet Bludge and Dixon at his office. On the way there, Wade thought back over the way friends had come in and out of his life in the years before he'd met Allenby. Worst, of course, were the friends who *changed*, turned into Scientologists or survivalists or conspiracy theorists or NASCAR fans, and wanted to drag you into the lunacy with them. He thought about the other friends he'd made or tried to make as an adult, how once you were with someone there were always so many complications: either you couldn't stand his wife, he couldn't stand yours, or the wives couldn't stand either of you or each other. He thought about his first friend in the world, David Roman, remembered the day he met him, age five, rolling a tire almost taller than he was up the hilly street they both grew up on, trying to get Wade to climb inside and roll down the hill into oncoming traffic with him, first of a million crazy misadventures that nearly sent them both to early graves. Buddies all through high school, together for hours every day, and then Wade had played it safe at San Francisco State while David went off to Vietnam in the last year of U.S. fighting there. David survived, came home, married the winner of the Meanest Woman in the World contest, while Wade settled for the runner-up. Now the two of them talked on the phone a few times a year, saw each other for a few minutes at Christmas if they were lucky. How was it, Wade wondered, that we let the people we loved get so far away from us for so long?

Wade remembered then, too, though, that when Angela had left him, David had called more often, come to see him with a second wife, a vast improvement, sane and sweet, shown him there was hope. Then on the darkest day of Wade's life, David had been there to listen again. Wade's mother had dropped a plate he had handed her to dry, trying to give her something to do, keep her busy with simple tasks, Wade there on the weekend to give his sister a break, give back to his mom a small measure of the love she had poured into his life. When the plate had hit the floor, his mother had looked down for a long time, then back up at him with a look of unbearable sadness. In a moment of sudden, brutal lucidity, she'd asked a question that had cut through him like a saber: **How long have I been crazy?** Wade had knelt to comfort her, wrap his arms around her in a long, hard hug; at length she'd hugged him back and said, with a trace of her old, familiar life-affirming smile, the other words he would carry to his own grave, the last he would ever hear from her: **You're a good boy. You remind me of my son.** Half an hour later she was gone.

David had cried with him when Wade phoned to share the news that night. Wade told himself now to give David a call when he got home, not wait for another funeral or another year to pass. Maybe get him together with Allenby; he knew they'd hit it off. What better gift to an old friend than to share a new one?

Bludge was waiting at the office when Wade got there. He handed Wade an envelope, his third of the day. What now?

"What's in here? I hope you haven't been redrafting that constitution for the Confederate Hammerskins."

"Just open it, okay?"

Wade opened the envelope. It contained another check made out to the Marcus Foster Fund. This one was for four thousand dollars.

Wade was stunned. "You already contributed. Can you afford—"

"I got the guys on the team to put in fifty bucks apiece. A few of them flaked, of course, and a couple checks bounced, but some guys put in more."

"Wow. They're in good company." Wade informed him about the contribution from the White House, could tell that Bludge was impressed even if he wasn't quite ready yet to party with the donkeys.

Dixon came in a few minutes later, deadpanned a glance at Bludge, muscles rippling in his T-shirt. Wade started to perform the introductions, but Dixon saved him the trouble, extending a hand toward the linebacker. "My friends call me 'Badass Motherfucker.'" He turned toward Wade. "I added the first name."

"Nice touch," Wade said. "Not too trendy these days, but—"

"It beats the hell out of LeDemetrius," Bludge said, as he accepted the handshake.

"Or Plaxico," Wade agreed. "Dixon has been doing some tutoring this semester," he told Bludge. "I thought maybe you could pick his brain a little bit before you start your community service project."

Wade had arranged, with Slate's approval, for Bludge to atone for his misconduct in the San Diego State game by tutoring children in a local low-income school district during the spring semester. Most of the kids he'd be working with would not be candidates for the European Heritage Club.

"I've been wanting you two guys to get to know each other anyway."

Dixon nodded, looked Bludge over again. "Because you thought we might be related, right?"

Bludge laughed, went with it. "I could see that. Could be my people used to own yours."

Wade told each about the other's connection with Marcus and then explained his plan for the two of them to share stewardship of the fund in his memory, be involved in selecting worthy scholarship recipients.

"Can I nominate myself?" Dixon immediately wanted to know.

Bludge grinned. "In that case, I withdraw my contribution."

Dixon blinked at Bludge's massive arms and chest, then looked at Wade: "Do I have your permission to kick this guy's ass if I have to?"

"You guys figure out what ground rules you want to set up for the fund and then get back to me, okay?"

Wade had been thinking about establishing a small scholarship fund of his own, in honor of his mother, to recognize students who helped others. Allenby's wager in his stead had certainly made that decision easier. He was planning to name Dixon as the first recipient, had meant to tell him today, but didn't call him back now as the prodigy walked off in conversation with Bludge.

Wade went to *Casablanca* instead: "Louis, I think this is the beginning of a beautiful friendship."

CHAPTER 26

The tide eventually turns and you always have
a chance to win.
                    —Joe Montana

And ruined love, when it is built anew
Grows fairer than at first . . . .
                    —Sonnet 119

Wade was still thinking about *Casablanca* when he turned on his computer. The greatest movie ever made, Bogie does the right thing at the finish line, ends on an epigram, and what does he get for his trouble? His girl in the sky with another guy, a cryptic smile to remember her by. Fuck. There was no justice in the world.

He checked his email, found another message from Jenna, this one marked URGENT as well as OFFENSIVE. She had sold an option on *Six Ways from Sunday*. She was rewriting the script to make the girls eighteen and over "so nobody follows your noble role model and winds up in prison getting cornholed." She would be returning his contribution to the budget soon, along with "a little something extra," and she promised him a share of the future profits if the flick hit the jackpot. She attached a clip downloaded from *Deep Throat*, suggesting it for his new screensaver, along with a recap of the balance sheet on that storied project: shot in less than a week for about thirty thousand bucks, the film had grossed something like six hundred million worldwide. Quite a bit more than *Casablanca* had pulled in, Wade remembered. Anything was possible. Maybe there was a smidgen of justice out there for him after all. Somewhere in Connecticut, Wade allowed himself to hope again, a certain special someone was freezing his nuts off.

He was about to leave his office, head for the bank to make a deposit and then for home, when Angela knocked and entered, still aglow, no need to guess how her follow-up interview had gone. Or maybe she'd heard from Berkeley and was getting an endowed chair there.

"So what's on for tonight, Wade?"

"You know, pretty much the usual: nowhere to go, nothing to do, no one to do it with when I don't get there. I'm considering installing a new screensaver, though."

"I hope your heart can stand the excitement."

Wade tapped his chest. "Not much left of this heart after the last time you broke it. I'm still picking up the pieces."

"'And all the king's horses and all the king's men—'"

"I hate that ending. Can't you come up with something more original?"

"I hope this weekend helped at least a little bit."

"This weekend was . . . something to remember you by?"

"I'm not taking the UC job, Wade."

"Oh. Back to UConn then?"

"Nope."

"Surely you're not—"

"Yep. Say hello to the new CSU Dean of Humanities. One-eighty K next year. Plus housing allowance, car allowance, travel allowance, of course, and—"

"Do you get to put a new window in your office, too?"

"The first thing I insisted on in the negotiations is that the chairman of the English Department is retiring. Say goodbye to Brownnose Brooks."

"And he thought *he* was going to be dean." Wade mimed applause. "You're off to a good start. Of course, he'll probably just try to go back to the classroom, unless—"

"Wait till you hear my next move."

"I thought we decided that crucifying him was going too far."

"I'm offering *you* the job."

"Oh. What makes you think I'm qualified to be department chair?"

"Well, for one thing, you've got the Berkeley pedigree, and if Allenby's pal puts out that book for you, you'll be one of the few in the department with a respectable publication."

"Don't get ahead of yourself there. Allenby's friend *is* publishing the book, but the reviewers may thrash it. Besides, why would I want that job anyway? The department chair is just a glorified scheduling clerk. Every time some nutjob cancels classes for a month or drops trou in the library, you have to negotiate with the union goons just to get him to show up and zip up."

"It'd be more money."

"I make enough money."

Wade paused. Had that sentence actually come out of his mouth? *There's no such thing as enough money* had been a tenet of his life for as long as he could remember. His haphazard employment history hadn't helped, nor had Brenda's preoccupations. Now, finally, he didn't have to worry any more from month to month whether there was enough in the checking account to buy a fucking tire. He was actually saving money every payday, and, with Allenby's guidance, investing some. He was no longer on track to perish a pauper. He had even made enough to send Brenda the money for the renewal of her teaching certificate, and there was reason to hope that she might someday be again among the gainfully employed and no longer in need of his support. Wade was far ahead of where any reasonable recent expectation would have placed him.

Angela wasn't impressed. "What, your ninety thousand per?"

"I got a raise. It's a hundred thousand now."

"Christ, Wade, there are community college teachers in this town making *two* hundred thousand a year."

"Teaching, what, thirty units a semester? Or pretending to?"

Angela nodded. "Well, yeah, a lot of it's online."

"Bully for them. There are people robbing banks in this town for a living, too. I'll get by." It was easier, of course, to hold the moral high ground when your road to it was paved with earnings from gambling and hornography.

"Well, if I can't entice you with a bigger paycheck, consider this: *you* could fire Brooks."

"*That*, at least, is worth talking about," Wade said. *If you wrong us, shall we not revenge?* "Maybe instead of firing him, I'll assign him five sections of Bonehead, starting at 7:00 a.m."

"See, I *knew* you'd make a kickass department chair. Vengeance *is* the noblest emotion, don't you think?"

"It's tempting," Wade admitted. "But I think I know a better candidate."

"Who? I'm *not* putting your protégé Dixon in charge before he starts shaving."

"Erica Wiley," Wade said. "She's been in the department forever, knows all the history, great teacher, gets along with everyone—and we're probably going to lose her to retirement pretty soon unless we give her something new to do."

Angela nodded. "Nice boost in her pension, too, if she does that job for a few years."

"Plus she'd be . . . what? One of three minority department heads on the whole campus? You'd be addressing that imbalance too."

"Good idea. I'll think about it," Angela said. "I'm sure there are other ways I can entice you back to the department. What if I offered you a chance to teach grad students instead of those knuckle-draggers you've been coaching?"

"Marcus was no knuckle-dragger," Wade reminded her quietly. "Neither was—is—Marvin Walker."

"God, I'm sorry, Wade. That was stupid."

He smiled to let her know she was forgiven. He'd thought about adding a Ronnie shot but let it pass when he saw her sudden chagrin. Was it possible he was finally maturing?

"Let me make it up to you." She returned the smile. "How about a seminar on . . . Sherwood Anderson and Gertrude Stein?"

"How about a poke in the eye with a hot tire iron? Which one's the good eye again?"

So much for maturity. Fulfilling while it lasted, though.

"Okay, okay"—she threw up her hands in surrender—"make it Faulkner and Fitzgerald then. Throw in Hemingway if you must."

"That's more like it," Wade said. "I'll . . . think about it."

"And, of course, don't forget, if you rejoin the Humanities Division, there'd be the opportunity for . . . private meetings with the dean."

She came closer, stepped into him, snuggled up, let him feel her breasts against his chest, with the usual effect.

Wade stepped back to downsize, let his eyes fall to her splendid, unreconstructed bosom. "The other night, when you were telling me about what Ronnie wanted you to—"

"I couldn't live with someone who's obsessed with superficial stuff like that."

"Are you telling me you left Ronnie because he wanted you to—"

"I left Ronnie for a thousand reasons. I came back to CSU for one reason: to be with you."

Wade opened his mouth. Nothing came out.

"I never loved Ronnie, Wade. My heart never found a home with anyone but you."

Wade's heart began making those frightening leaps and lurches again. He hoped the coronary unit at the local ER was fully staffed and standing by.

"You sure it wasn't partly a power trip that brought you back, getting to be dean?"

"You think I can't get a dean job somewhere else?"

Berkeley, Wade thought. She could be in fucking Berkeley. "I think you can get . . . anything you want."

"Good. I'm glad we understand that."

"You should understand *this*, though. I like the job I have, *and* I have several other options with Allenby, so I don't know if I'll be—"

She stepped into him again, shushed him, drew him close. "Are *you* sure you're not just afraid you can't handle having me for your boss?"

He looked into her eyes, put his arms around her, pulled her tight, studied her flawless face, her thrilling form, touched her forehead tenderly with his own, started to kiss her—then pulled back. "You know, before you go too far down that road, you might want to check into how things worked out for the last woman who tried to be my boss."

She shoved him away, shook a mock fist in his face. He reached up, curled her hand into his own, pulled it down, brought her chest-to-chest again.

"This might seem like a funny thing for a guy like me to ask a girl who's been at Columbia and Stanford and UConn and all, but—"

Could he do it? Could he finish the sentence? Was he really ready to say this, try it again?

"Come on, CSU. You can do it. I'm wide open in the end zone."

Wade nodded, stepped back, took a deep breath, locked eyes, ignored the odds, let it fly: "Did anyone ever tell you you've got a good head on your shoulders?"

THEMES IN *DESPERATION PASSES*

Although written mainly in a humorous style intended to be entertaining, *Desperation Passes* contains a number of issues suitable for classroom or reading group discussion, these among them:

The skewed values of universities that pay huge salaries to football coaches and administrators compared to the pay rates for teachers, tutors, and soldiers.

The literacy levels and graduation rates of student-athletes.

Ending a marriage versus striving to salvage it. When is it time to get out?

Forgiving an unfaithful lover and trying again to make a relationship work.

Unintended pregnancy and the options of abortion, early marriage, or adoption.

The controversy over Affirmative Action hiring policies and the emphasis on "diversity."

Racial discrimination against coaching applicants.

Racial tension among teammates and the possibilities for changes of attitude.

The controversy over use of the word "nigger."

Excessive drinking on campus and its consequences.

Sex crimes on campus and the struggle to report and respond to them.

The role of pornography in American society and the background of porn performers.

Casual sex and its implications, including blackmail.

Recent generations' ignorance about history, especially World War II.

The debate over America's use of atomic bombs to end World War II.

American military tactics in Vietnam and in the War on Terror.

Judgments of individuals who participated in war and killed civilians.

Domestic violence and its impact on people's lives.

Violent behavior and its consequences among young American minority males.

Punishment versus forgiveness of student-athletes' misconduct, and the consequences of decisions in these cases.

Suicide as a response to bankruptcy and public humiliation.

President Obama's leadership as a model for reconciliation, compromise, and progress.

Men's acceptance of (or reluctance to accept) women in leadership roles.

DISCUSSION QUESTIONS FOR
DESPERATION PASSES

1. The novel opens with a reference to the enormous salary paid to Nick Saban when he jumped to the University of Alabama, where he has subsequently won multiple national championships. How do you feel about the payment of vast salaries to football coaches compared to the pay for others in our society, including teachers, tutors, and the soldiers who put their lives on the line to defend us? Is there a defense for paying big salaries to coaches? What about the salaries of university presidents? Is it appropriate that a public university president should be paid more than the Chief Justice of the Supreme Court?

2. When you met A.J. Dupree and Thaddeus Marston, how did you feel about their inclusion in the population of college students? Are they prepared to succeed academically? What is the justification for their enrollment? Should universities be required to field teams with legitimate college-level students? For whom is college intended? What is the purpose of education?

3. Wade refers to his father's decision to leave his mother and its impact on his own failure to end his own unsuccessful marriage in time to pursue his first opportunity to make a life with Angela. How do your own experiences or observations connect with these decisions? Is marriage "until death do us part," or is divorce sometimes the appropriate solution? If a partner in marriage succumbs to drug addiction, as Wade's wife Brenda did, how long is a partner obliged to stay to try to help? How long do you think you would stay before giving up if your partner didn't change? Is "unconditional love" a realistic concept?

4. Wade refers to Angela's leaving him to return to Ronnie, a previous lover, yet throughout the novel he is hoping to reconnect with her. Is forgiving an unfaithful lover and trying again to make a relationship work a realistic goal, or is it better to move on?

5. Allenby's sophomore stepson Prince Pembleton unintentionally impregnates his girlfriend, Jennifer, and they contemplate marriage. How did you feel about their prospects for a successful family life? What other options do you think they should consider?

6. Wade reveals that his job as a counselor was rushed through an approval process, and he is subsequently required to reapply for it. He vents his anger over the requirements for "diversity" in current hiring policies. How do you feel about these requirements, about Wade's reaction, and about the tactics used by Angela to circumvent the issue in Wade's case?

7. Although representation has improved dramatically in recent years, the ratio of African-American coaches to players is still very low. How did you respond to Sherman Slate's job interview? What did he do or say that earned him the job? Would you have hired him? What about the attempt by Coach Lytle to keep his job? Were you persuaded by his argument that he deserved another chance?

8. How did you feel about Bludge when you met him? Did you feel any sympathy for any of his extreme positions? Why do you think Marcus was willing to try to give him another chance? How did you feel about the outcome of their interaction after Bludge's crucial mistake at the end of the bowl game?

9. Several characters in the novel, including Bludge, who is white, use the word "nigger" freely. How do you feel about their usage of the word? Is it okay for some but not for others? Do you use the word yourself? Do you say anything when you hear other people use the word?

10. What was your reaction to the description of the fraternity party? How did you feel about what happened to Larashawndria there? How much responsibility do you think she bears for the situation she found herself in? Have you ever been in a similar position or known someone who was? What responsibilities do colleges and universities have to curtail the culture of binge drinking on campus and its consequences?

11. How did you react when, along with Wade, you met Jenna Jones? How did her revelations about her background

affect your response to the activities she has embraced? Do you think she has other options besides pornography?

12. What was your response to the relationship between Wade and Yoshi? Do you think Wade figured anything out about this during his conversation with Larashawndria? Did he deserve the blackmail Yoshi threatened him with?

13. Wade savagely ridicules his current boss Delia Herman and his former boss Gordon Brooks. Why do you think he despises them so much, and did he succeed in making you despise them as well? Have you ever worked for someone that you couldn't stand? How did you handle the situation? Compare or contrast yourself with Wade.

14. Wade also ridicules online classes and those who teach them. How did you react to his dismissal of this form of education? How have your own experiences of online versus face-to-face classes, or those of others you know, affected your opinion on this issue?

15. Were you surprised when Dixon revealed the ignorance of Dupree and Marston about World War II? How much did you learn about this historical event yourself in high school? What is the importance of understanding this war in order to understand issues in our contemporary world?

16. Wade and Yoshi briefly debate the ethics of America's use of atomic bombs to end World War II, and Wade refers to bombings again in a conversation with Allenby. What is your understanding of the reasons for Truman's decision to drop bombs on Hiroshima and Nagasaki, and do you agree with the decision? Why or why not? [Note for further reading: Paul Fussell's essay "Thank God for the Atom Bomb."]

17. What was your response to the conversation that Wade and Allenby had about American military tactics in Vietnam and in the War on Terror? How do you feel about America's decisions to intercede militarily in Vietnam and in the Middle East?

18. Allenby makes a startling revelation about his own participation in the war in Vietnam. Did this change the way you viewed him? How many other American soldiers do you

think may have had similar experiences in Vietnam or in Iraq or Afghanistan?

19. Domestic violence surfaces as a theme both in Angela's relationship with Ronnie and in Dupree's childhood experiences. Why do you think Angela went back to someone who struck her? Did Dixon's revelations about the way Dupree's mother abused him change your perspective of him at all?

20. Coach Slate refers at the funeral to the alarming homicide rate among young African-American males. Have you or has anyone you know been affected by this type of violence? What do you think are the causes of killings among minority males, and what do you think we should be doing about it?

21. How did you feel about the decisions that Coach Slate made regarding who could play in the bowl game and the outcome of these decisions? How do you feel in general about the ways that athletes are punished (or not punished) for their misconduct and/or crimes? What policy would you like to see our society follow in this regard?

22. What was the impact of Wade's encounter with Buck Mason in jail? How did you respond to Buck's comment that he "wouldn't change a thing" in his life? How do you feel about Buck's prospects for rehabilitation?

23. How did you feel about the fates of Coach Lytle and Delia Herman? Did they get what they deserved? Why do you think Herman may have taken such an extreme step?

24. Chapter 25 has an epigraph that includes an excerpt from a speech by President Obama. In what ways was his leadership referenced as a model for reconciliation, compromise, and progress in the novel? Did you agree or disagree with Wade and Allenby's enthusiasm for Obama's leadership?

25. The end of the novel raises a question about the future for Wade and Angela. Will they be able to put the past behind them and make their relationship work? Will he be able to work for her? Which of the job opportunities available to him do you think he will take, and how do you feel about their chances as a couple going forward? How did you respond to Allenby's decision regarding his wife and Erica Wiley?

26. This novel blends a comic style with some serious scenes, include a killing, a funeral, and a confession of war crimes. Does the combination of comedy and tragedy work or not? Why?

27. The novel emphasizes the interracial friendship between Allenby and Wade and offers the prospect of another between Bludge and Dixon. Has race played a role in the friendships which you have formed? Have you or others you know faced any challenges in forming friendships with people from ethnic backgrounds different from your own?

28. How do the epigraphs at the beginning of each chapter set the tone for what follows? Which ones seemed most relevant to you? Were there any that you found surprising? Were there any that did not seem relevant?

29. What impact do the novel's many allusions have? Among the many references to literature, movies, television, political issues, and historical figures, which references seemed most important to you? Why? Can you identify any other literary techniques that this author used?

30. Which character in the novel did you ultimately find most sympathetic, and which one was least sympathetic? Why?

31. What was your favorite scene in the novel? Why? If you could edit out one scene, which one would it be? Why?

32. If you could change one choice that a character in the novel made, what would it be? Why? What would have been the improved consequences of a different choice?

33. What do you think is the most important theme in the novel? [You may wish to review the list that precedes these questions.] Which characters do you associate most clearly with this theme?

CHAPTER-BY-CHAPTER QUESTIONS FOR DISCUSSION

Chapter One (pages 1-13): Questions for Discussion

1. How do details from the opening exchanges of dialog between Allenby and Wade help to establish their differences as well as their shared interests?

2. What is the significance of Allenby's question to Wade about the status of the assistant coach who intercedes between Marcus Foster and Coach Lytle? Compare his concern with concerns for hiring of minorities and women in other professions.

3. What is the point of Wade's references to Lincoln, McClellan, and Westmoreland, and of Allenby's non-response?

4. How would you characterize the relationship between Wade and Angela based on their opening exchange? Compare other depictions of embattled romances you are aware of.

5. Comment on the characterization of Coach Lytle and of the depiction of the football game being played in Chapter 1. What issue surfaces immediately in connection with the depiction of the coach, and how do you feel about his public pronouncements?

6. What complications has Allenby taken on in his personal life, and how do you feel about them? Compare his domestic arrangements with others that you have experienced or observed.

7. What is the impact of the revelation at the end of the chapter? Does it change perceptions of the connection between Allenby and Wade?

Chapter Two (pages 14-20): Questions for Discussion

1. How do the epigraphs at the beginning set the tone for this chapter?

2. How would you describe Allenby's relationship with his wife based on his comments about their marriage? Compare his remarks with what you have observed or experienced about the

impact of male or female obsessions within relationships.

3. How did you respond to Allenby's assertion that "American women are shopping for jewelry and shoes"? What was Wade's internal response?

4. Find the source of the quotation, "'Tis' the times' plague when madmen lead the blind" and explain why Allenby applies it to the relationship between his stepson and his bride-to-be.

5. Allenby says that Wade should be "scared" by his relationship with Yoshi. What was your response to the initial scene between her and Wade?

Chapter Three (pages 21-26): Questions for Discussion

1. What has taken the place of religion in Wade's life? How did you respond to his description of the response by his mother's church to her dilemma? How do you balance what your parents have taught you about religion and what you have decided for yourself?

2. How did feel when you read Coach Lytle's remarks about the new job he is taking and his reasons for taking it? How do you feel about the salaries that are paid to college coaches? What other salary inflation can you compare this to?

3. What is the role of television in Wade's life, in this book, and in your life? Do you agree with what Erma Bombeck said in the second epigraph? Is television a "Vast Wasteland" or a wonderful vehicle for delivery of entertainment and education?

4. How did you respond to the information about the arrest of two players from the CSU team? What do you think should be done about the epidemic of inappropriate behavior by professional and college athletes?

5. How did you react to the phone conversation between Wade and Angela at the end of the chapter? Should he allow himself to become interested in her again or just put the past behind him and move on?

Chapter Four (pages 27-33): Questions for Discussion

1. How did you react to Wade's description of Delia Herman? Compare his response to her with your own response to a boss you have reported to.

2. What was your reaction to the emphasis on clothing, both Herman's and Wade's, in this chapter? Do "clothes make the man [or woman]," or is this concern mainly irrelevant to you?

3. How did this chapter's references to expenditures on campus compare with your response to what you have seen money spent on at other campuses?

4. As you learn more from Wade's descriptions of Dupree and Marston, what are you feeling about their place on campus? Are these real college students or "athletes masquerading as students?" How does their behavior compare or contrast with the behavior of student-athletes you have known? For whom do you think college is meant?

5. Why do you think Herman appoints Allenby to chair the committee to hire a new football coach? And why do you think Allenby wants Wade to serve on the committee with him? How, in your experience or observation, does the selection of committee members affect the results that the group produces? Think about the first epigraph, from Dave Barry, and consider this: are committees and meetings always a waste of time, or can they produce meaningful results?

Chapter Five (pages 34-44): Questions for Discussion

1. What does Wade's attitude toward exercise indicate about him? Compare or contrast your own attitude in this regard.

2. How did you respond to Erica Wiley's articulation of her preference not to have children? Do you consider this a valid choice, or do you think people who bypass this role in life are selfish and/or are missing an irreplaceable experience?

3. How did you react to Wade's description of the latest atrocities committed by parents?

4. Erica tells Wade that for women there is usually an emotional component to sexual relationships. Is this outdated nonsense or still largely true?

5. How did you respond to the description of the classes taught by Professor Hotchkiss? Would you sign up for a class like this?

6. What was your reaction to meeting Dixon James? How would you feel about being graded on your papers by someone at his stage of life and education?

7. What was your reaction to Wade's description of the educational standard at CSU? Do you think he is exaggerating or speaking relatively accurately?

Chapter Six (pages 45-54): Questions for Discussion

1. How do the epigraphs for this chapter establish its tone? Which of the two epigraphs has more impact on you? Why?

2. What impact did the statistics rattled off by Allenby and the comment quoted from Professor Lapchick have on you? How do you account for the imbalance of opportunities for minorities in coaching positions?

3. What accounted for Wade's taking an interest in politics after many years of non-participation? Do you agree or disagree with Obama's policies? Why? How do you feel about Wade's objection to Obama's "fallback into holy water"?

4. How does Allenby's personal athletic history as described in this chapter fit into the themes of this novel? How is the importance of quarterbacking in football, like pitching and catching in baseball, relevant to this history?

5. You finally meet Dupree and Marston in this chapter after hearing in advance of their misadventures. How did you react to meeting them? How did you feel about Marston's comment on the value of online classes?

6. Describe the interaction that occurs when Dixon James meets Dupree and Marston. How do you like his chances of helping them?

Chapter Seven (pages 55-64): Questions for Discussion

1.   What was the impact of the inclusion of Tom Brady, Clint Eastwood, and Jack Nicholson in the discussion of fatherhood roles? Does the celebrity culture influence our standards about behavior as parents and in other roles?

2.   What were your chief impressions of Prince Pembleton and Jennifer when you met them? What do you think are their prospects for a successful marriage?

3.   How will Pembleton and Jennifer fare as parents? What options are mentioned in the chapter, and what do you think they should do?

4.   On page 61, Wade feels "a flicker of pity" for Pembleton. Did you share it? Why or why not?

5.   How do the exchanges between Wade and Yoshi at the end of this chapter influence your expectations about the future of this relationship?

Chapter Eight (pages 65-72): Questions for Discussion

1.   Which of the epigraphs prefacing this chapter had more impact on you? Why?

2.   Did white student-athlete Chris Blodgett's (Bludge's) use of the word "nigger" shock or offend you? How do you feel about his argument for his right to use it? How do you feel in general when you hear this word used? Do you ever use it yourself? Do you ever tell others that you object to it?

3.   What impact did Bludge's story about his younger brother have on you?

4.   Describe Wade's previous attempts to be involved as an advisor to student organizations. What conclusions does he appear to have drawn from these experiences?

5.   What did you think about Bludge's plan to start a European heritage club? Is there a place for this on campus or not? How did you feel about the way Wade handled Bludge's invitation to serve as advisor? How would you feel about the appropriateness of campus clubs organized not on the basis of

color but of nationality: Irish, Scottish, French, etc.?

6. Why do you think Bludge said that Coach Lytle is a hypocrite? What expectations does this charge arouse?

Chapter Nine (pages 73-84): Questions for Discussion

1. This chapter begins with an epigraph describing William Wilberforce. Why is his inclusion in this novel appropriate?

2. What do you think is the point of including the second epigraph, from Miles Davis?

3. How did Sherman Slate succeed in impressing the interview panel? Which of his responses did you find persuasive?

4. "There's a black man in the White House," Allenby reminds Wade. "Anything is possible." Do you think that Obama's election signified a profound change in American culture, or have we reverted to business as usual?

5. How did you respond to Coach Lytle's reversal of his decision to leave CSU? What do you think is behind it?

Chapter Ten (pages 85-94): Questions for Discussion

1. What is the irony of quoting Joe Paterno in the first epigraph?

2. As you met Marcus Foster with Wade, how did you size him up? What characteristics stood out? How does he provide a contrast to Dupree and Marston? Do some research and speculate about the significance of the choice of a name for this character.

3. "Find a good woman and treat her right," Marcus declares, quoting his high school coach. Wade compares this with his mother's advice: "Marry a girl with a good head on her shoulders." Are these homilies corny and outdated or are they valid?

4. In reviewing Marcus's role as a peacemaker in the San Diego State game, Wade and Allenby talk about the role Willie Mays played in breaking up a fight between the Giants and the Dodgers. How common is it in your experience for people to step in to stop a fight rather than adding to the hostilities?

What examples can you supply from your own experience or observation?

5. What was Wade's response, and what was yours, to Coach Lytle's answer to the interview question about his record on hiring minority coaches?

6. "You don't mess with success," Lytle declares at the end of the chapter. Has he made his case convincingly? How does he appear to be defining "success," and how would you define it for someone in his position?

Chapter Eleven (pages 95-109): Questions for Discussion

1. What was your reaction to the conversation between Delia Herman and Wade about the role of "diversity" in hiring processes? Has the focus (or lack thereof) on diversity in hiring ever had an impact on you or on someone that you know?

2. When you met Clara Shelby, did you find her refreshing or revolting? Why?

3. How did you react to Yoshi's declaration of interest in taking over Wade's job? "That was just sex," Yoshi tells Wade when he wonders how she could pursue his job after they were intimate, contravening what Erica Wiley had said to Wade about women's emotional connection to sex. Which woman do you think is expressing a more prevalent viewpoint? Is the difference in age between Erica and Yoshi relevant? Connect discussion of this question to the first epigraph in this chapter.

4. How would you describe Wade's relationship with his former, and possibly future, boss Gordon Brooks? Compare Wade's response to Delia Herman, and, again, compare or contrast your own feelings about people you have worked for.

5. How did you feel about the offer that Brooks made to Wade? Can you compare this to any of the stories you have heard about "freeway flyers" teaching on college campuses? Connect discussion of this question to the second epigraph in this chapter.

6. During his conversation with Angela at chapter's end to enlist her support to keep his job, Wade again raises the issue of the domestic violence that she endured from Ronnie Parker.

Why would an educated woman like Angela put herself in this position? Has domestic violence been an issue in your life or in the lives of others you know? How has it affected you? How have you responded?

Chapter Twelve (pages 110-121): Questions for Discussion

1. The chapter begins with a description of Wade's reading preferences. What do they tell us about him? Compare your own preferences for reading materials.

2. What details emerged in Wade's further interrogation of Dupree and Marston? How did their revelations affect your judgment of Coach Lytle?

3. What is the significance of Wade's description of the composition of the women's volleyball team? Do you have any athletic experiences or observations that relate to his perceptions?

4. Wade confesses to a sexist bias in describing his response to female athletes. How does the second epigraph for this chapter relate to this confession, and how do you respond to his bias? Does his account of the sports he attempted himself influence your judgment?

5. What impact did Dixon's account of his attempts to tutor Dupree and Marston have on you? Were you surprised by the degree of their ignorance about World War II? How much did you learn about this event in your own high school history classes?

Chapter Thirteen (pages 122-132): Questions for Discussion

1. This chapter opens with a description of an attempt at an abortion by Pembleton and Jennifer. What was your reaction to reading about it? Can you compare it with any other situations or experiences that you have learned about?

2. What was the point of Wade's description of the negotiations over the purchase of coffee at Starbucks with Larashawndria?

3. How did you feel about Larashawndria's description of

the fraternity party and her interaction with others there? Is her account consistent with what you have experienced or heard about fraternity parties? How much responsibility do you think she bears for what happened to her there?

4. Did Larashawndria's description of her background and her goals change the way you viewed her in any way?

5. How did Wade finally succeed in breaking through the wall Larashawndria put up between them?

6. The epigraph for this chapter suggests that women's lives are unbearable. Do you agree or disagree? Consider Larashawndria's experiences as a college student in responding.

Chapter Fourteen (pages 133-145): Questions for Discussion

1. Joe Paterno is back in another epigraph. What attitude toward the sexual behavior of his team's athletes is implied by what he says? What do you think of this attitude? It is reasonable or unreasonable for a coach to take this approach?

2. Jenna Jones is supporting herself in part through a pornographic website. How do you feel about this option for paying her way through college?

3. When you met Jenna, were you repelled, attracted, amused, or none of the above? Describe your response. Do you think she is intelligent or not?

4. What was the significance of the references to the Clinton/Lewinsky scandal, and to Hillary Clinton, in the context of this novel's plot?

5. How do you feel about the way that Wade handled Jenna's visit to his office?

6. Jenna's revelations complete our picture of Coach Lytle. What do you think his fate should be?

7. What is the significance of the exchange between Wade and Allenby at the end of the chapter?

Chapter Fifteen (pages 146-160): Questions for Discussion

1. How did Wade handle the aftermath of his interview with

Jenna? Were you surprised or disturbed by any of his actions?

2. Allenby encourages Wade to submit his dissertation for possible publication. How does this gesture add to the definition of their friendship? How does the prospect of publication fit into the "desperation passes" theme of the novel as a whole?

3. How do Wade's encounters with Delia Herman and Gordon Brooks in this chapter extend themes introduced in his earlier interactions with them?

4. Online education comes under attack again in this chapter. Compare your own experiences with online education if relevant.

5. Explain how Angela solved Wade's problem with the possibility of losing his job. How did her intervention in his behalf influence your feelings about their relationship?

Chapter Sixteen (pages 161-176): Questions for Discussion

1. How did you respond to Marcus's request for Wade's help in talking to his coach? Why do you think Marcus wants to help Bludge? Connect to the epigraph from Johnny Unitas and consider the reversal of races involved [Unitas was white and Samples was black].

2. How did you react to the brief discussion of religious faith between Marcus and Wade? What ideas expressed by either of them do you agree with or disagree with?

3. Describe the dynamic of the meeting that occurs among Slate, Marcus, Allenby, and Wade. Whose words carried the most weight for the other characters? Whose words made most sense to you? What do you think the punishments under discussion should have been?

4. What impact did the conversation about comparing football and war have on you? Whose point of view seemed more persuasive to you? Why?

5. Did Allenby's revelations about his own role in the war in Vietnam change your view of him? Why or why not?

Chapter Seventeen (pages 177-193): Questions for Discussion

1. What impact did Allenby's story of being attacked in Texas have? How much have sports and/or American society changed since the date of the attack he mentions?

2. "Why would he stand up for me?" Bludge asks Wade about Marcus. Wade lets Bludge try to figure it out himself. What do you think?

3. What did you think of the decision that Coach Slate made to suspend Marston and to let Bludge and Dupree play in the bowl game?

4. How did you react to Angela's surprise arrival at Wade's hotel? What elements of their interaction in the hotel room define their relationship?

5. Comment on the role that television plays in this chapter, and compare Wade's viewing habits with your own. What did you think of his idea for a new TV show, and how would it compare with other shows that are currently broadcast?

6. What is the point of including the epigraph from Theodor Seuss Geisel in this chapter?

Chapter Eighteen (pages 194-208): Questions for Discussion

1. The connection between sports and religion, initiated in Chapter 3, resurfaces here. What did you think of the explanation that Wade gave for his own loss of religious faith? Compare or contrast the impact of similar events on your own faith or lack thereof.

2. How do strategic maneuvers in the game reflect the philosophy that Coach Slate spoke of in his interview? Comment on the significance of the first epigraph.

3. What was your response to the conversation between Wade and Allenby about excessive celebrations by athletes? Do you agree with them, or are these just part of the fun of the game?

4. What is the significance of Angela's arrival at the game and of her bringing her "companion"?

5. How did the description of the end of the game, particularly the roles played by Dupree and Bludge, affect you?

Chapter Nineteen (pages 209-216): Questions for Discussion

1. How did you feel about Wade's critique of the educational standard for USC's football players? Is this just sour grapes, or does he have a legitimate point?

2. What impact did Slate's post-game speech have on his team? On you?

3. Analyze the interaction in the locker room between Marcus and Bludge. What do you think caused a change to happen?

4. How did you react to the conversation between Wade and Bludge after Marcus's departure to the showers? Is the humor in their exchange permissible or disturbing to you?

5. Describe the impact that Marcus's fate had on Wade. What impact did it have on you? Why do you think the chapter ends this way? Is the inclusion of this tragedy in what is largely a comic novel acceptable or out of place?

Chapter Twenty (pages 217-226): Questions for Discussion

1. What was your reaction to the details of the shooting? Whom do you hold accountable? Can you connect Marcus's fate with any others you know about?

2. What was the most important message in Coach Slate's address at the funeral?

3. How did you respond to Bludge's speech at the funeral? Do you think he has learned something? Compare your response with Allenby's.

4. Did Dixon's comments about A.J.'s background influence your feelings about him? Compare your response with Wade's.

5. How does the exchange between Angela and Wade at the end of the chapter affect your feelings about their relationship? Is there a basis here for understanding Angela's attraction to Wade?

Chapter Twenty-One (pages 227-234): Questions for Discussion

1. How did you react to the revelations about the financial arrangements for his own salary and benefits negotiated by the CSU president? Compare the first two epigraphs. How do you feel about the payment of substantial salaries, from public tax funds to which you contribute, to college and university officials while tuition and other expenses for students increase every year? What does the president's behavior suggest about the divide between the haves and have-nots in American society? How do we solve this problem?

2. Compare or contrast the marriage proposals put forth or discussed in this chapter.

3. What do you think is the significance of Wade's reminding Angela of her history at Stanford?

4. Wade and Angela also review her history with Ronnie Parker. How does she attempt to explain going back to him? Compare your own experiences with or observations about women who stay in relationships with abusive males.

5. What does Wade's dream about a wedding ceremony reveal about him and about his prospects with Angela?

Chapter Twenty-Two (pages 235-240): Questions for Discussion

1. "Wade was okay with cops." Compare or contrast your own feelings about and/or experiences with law enforcement officers with what happens to Wade in this chapter.

2. Wade's neighbors get involved in the scene of his arrest. What was your reaction to the depiction of Mrs. Partridge?

3. Wade's other neighbors, Julio and Simon, also appear in this chapter. Is Wade homophobic? The author has defended his portraits of Julio and Simon by saying that since the novel ridicules the excesses of heterosexual behavior, the excesses of homosexual behavior should be equally fair game. Do you agree or disagree?

4. At the end of the chapter Wade's crime is revealed. What did you think of the basis for his arrest?

Chapter Twenty-Three (pages 241-251): Questions for Discussion

1. How does the opening epigraph from Tupac set the tone for this chapter?

2. In jail Wade reencounters one of his former students. What did you react to in the characterization of Buck Mason? Did he remind you of anyone you know or have heard about? Did any elements of his story or his philosophy surprise or repel you?

3. How did Wade's interaction with Buck affect your feelings about Wade's teaching career and/or about his personal characteristics?

4. What is the significance of the conversation between Wade and Erica after she comes to retrieve him from the jail? How did you feel about what you learned about her past? Why do you think she says to Wade, "Listen to your mother"?

5. What was your reaction to Delia Herman's fate? Is the playful tone Wade and Allenby take about it inappropriate? Why or why not?

Chapter Twenty-Four (page 252-258): Questions for Discussion

1. How did you feel when you read about the CSU president's double-dipping? Is the Board of Trustees justified in firing him for this?

2. Allenby, earlier offered the position of athletic director, now refers to "other plans" that CSU's Board of Trustees may have for him. What job do you think he will/should take? Why?

3. Angela compares the experience of being arrested along with Wade to the arrests of Martin Luther King and Rosa Parks. How and why does Wade deflect this comparison?

4. Angela supplies more details about her past attraction to Ronnie: "Women like muscles. It's the way we're wired." Compare or contrast your response to what she said with Wade's.

5. How does Angela's explanation of what Ronnie wanted her to do account for the decisions she is making now?

Chapter Twenty-Five (pages 259-273): Questions for Discussion

1. What do you think is the intent behind the pairing of the epigraphs for this chapter?

2. This chapter wraps up a lot of loose ends, beginning with the plan for Jennifer's forthcoming baby. What did you think of the resolution of this subplot? What do you think you would do in her situation or in Pembleton's?

3. Comment on Wade's plan for foreign policy and compare it with his earlier plan for attacking al Qaeda. Is there method to his madness?

4. Wade's good fortune at the novel's end (winning a bet, getting a book published, earning a raise and a possible promotion) is largely the result of his relationship with Allenby. How does Allenby respond when Wade asks if their friendship is reciprocal? What did you think of this response and/or about Wade's further deliberations on friendship? How successful have you been in maintaining friendships that have mattered to you at earlier points in your life?

5. How did you respond to Wade's attempt to console Allenby over Marcus's fate?

6. Why do you think Allenby passed up the chance for a relationship with Erica? What do you think about his decision?

7. How does the story of the end of Wade's mother's life affect your feelings about Wade's relationship with her and her influence on him?

8. Why do you think Wade brings Dixon and Bludge together at the end of this chapter?

Chapter Twenty-Six (pages 274-279): Questions for Discussion

1. What is the significance of the references to two memorable films of very different types at the beginning of this chapter?

2. Angela, now a dean, offers Wade a chance to come back to the English Department, after Allenby has offered him some other options. Which job do you think he will or should take?

3. "I make enough money," Wade says to Angela. Comment on his discussion of his own economic history and then compare your own economic history and expectations. How much is "enough money"?

4. How do the fates proposed for Gordon Brooks and Erica Wiley wrap up their characterizations in the novel?

5. The novel ends with Wade's line to Angela, echoing words he'd often heard his mother say: "Did anyone ever tell you that you've got a good head on your shoulders?" Some readers have said that the last line of this novel should be a more explicit marriage proposal. Do you agree or disagree? Why? Is Wade foolish to take a chance with someone who has hurt him before?

AN INTERVIEW WITH THE AUTHOR
OF *DESPERATION PASSES*

1. Your first novel, *Nobody Roots for Goliath*, was largely about the relationship between a black student-athlete, Marvin Walker, and a white college teacher, Malcolm Wade. In *Desperation Passes* you again show Wade, now a counselor, interacting with black student-athletes. Where did this interest come from?

I was a child in Redwood City when Willie Mays came west from New York with baseball's Giants in 1958, and a few years later Wilt Chamberlain came to San Francisco with basketball's Warriors. My favorite football player of that era was Jim Brown. All three of these players seemed to me like gods come down to earth to mingle with the mortals and show us how their games should be played. So I've had the fascination with the major sports and their superstars from almost the beginning of my life. I'm not exactly sure how much it mattered to me then that all three of these great players were black, but I do remember having friends in my neighborhood who rooted for the Yankees, even though they were in New York, instead of the Giants, because Mickey Mantle was white and Mays was black. I instinctively abhorred the reason for that preference, probably because of the values that my parents had instilled in me. Once I became a college teacher, I saw the African-American athletes in my classrooms carrying forward the legacy of my earlier heroes, but I also recognized (even when these students sometimes did not) that they were unlikely to earn their livings as athletes, so I have taken particular interest in helping them to meet their academic goals and in writing about the challenges that they face.

2. Some of the student-athletes you depict don't seem to be qualified to be college students. Would it be fair to say that you have reservations about including students like A.J. Dupree and Thaddeus Marston from *Desperation Passes* in the college population?

I have some ambivalence on this subject. On one hand, there is some resonance for me when someone like Gerald Gurney, a professor at University of Oklahoma who formerly worked as an advisor to athletic programs, says, "I believe the value of a college education is to teach students to think critically. It shouldn't be for remedial reading." On the other hand, I'm a great believer in the transformative possibilities of a college education, and I don't mean just in the classroom. If we're ever going to create an egalitarian society, we have to use the campuses to promote opportunities to better themselves for people who have historically been denied them. At the same time we somehow have to make sure that students coming to college without adequate preparation aren't just waved through the system with a meaningless degree or discarded after a knee injury and fifty units of pap classes. When former UCLA basketball player Ed O'Bannon testified in court, "I was an athlete masquerading as a student," he was speaking for many others, and unfortunately, speaking in particular for many African-Americans recruited to play basketball or football.

3. Head coaches come in for their lumps in both of your novels. What was the basis for these portrayals?

It's true that I ridiculed an insensitive coach in *Nobody Roots for Goliath,* and in *Desperation Passes* Coach Lytle is obviously despicable, but I tried to balance those portraits with Sherman Slate and Marilyn Porter, who bring into the second novel some of the values of the coaches I've known and admired. Most of the coaches I have known have been people of high character who wanted to set a strong example for their players, so I'll acknowledge that I've gone outside of my own experience and into some sordid headlines to characterize Lytle. In addition to the absurdly escalated salaries being thrown at hypocrites like him, the lack of opportunities for black coaches in college sports, even though black students constitute a high percentage of the athletes, is something else I wanted to focus on in this book.

4. Your own novels are set in academia and seem to take a pretty dim view of the supervisors who work in that environment. Is this based on personal experience?

The academic administrators I was exposed to in a small private college were generally not suited for the tasks they were handed. In some cases they were faculty who had been promoted because they had a PhD, even though the subject of their research had nothing to do with management skills. There was also an awful lot of sycophancy involved in securing promotions in the management chain there. The elevation of Gordon Brooks, who appears in both of my novels, reflects these issues. Since I moved to the public sector, I've been fortunate to have direct supervisors who are capable, reasonable people, but I've also seen absolutely catastrophic hires at higher levels, as is reflected in the depictions of Delia Herman and the nameless president in *Desperation Passes*. As with the coaches, the inflation of salaries for academic administrators is certainly an issue that alarms me, and it ought to alarm anyone whose taxes are supporting lavish lifestyles for folks who should be satisfied with half the salary and the opportunity for public service at a high level. We now have coaches and administrators fired from multiple jobs for manifest incompetence but collecting hundreds of thousands or even millions of dollars in salary, for not coming to work, because of the buy-out clauses boards of trustees have agreed to—while tuition increases every year for students, and faculty and staff go for years without even cost of living adjustments, let alone raises.

5. Readers are bound to wonder how much of your protagonist Wade is based on your own life, and about the basis for the characterization of his great friend, Allenby. Where did these characters come from?

I was lucky enough to land a post-graduate fellowship and to go fairly smoothly into full-time college teaching at an early age, so I didn't have the career issues that beset Wade, but I've known many highly qualified "freeway flyers" who could just as easily have been given the jobs I got. And I could just as easily have spent twenty years cobbling together a menial income as Wade did, so I've tried to project a view of academic life from someone who has had that path. The way Wade's life most resembles mine is in having a mother whose kindness defined his world. Allenby is partly my father, partly Obama, and partly a figment of my imagination, an unabashedly idealistic portrayal of what is or ought to be possible in this country for a visionary of any color who works hard and treats others with respect.

6. At the end of *Nobody Roots for Goliath*, Wade spurns an opportunity to resume his tempestuous affair with Angela Hardy, but when she reappears in *Desperation Passes* after his divorce, he jumps at the chance to try again with her. Isn't their relationship a recipe for disaster?

That's probably a fair appraisal of most of the romantic relationships I've observed. I'm a huge fan of the screwball comedies that Howard Hawks directed, and antagonistic romance has always seemed more interesting to me than the sappy-ever-after type of story line. The Burton-Taylor collaborations, especially *The Taming of the Shrew* and *Who's Afraid of Virginia Woolf?*, also really inspired me. If George can hang in there with Martha after all they've been through together, maybe there's a glimmer of hope for Wade and Angela.

7. You mentioned movies as an influence. What writers have most influenced your own writing?

I just referred to the film version of *Who's Afraid of Virginia Woolf?*, and Edward Albee's play—in my opinion, the greatest American play—is one of the two most influential works in my life. The other is Kingsley Amis's wonderful campus novel, *Lucky Jim*. Allenby's role in solving the wide array of Wade's problems at the end of *Desperation Passes* is intended as a nod to the deus ex machina ending of *Lucky Jim*—an homage that I admit might work a little better if a few more contemporary readers were familiar with that great book. What I'm shooting for is a kind of cross between the styles of those two masterpieces, with of course the difference of a focus on sports within the campus culture. My reliance of dialog to carry the narrative comes largely from my admiration of Albee (and from those screwball comedies), while Amis opened my eyes to the possibilities of using a character's unspoken thoughts as a sardonic commentary on the inane utterings of others. A couple of other writers who have influenced me with their use of humor and dialog are David Lodge (*Changing Places*) and Richard Russo (*Straight Man*).

8. Any other important literary influences?

Like a million American boys before and after me, I read Thomas Wolfe at fifteen and decided I was going to be a writer. In graduate school I worked on Faulkner and Conrad, and I'd still put Faulkner at the top of the heap among all novelists, the closest anyone has come in that genre to what Shakespeare achieved in his plays. If I'm looking to read for pleasure, though, I'll confess I'm more apt to pick up Hemingway or Elmore Leonard. Among the current writers, I really admire Jess Walter, Nick Hornby, Tom Perrotta, Jonathan Tropper, Scott Lasser, and Zadie Smith, in addition to Lodge and Russo, who are still going strong.

9. What advice do you have, based on your own experiences, for aspiring writers?

Samuel Johnson famously said, "No one but a blockhead ever wrote except for money." I made five hundred dollars from my first novel, after working on it for twenty years, so I guess that qualifies me to speak for the blockhead contingent. I would say, "Write because it matters to you. Work hard to make your writing the best it can be, but don't expect a quick payoff." The old standby, "Don't quit your day job," still seems like sound advice to me. If making a living is a goal, then finding and keeping a job that pays the bills is a pretty good place to start. Almost anyone who is motivated to do so can find time to read and write outside the hours required for a job, and the workplace itself may provide a compelling subject for writers. Reading compulsively for years—and I don't mean just comic books and vampire novels—seems like an obvious requirement for anyone who wants his or her own writing to be considered.

10. Any other advice based on the experience of getting your second novel into print?

Until you have tried to write a novel yourself, you have no idea of the amount of work and stress involved, the thousands of hours of thinking, writing, rewriting, agonizing, contemplating suicide (or, if distractions have been especially annoying, homicide) that go into it. And that's the easy part. Once you've torn your life apart to write the book, getting someone to read it is when the real work begins. For most writers, finding an agent, a publisher, or an audience for their book will prove far more daunting than writing it.

My first book was published because Robert Katz honored his commitment after purchasing it, even though his partner at Willowgate Press became ill and had to withdraw from their venture. The positive review of *Nobody Roots for Goliath* that James Cox published in *Midwest Book Review* inspired me to try again, and *Desperation Passes* appears in print now because of Marian Jacobs' generous funding and the dedication of two people, Paula Sheil and Robert Reinarts. I'm confident that both of them would join me in saying that launching a new small press is exciting, rewarding—and not for the easily discouraged. They have had to battle through many layers of bureaucracy and many other obstacles to get this novel into print, and I'm more aware than ever now that the writer is just one part of the complex process that goes into producing a published book.

ACKNOWLEDGMENTS

Publication of this book and the establishment of Tuleburg Press were made possible by a grant from the Marian Jacobs Literary Forum, a branch of the Stockton Arts Foundation. I wish to thank Ms. Jacobs and all of the members of each organization, especially Paula Sheil and her husband Fred, Robert Reinarts, Tama Brisbane, Bruce Crawford, Jose Cantu, Wendi and William Maxwell, and Jennifer Torres-Siders. I thank Paul Marsh, Travis Silvers, Sara McDougall, Michelle Green, and Tara Cuslidge-Staiano for their assistance with the launching of the press, Debra Hyman for consulting on the design of the book, Michael Oliva for the cover design and art, and Diane Smith and her staff at Tokay Press for the printing.

This novel originated many years ago as a short story in a high school English class not so much taught as transfigured by the extraordinary Virginia O'Hagan, later Virginia Herbert. I regret that Virginia died in December of 2014, a month shy of what would have been her 96th birthday, but I am grateful that I was able to share my manuscript with her prior to its publication, and I thank her again for the unparalleled passion and inspiration that she brought into her students'—and former students'—lives every day. I thank also every other teacher whose classroom I passed through, especially Tom Lorenat and Dan Silva at San Carlos, Robert Knighton, Robert Kreiter, and Howard Lachtman at Pacific, and Terry Doody and Robert Patten at Rice University, along with, in memory, my friend and mentor Walter Isle, who pointed me on my path when he said to me in Houston one day, "There's a book called *Lucky Jim* by a writer named Kingsley Amis that I think you would enjoy."

I was fortunate to be an undergraduate at Pacific during a period when its football program flourished and produced a number of players and coaches who would make their mark in the wider world. I am grateful to several of the players on the team who went out of their way to befriend a geeky freshman and to encourage my lifelong interest in their sport: Charles Alexander, Wilson Meier, and William Cornman (still the most elusive punt returner I have ever watched) were especially considerate, and I have not forgotten their generosity.

The inspirational coach to whom Marcus Foster refers in these pages is modeled after my distinguished former Menlo College colleague and two-time Rose Bowl veteran Ray Solari. I also had the good fortune to pick the brains of a new generation of coaches in locker room conversations with Gary Barlow, Marvin Jackson, Jesus Reyes, and Todd Herrington; I thank them for their insights, and I apologize for any football-related errors, which are solely mine. I drew some further inspiration from the epic performance by Armanti Edwards in Appalachian State's historic victory over Michigan at Ann Arbor in 2007. I have obviously taken some liberties in blending a fictional college football team into a recent season when the real USC team was banned from bowl participation. I also note for the record here that upon return from its ban, a USC team ranked number one in the preseason polls finished the season with a record of 7-6 and a defeat in the Sun Bowl by an unranked team with seven losses.

It might surprise some people to know how much a word of appreciation or encouragement can mean to those of us who flail away at fiction. Many friends and colleagues have offered their support. Knowing I will leave out many who deserve mention, I offer thanks to Will Agopsowicz, Sheli Ayers, Lynn Beck, Bob Bini, Joe Bisson, Barbara Broer, Rob DeWitt, Mike Duffett, Elinor Fox, Lesley Fujii, June Gillam, Dave Gouker, Greg Greenwood, Kathy Hart, Brian Katz, Robert Katz, Navneet Kaur, Roger Lang, Mary Little, Nancy Mangum, Matt Marconi, Mary Fae McKay, Dick Moore, Diane Oren, Mary Ann Paz, Hubert and Patricia Powell, Lowell Pratt, Rick Rapoza, Bob Rennicks, Rich Resse, Richard Rios, Jack Saunders, Gary Scott, Mark Slakey, Mike Thibodeaux, Marilyn Thomas, Jeff Topping, and James Van Dyke. I especially thank Mary Ann Paz, who saved my soul if not my life, by letting me participate in her volleyball classes for many years after I came to Delta College; Candace Andrews for reviewing my first novel; Ginger Holden for assigning it to some of her students (and risking being burned at the stake by the fundamentalists among them); Sam

Hatch for editing *Desperation Passes* and offering his ideas to improve it; Anna Villegas for her inspiration and support; and Linda Nugent for suggesting to me that Wade and Angela should give it another shot. Old friends who kept in touch across many years also made a big impact on my efforts to produce this book. I thank Tom Bachus, Gordie Burton, Jerry Fripp, Robing Fryer, Jay Goldsmith, Rick Karr, Jeff Ludvigson, Evangelia Panagopoulou, and Mark Shilstone for their encouragement, and Bob Zachary for pointing out a good spot to get shot in San Antonio. I especially thank Dave Humber, for his support of my first novel and for writing what many readers have told me was their favorite review of it. My siblings played important roles as well: my brother Ian by setting the gold standard for a work ethic, my sister Marilyn by taking wonderful care of our mother in her declining years, and my brother Todd by helping all of us to cope with the challenges confronting us. Todd also inspired the language of this book's dedication to our mother. My sister-in-law Nancy gave me the boost I needed to finish this book when I got stuck.

Like most aspiring writers, I have encountered from the world's high and mighty mostly rejection and occasionally outright scorn, but I choose to focus on the handful of more uplifting responses. Pulitzer Prize winner Michael Chabon sent me a handwritten note upon the publication of *Nobody Roots for Goliath*. Peter Riva, agent for the estate of Stieg Larsson, kindly telephoned me with encouragement and advice after reading an early draft of *Desperation Passes*. And I had the great honor of meeting and spending a few private moments with Willie Mays, who could not have been humbler or more gracious when we spoke. The dialog I have given to Allenby here essentially duplicates the conversation I had with #24. To those who have assailed him for failing to take a more polemical role in the Civil Right Movement, I commend the biography by James S. Hirsch, especially the pages documenting Mays's role in bringing black and white soldiers and teammates together when he served in the Army, well before Rosa Parks and Martin Luther King, Jr. became household names. There is more than one way to advance the cause of brotherhood. And to those who are wondering what a baseball Hall of Famer is doing in a novel about football, please consider this: while no one would wish that he had forsaken our national pastime, imagine what Willie Mays could have accomplished as a college or NFL quarterback if that opportunity had been available to him!

I thank Professor Richard Lapchick of the University of Central Florida and his former assistant Kelvin Ang for their help with my research for this novel.

I also commend to readers *Johnny U: The Life and Times of John Unitas*, by Tom Callahan, probably the best sports biography I have ever read. And I thank Bruce Jenkins and Scott Ostler of the *San Francisco Chronicle* for many years of spirited columns that continue to demonstrate the possible intersection of literacy and sport.

Finally, I need to give most thanks to those who have helped most with the publication of this book. Neither *Desperation Passes* nor Tuleburg Press would exist without the dynamism of Paula Sheil—mentioned above, she more than deserves mention again. Her energy, enthusiasm, optimism, expertise, and outreach to others in our community galvanized everyone else involved in making this happen. Robert Reinarts, honored at the 2014 San Francisco Writers Conference for his novel *Charon's Daughter*, did much of the heavy lifting to get Tuleburg Press established. Shaheen Ayaz, who came into my life as my parents were leaving it, lifted my heart at a time when I most needed it. And Joan Bailey, my beloved partner for many years and my best friend, was my first reader for this book, as she has been for everything else I have ever written. Knowing I could make her laugh was the motivation that kept me at the keyboard when all else failed, and for her unflagging encouragement and support, I owe her more than I can possibly say.—Phil Hutcheon